אשר ו/קצי

20.10.00

THE CHANGING LAND
BETWEEN THE JORDAN AND THE SEA

Aerial photographs from 1917 to the present

by Benjamin Z. Kedar

Men, airplanes and hangar of the 1st
Squadron, Australian Flying Corps, near
Julis. One of Frank Hurley's color
photographs, January 1918. [AWM B-1644]

THE CHANGING LAND
BETWEEN THE JORDAN AND THE SEA

Aerial photographs from 1917 to the present

by Benjamin Z. Kedar

YAD BEN-ZVI PRESS • MOD PUBLISHING HOUSE

Design: Yehuda Salomon
Photography: Moshe Milner
Production Chief: Arik Ben-Shalom
Typesetting: Irit Mana
Graphics: Plus Publishing Ltd.
Color Separation & Plates: Total
Graphics Ltd.
Printing: Meiri Printing Ltd.

ISBN: 965-05-0975-5

Page 1:
The Valley of Jezreel, 1918:
A German plane above a caravan
[M 2747]

Acknowledgements:

Many are those who helped me to prepare this book, a revised and expanded version of the Hebrew original first published in 1991. Dr Gerhard Heyl, Dr Achim Fuchs and Gertraud Rüdiger of the Bayerisches Kriegsarchiv in Munich repeatedly allowed me to prepare copies of the glass negatives of Fliegerabteilung 304, and Gert Zeller, photographer with the Bayerisches Hauptstaatsarchiv, painstakingly produced the required enlargements. Joyce Bradley and Matthew J. Woodhead of the Australian War Memorial in Canberra, and Jane Carmichael of the Imperial War Museum, London, helped me to locate photographs preserved in their collections, as did staff members of the Public Record Office at Kew and the Heeresgeschichtliches Museum in Vienna. Judy Collins of the EROS Data Center in Sioux Falls, South Dakota, provided copies of NASA images. In Jerusalem, Dr. Dov Gavish, curator of the Aerial Photographs Unit of the Hebrew University's Department of Geography, Yoram Mayorek and Reuven Koffler of the Central Zionist Archives, Shimon Rubinstein of Yad Izhak Ben-Zvi, Menahem Levin and Dr. Yohanan Cohen-Yashar of the Municipal Archives, Rafael Weiser and Shlomo Goldberg of the Jewish National and University Library, kindly allowed me to have several of their photos computer-enhanced in Tel Aviv. Dr. Moshe Krakowsky of the Soil Survey, Land Evaluation and Remote Sensing Department of the Ministry of Agriculture, Tel Aviv, was always generous with his time and advice, helping me to locate numerous aerial photographs taken from 1944 onward, and Ram Zeidenberg, the department's director, gave his permission to have them enhanced by computer. Haya Kurz and Yossi Sherman, of the Survey of Israel, Tel Aviv, helped me to locate other photos of that period. Amira Stern, Director of Archives at the Jabotinsky Institute, Tel Aviv, allowed me to reproduce the photo showing Col. Margolin and Lt. Jabotinsky.

Ruth Schell of Ludwigshafen entrusted me with the album of Fritz Groll; Nanna Steiner of Munich and Knud U.K. Steiner of Espoo, Finland, gave me the photographs assembled by their father, Erich Steiner, as well as some of his documents and memorabilia; Elisabeth Rengstorf of Münster entrusted me with the aerial photographs collection of her late husband, Professor Karl Heinrich Rengstorf; Helmut Felmy of Bad Soden lent me photographs from the collection of his father Hellmuth Felmy; Susanne Kollmar and David Rüegg of Munich allowed me to use photographs from the album of Adolf Schreiber, Ms. Kollmar's grandfather. (It was my friend Dr. Hannes Möhring of Tübingen who succeeded in locating Herr Schreiber's descendants). Joachim Raich of Stadtbergen copied for me two watercolor paintings from the album of Hilwa von Heemskerck, Munich, and kindly extended other help. Dr. Ernst Schmittdiel, Erlangen, allowed me to use the World War I diary of his father, Heinrich Schmittdiel. The Süddeutscher Verlag, Munich, granted permission to use a photograph from a book by E. Berghaus. Nimrod Leef of Jerusalem allowed me to reproduce aerial photographs from the collection of his father, Zalman Leef, as well as some ground photos from his albums. Valentine Vester gave me the permission to reproduce photos from the album of the American Colony, Jerusalem. Dr. Miriam Zurr of Giv'atayim placed at my disposal photos belonging to her late husband, Emanuel Zurr. My friend Prof. Alex Carmel of Haifa University brought me the Rengstorf photos from Münster, placed at my disposal a World War I aerial photo of Haifa from his private collection, and was always ready to extend help and advice.

Otniel Schneller of the Israeli Ministry of Transportation and Dr. Doraid Mahasneh, the then director of the port of 'Aqaba, evolved–shortly after the signing of the Israeli-Jordanian peace treaty–a procedure that ultimately allowed our crew to enter Jordanian air space to take photos of the Gulf of 'Aqaba. Ze'ev Hoch of Tiv'on volunteered to pilot our plane on this and other occasions. Professor Yoav Gelber of Haifa University and Professor Benny Morris of Ben-

Gurion University in the Negev checked my description of the events that took place in 1948 in the localities whose aerial photographs are reproduced in the present book; Morris was always ready with advice and comments on sundry other issues as well. Professor Alon Kadish kindly put at my disposal his still unpublished study of the Israeli conquest of Lydda in July 1948. Clarit Ziegler of the Israeli Central Bureau of Statistics, Jerusalem, and Nader Abdel Fattah of the Palestinian Central Bureau of Statistics, Ramallah, helped me to collect demographic data.

Tamar Soffer, chief cartographer of the Hebrew University's Department of Geography, exhibited uncommon patience when asked to enter ever new details into the maps she had prepared. Jürgen Keil, formerly director of the Goethe-Institut in Tel Aviv, alerted me to the existence of Erich Steiner's collection and brought me the first batch of it from Munich. Mordechai Lewy, formerly Israeli consul in Berlin obtained information about Steiner's career and through the good services of Dr. Andrzej Drzycimski of Gdansk-Wrzescz I received information about Steiner's death in 1943. Mother Juliana, abbess of the Russian Convent of the Ascension on the Mount of Olives, graciously gave her permission to ascend the convent's belfry (the 'Russian Tower') and shoot a photo of Jerusalem comparable to the one found in Steiner's collection. Avi Flor and Dani Recanati, then of Isfar, Tel Aviv, produced stills from a WW I Australian film. I am indebted for various pieces of information, or assistance extended, to Christa Becker (Munich), Dr. Meron Benvenisti (Jerusalem), Dr. Gideon Biger (Tel Aviv), Andreas Bönte (Munich), Prof. Ilan Chet (Rehovot), Prof. Gabriel Cohen (Tel Aviv), Amos Dolev (Tel Aviv), Uri Dromi (Jerusalem), Leah Engel (Jerusalem), Nili Graiser (Tel Aviv), Feisal al-Husseini (Jerusalem /'Ein Siniya), Dr. Vered L. Kenaan (New Haven/Tel Aviv), Ben-Zion Kessler (Kedumim), Dr. Avner Levy (Jerusalem), Rachel Kangisser (Jerusalem), Prof. Shaul Krakover (Beer Sheba), Dr. Marlene Pollock (Munich), Yaacov Saar (Jerusalem), Gershon Shafat ('Eyn Tzurim), Aviva Shwartz-Yehoshua (Tel Aviv), Prof. Moshe Sharon (Jerusalem), Shelomo Sheva (Tel Aviv), Dr. Gabriel Silagi (Munich), Orly Stern (Tel Aviv), Daniella Talmon-Heller (Jerusalem), Ofra and Gabriel Treidel (Kinneret), Prof. Ra'anan Weitz (Jerusalem) and Dr. Jay Winter (Cambridge).

Dr. Zvi Zammeret, director of Yad Izhak Ben-Zvi, Jerusalem, and Yossi Perlowitz, director of Ministry of Defence Publishing House, Tel Aviv, demonstrated a patience and forbearance quite uncommon among publishers, as did their deputies, Hana Biderman and Yishay Cordova. A fellowship of the Alexander von Humboldt-Stiftung enabled me to visit repeatedly the Bavarian State Archives, Munich. A grant of the Research Institute for the History of the Jewish National Fund helped with the book's publication. Evelyn Katrak (Jerusalem) attempted to improve my English.

Special thanks are due to Dr. Dov Gavish for his advice and criticism; to Moshe Milner, prince of aerial photographers, who took all color aerial photos and most of the color ground ones; to Yehuda Salomon, the designer, who took it upon himself to study the book's subject in depth, developed a procedure for taking the new aerial photos in ways that promised correspondence with the World War I ones, and insisted on repeated flights until a reasonable correspondence was attained; and to Professor Nurith Kenaan-Kedar, my mentor in matters of form, color, and passion.

Mount Scopus,
September 1998   B. Z. K.

To my sons
Arnon and Jordan

Officers of German Squadron 300 regard an airplane with three men aboard stirring up dust at take-off. Hellmuth Felmy, the squadron commander, is second from right.
[F 34]

Table of Contents

Men of Bavarian Squadron 304 drag a damaged airplane while their officers walk by. [M 1261 I]

Old Jaffa, densely perched above the harbor, is left of center; the town's new quarters spread southward and northward along the coast. The Jewish suburb of Tel Aviv stands out on the sands at center. The trapezoid enclosure on the sand dunes, near the midpoint of the photo's right margin, is Tel Aviv's cemetery. (The glass negative of this German photo, taken on 22 November 1917, 13:10 hours, is damaged). [M 85] For a present-day view of the same area see pp. 10-11.

From Adolescent Fantasy to
'Candid-Camera' History

Our photo, taken on 8 February 1997, 10:40 hours, shows Jaffa and Bat Yam on the left and a part of Tel Aviv in the center and on the right. The Ayalon Freeway stands out in the lower left corner. The trapezoid cemetery is now surrounded by buildings.

Gustaf Dalman, 1855-1941. [Stange, Religionswissenschaft *(see n. 2)]*

The present book amounts to a belated realization of a youthful fantasy. As a teenager in Tel Aviv of the mid-1950s I often wondered whether the town was indeed built on sand dunes, as was repeated so frequently and with such pride. I had my doubts. Of course, I had often seen the famous photograph of 1909, which shows Tel Aviv's founders witnessing, at the foot of a sand dune, the allocation of the first building plots; but I had also noticed that when municipal workmen dug up parts of a pavement or street, they did not always lay bare a sand bedding. True, when they broke ground near my high school on Mazeh Street, close to Tel Aviv's original nucleus, sand was revealed; but to the north and northeast the workmen usually uncovered light brown or reddish soil. And the sand issue was only one of many that bothered me. At the time I had been in Israel only about six years, and the oldtimers' often condescending talk about the desolation of the country as they had found it aroused in me an uneasy amalgam of awe and envy. I tried very hard to visualize that desolation. In daydreams I yearned for a time machine that would allow me to hover above the country, say, 100 years earlier and see it for myself at a stage that even the hoariest oldtimer could not have witnessed. Of course, such a machine would also have enabled me to settle the sand issue once and for all by a single glance at the area where Tel Aviv was to arise.

While studying history in Jerusalem in the early 1960s, I chanced upon a book in the then new National Library that brought me tantalizingly close to a realization of those adolescent fantasies: Gustaf Dalman's *Hundert deutsche Fliegerbilder aus Palästina*. Published in Gütersloh, Germany, in 1925, the book contains 100 aerial photographs of Palestine, most of which were taken in 1917 and 1918 by airmen of a German unit – the Bavarian *Fliegerabteilung* (that is, Air Squadron) 304 – which formed part of the Turkish-German force then trying to check the northward advance of the British under General Allenby. These photographs show many parts of the country as they looked at the close of 400 years of Turkish rule over Palestine. I was especially struck by a photograph, dated 3 December 1917, showing the Castel-Abu Ghosh stretch of the main road from Jerusalem to the coast. The photo, taken from the east, disclosed that the road followed almost precisely the same winding route with which I was familiar (today's four-lane highway was constructed only in the early 1970s), but the surrounding mountains were almost as barren as parts of the central Negev or Samaria today, with no hint as yet of the forests through which the road was later to run. The road's bend at Abu Ghosh was as I knew it, but instead of the sizable Arab-Israeli village that was to fan out on both sides of the road, the German photograph of 1917 showed a single cluster of houses on a slope to its south (see photo below).

The road from Jerusalem to Jaffa, 3 December 1917, 13:45 hours, alt. 2,200 m. [M 739]

Of course, one can learn about the course of the Turkish Jerusalem-Jaffa road, or about the size of Abu Ghosh in 1917, from contemporary maps. But a map and an aerial photograph differ immensely. A map contains only that selection of features which a cartographer considered significant; an aerial photograph shows all the details, some of them fleeting, that a camera's lens recorded mechanically. A map translates reality into conventional signs; an aerial photograph allows us to observe reality directly. A map is two-dimensional; an oblique aerial photograph – and most of the photos taken by Squadron 304 are oblique – has a touch of third dimension. A square centimeter of a map can be absorbed at a single glance; a comparable square of an aerial photograph yields ever more details when studied with the help of a magnifying glass, or when enlarged in a laboratory or on a computer screen. As an investigative tool, the aerial photograph is more powerful – it may help us comprehend the structure of an entire habitat, just as it allows us to peer into a walled court. In short, as the French ethnologist Marcel Griaule once put it, the aerial photograph is a talking map. I suspect though that the widespread fascination with aerial photographs can be accounted for not only by these practical advantages, or by the technique's relative novelty, but also by the resemblance of the panoptic overview from the air to primordial notions of beholding the earth from on high. The same appears to be true, *a fortiori*, of satellite images.[1]

Dalman, an eminent biblical scholar interested in the material culture of Palestine in antiquity, especially in the time of Jesus, did not include in his book aerial photographs of the new Jewish villages and residential areas existing in 1917-18 (though in his early years as a Protestant missionary he had written down Galician- and Russian-Jewish melodies, and he had later reported on the Jewish settlement of Palestine that began in 1882.) The 100 photographs he published in 1925 aimed at providing "a proper acclimatization in the land of Jesus and the prophets," as he believed that nothing allows for a better perception of a tract of land, and of the location of settlements and roads in it, than an aerial photograph.[2] Hence, young Tel Aviv appears in Dalman's book just once, a grouping of regularly spaced dots occupying a few square millimeters on a photograph that shows the town of Jaffa and its surroundings. I was disappointed, although by that time I had already ascertained from old maps which parts of Tel Aviv were built on sand and which were not. One of Dalman's collaborators stated, however, that as of 1925, 2,662 photographs taken by Squadron 304 were extant in the Bavarian War Archives in Munich. Of these, 1,406 were briefly described in the catalogue appended to Dalman's volume, and I learned from these descriptions that several photographs showed Jewish settlements, and that a few of them showed Tel Aviv. I made a mental note to check some day whether the photographs had survived World War II. Being at that time already interested in the Crusading Kingdom of Jerusalem, it occurred to me that the German photographs might also reveal traces of Frankish fortifications that had subsequently disappeared.

Years later, in 1976, I spent a sabbatical in Munich, my grant earmarked for a study of European approaches to the Muslims in medieval times. But I had not forgotten the German World War I photographs. Having ascertained that the entire collection was intact, I went on one of my first days in Munich to the small brick house in the northwestern part of the city in which the Bavarian War Archives are located. The director, Dr. Gerhard Heyl, had a surprise in store: about three years earlier he had had a visit from an old man, Fritz Berthold, an erstwhile officer with Squadron 304, who had deposited with him the typewritten war journal of the unit, copies of weekly reports to the Turkish-German general headquarters at Nazareth, circulars, aerial and ground photographs, and other documents – all of which allowed for a detailed reconstruction of the squadron's activities during the eleven months it was stationed in Palestine. One of the more interesting documents is the original typewritten report about a reconnaissance flight over the northern Negev on 8 November 1917, with *Oberleutnant* Berthold serving as observer. The report divulges that the flight took off from the 'airport' at 'Iraq al-Manshiya (the Arab village on the site of which the Jewish town of Qiryat Gat now stands), that it lasted 85 minutes, and led Berthold to the conclusion – a correct one – that the British, who had breached the Gaza-Beersheba front a few days earlier, intended to advance along the railroad leading from Beersheba northward, and not along the road leading northeastward to Hebron (see photo right).

The large, heavy glass negatives of Squadron 304 are kept in the Archives' storage rooms, and it was only later that I was allowed to see them. But the boxes containing their contact prints were soon placed on my table in the almost empty reading room. The prints are of excellent quality and usually much sharper than the reproductions in Dalman's book. It appears that almost every photograph was meticulously labeled by the German airmen a short time after the picture had been

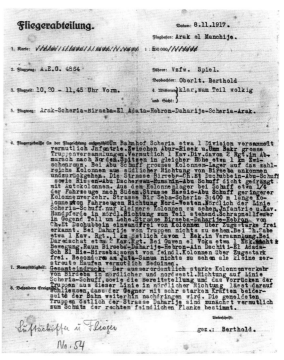

8 November 1917: Berthold's report on his flight over the northern Negev and the Judean Mountains. [M Luftschiffer und Flieger, No. 54]

Squadron No.	Ordinal No.	Date	Hour	Main Locality	Altitude	Focal Distance

Lateral Deflection

Vertical Deflection

taken: the upper margin gives the number of the squadron, the ordinal number of the photograph, the date and hour of the shot, the name of the main locality appearing on it, the height from which the shot was taken (there are a few mistakes concerning the last two data), and the focal distance of the camera. An arrow pointing northward is usually incised on the negative itself. In some of the photographs one may discern, in the right margin, the automatically recorded readings of the camera's lateral and vertical deflection at the time of the shot. A large proportion of the photographs focus, as one might have expected, on military targets. Some testify to the considerable size of Arab villages in the southern part of the coastal plain, while others show the Jewish villages of Rishon le-Zion, Nes-Ziona, Rehovot, Gedera, Petah Tiqva, Kfar-Sava, as well as Merhavya, where Squadron 304 was stationed for about ten months. The Bavarian airmen took several ground pictures of the Jewish pioneers of Merhavya, especially of its more attractive women. The most striking photograph is that of a dark-haired girl in an embroidered, wide-sleeved peasant dress, her face radiating quiet resolution. A conscientious Bavarian aviator had inscribed the name *Riffka* on the upper margin, which some sixty years later enabled my friend Alex Carmel to locate Mrs. Rivka Geffner in a Haifa home for the aged. A copy of the German photograph was on her desk, and she distinctly remembered that the officer who took it kept remarking on her astonishing resemblance to his wife back home in Bavaria.

None of the photographs focuses exclusively on Tel Aviv, but the tiny township appears on several shots of the Jaffa region. I wondered whether it would be possible to enlarge from one of them the quadrangle containing Tel Aviv. Dr. Heyl promised to help. It took some time to obtain the necessary permits, but finally I was notified that the glass negatives had been transferred to the photographic service of the Bavarian Archives in central Munich and that I would be permitted to be present while the enlargements were being prepared. Gert Zeller, the photographer, invited me into the darkroom to show him the exact part of the photograph I wanted enlarged. I chose a photograph of the Jaffa area and pointed to the cluster of streets intersecting one another at right angles which at that time was Tel Aviv. Zeller applied pressure to the instrument's mounting, and the cluster slowly began to grow on the screen before us. Here was a ludicrously short Herzl Street, Tel Aviv's main thoroughfare, flanked by a dozen of houses on either side, and leading to the fortress-like *Gymnasia Herzlia*, the world's first Hebrew high school. Here was a scrawny Rothschild Boulevard, consisting of three rectangles in all, with a

Rivka of Merhavya. [M 1267d]

Tel Aviv and vicinity, 12 January 1918, 10:30 hours, alt. 2,200 m. [M 93a, original size]

few trees in the southernmost of them and three parallel lines of shrubs sticking out of the sand in the northernmost. Each and every house and garden had become distinctly visible, but still the township on the screen continued to grow, surrounded by sand on three sides. When the gate and windows of the high school became discernible, further enlargement was impossible (see photos on p. 14 and below, and pp. 92-93) and Zeller stopped the machine. The darkroom grew silent. "What place is that?" asked Zeller, sensing my emotion. "That," I replied, "is Tel Aviv as it looked 60 years ago. A view that no one, not even the German airman who took the picture, has ever seen before now."

Another blow-up allowed to discern remains of La Fève, an important Frankish castle erected by the Knights Templar, which guarded the main crossroads of the Jezreel Valley. In 1183 the castle served as a staging point for the entire Frankish army that was facing Saladin, and in 1799 the Turks, in an attempt to halt Napoleon's soldiers, positioned infantry and light cannon behind the ruins of its walls. Today one can see almost nothing of the Frankish castle, covered as it is by Merhavya's houses and lawns. But one of the German aerial photographs shows clearly the hill of La Fève, flanked by the modern houses of Merhavya's original open court to the east and the tents of Squadron 304 to the west. An enlargement of the quadrangle showing the castle's remains, and the ditch surrounding them, was of help for a survey of this Frankish site (see photo right).[3]

Remains of the Crusader castle of La Fève (at center) and the houses of Merhavya (at bottom). [A section of M 527, enlarged three times]

Now that I had at my disposal a time machine of sorts, it occurred to me to juxtapose the earliest views, the aerial photographs of 1917-18, with their present-day parallels – new shots of the selfsame areas, to be taken from about the same height and angle. The more exact the correspondence between the old and new photographs, the more precisely would they divulge the nature and extent of the changes that had taken place. The time machine might thus allow for exercises in visual history, with scenes of the past directly observed and instantly compared with their present-day counterparts and derivations. Such comparative observations might bring us somewhat closer to what Sigmund Freud believed to be attainable only by a flight of imagination: namely, to face simultaneously various phases in the history of a locality, so that "the observer would perhaps only have to change the direction of his glance or his position in order to call up the one view or the other."[4]

It dawned on me almost immediately that such visual exercises might provide new answers to the interrelated, emotion-laden questions about the state of Turkish Palestine during the initial stages of Jewish colonization, and about the impacts of Zionism on the country's physical layout.

The first of these issues was eloquently raised, back in 1891, by the leading Zionist thinker Ahad Ha-'Am. In his article *Emet me-Eretz-Israel* (Truth from Palestine) – written, in Hebrew, aboard an Odessa-bound steamer immediately

Tel Aviv, 12 January 1918. [A section of M 93a, enlarged three times]

Capt. Frank Hurley in the observer's seat of an airplane, Palestine, 1918. [AWM P-1184/26/19]

after his first visit to the country – he shocked many of his pro-Zionist readers in Europe by pointing out that

> outside of the country we are accustomed to believe that Palestine is today almost entirely depopulated, a desert unsown, and whosoever wants to buy land there, may come and do so according to his heart's desire. But in reality this is not so. Throughout the country it is difficult to find arable land that remains untilled; only sandy fields or stony mountains, fit merely for tree planting, and this too only after having been cleared and prepared with much work and at great expense – only these are not cultivated, because the Arabs do not like to take much pains at the present for the sake of a distant future.[5]

Both of the conceptions that Ahad Ha-'Am so lucidly confronted have remained with us to the present day. The conception he attacked – namely, that Turkish Palestine was a largely desolate, uncultivated tract of land – is fundamental to Zionist and Israeli argumentation, which stresses that Jewish pioneers made a desolate country bloom, while the conception he so forcefully put forward is close to the one propounded by Palestinians and other Arabs. (Indeed, it is noteworthy that at the Arab-Israeli Peace Conference which took place in Madrid in 1991 – that is, one hundred years after the publication of Ahad Ha-'Am's article – the two conflicting conceptions were presented, or alluded to, in the opening speeches of the Israeli prime minister and the chairman of the Palestinian delegation.)

The longer I studied the aerial photographs stored in the Bavarian War Archives, the more I became convinced that they offered a clear-cut, indisputable answer about the extent of cultivation in the sizable areas they covered, and that their publication might therefore serve as a sobering antidote to ardently held generalizations. True, an aerial photograph is not self-explanatory, but the reproduction of reality it provides is so easily comprehensible that it needs little elaboration and, unlike a written account, this mechanically produced visual text is above suspicion of selection, manipulation, or prejudice as far as the terrain it covers is concerned. This, I mused, would also be true of a pair of aerial photographs covering the same area, with each taken in a different period. Here, too, the spectator would be able to observe similarities and differences for himself, neither aided nor hampered by extensive verbal explanations, with the two shots interpreting one another, and allowing, among other things, for a direct study of Zionism's multifaceted impact. A series of such paired photographs would amount to a promising historical source – limited in scope, because the views from the air disclose changes in only some material aspects, but candid and hardly assailable as far as these aspects go. In an age in which the feasibility of an unbiased account has been so widely called into question, the photographs may tell a uniquely objective if rudimentary story.

It took some fifteen years to realize this project. In the meantime I learned about other collections of aerial photographs taken in Palestine during World War I. Yehoshua Ben-Arieh, my colleague at the Hebrew University, informed me that in the 1920s the geographer Abraham Brawer had deposited in Jerusalem's National Library more than 1,300 copies of aerial photographs then kept in the archives of Munich and Potsdam.[6] I learned also about aerial photographs taken by the Germans' enemies at the time. In the Imperial War Museum in London I was able to see a small number of the many photographs taken by the British, and when I asked the whereabouts of the rest, I was told: "Please do understand that ours is a small island; we cannot keep just everything." The Australians, who also photographed Palestine intensively from the air during World War I, dwell on a larger island; be that as it may, many aerial photographs are kept at the Australian War Memorial in Canberra. Dov Gavish, head of the aerial photography unit at the Hebrew University, allowed me to use photographs he received from Australia, and I ordered others from Canberra. These included the color shots that Captain Frank Hurley, the official photographer of the Australian Imperial Force in the Middle East, took in Palestine in January 1918, probably the earliest color photographs ever made of the country. Gavish also told me of several drawers packed with aerial photographs in the archives of the Israel Antiquities Authority. It turned out that most of them were photomosaics – that is, a number of vertical aerial photographs glued together to form a sequence – which the British had prepared during the last year of World War I. These mosaics show the line of Turkish fortifications west of Jerusalem, the many fields alongside the road linking the Arab villages of At-Tira and Qalqiliya, the road from Jenin to El-'Affule, the western part of the Sharon plain with its large winter swamps, and much more. Since the photographs had been stacked in narrow drawers for many years, many of them were faded or decayed, and only a few were fit for reproduction.[7]

In an especially good state of preservation is the mosaic showing the Jaffa area at noon of 19 November 1917 – that is, just three days after the Wellington Regiment of the New Zealand Mounted Rifles Brigade occupied the town (see photo below). The shoreline can be seen near the mosaic's left margin; the Arab quarter of Manshiya, consisting of small houses and narrow but straight lanes, lies somewhat east of the coast and parallel to it, with the white rectangle of the Hasan Bek Mosque clearly discernible between the quarter and the sea. Tel Aviv appears in the right-hand part of the photograph marked 'M2099,' and the large but squat U of the Herzlia High School and the straight, wide streets around it immediately stand out. Trenches can be observed along the seashore as well as on the sand dunes in the mosaic's upper right corner – that is, in the area where Tel Aviv's future main thoroughfare, Allenby Road, was to be. But the British photographer

Tel Aviv and Manshiya, 19 November 1917, 12:00 hours. [IAA, Unnumbered mosaic]

Fritz Groll in Samakh. [G-2, 1]

Hauptmann Erich Steiner. [S]

does not appear to have worked systematically, for Tel Aviv's southeastern part as well as the southern extremity of Manshiya are missing. This is one reason why I prefer the Tel Aviv enlarged from the German photograph to the Tel Aviv on the British mosaic. But there is a weightier reason. The photographs of which the mosaic is composed are vertical and cover small areas, and the distortion of the terrain is therefore negligible; as they were shot at noon, shadows are minimal; they are undoubtedly preferable for the preparation of maps, as they share with them the cold two-dimensionality that presents streets as double-lines and houses as planes. The German photograph, in the contrast, is oblique and therefore enables us to view Tel Aviv as if from a nearby mountain or a low-flying airplane: the houses have not only roofs, but also facades, stories, volume. Moreover, the German photograph was taken in the morning, and therefore all the houses, trees, and fences cast shadows. In short, the British mosaic is merely a series of aerial photographs; the German shot has the touch of a living picture.

Additional sources subsequently came to light. In 1988 I learned about the private collection of Fritz Groll, head of the photography and survey unit of the German Squadron 300, who served in Palestine from 1916 to 1918. Groll's adoptive daughter, Marga Schraffenberger, donated two subsidiary albums to the Jerusalem Municipal Museum; and I was able to study the main collection in her apartment in Landau/Pfalz, close to the German-French border. Groll's albums contain aerial photographs of localities in the north of Palestine – for example, Bitanya and Kafr Kanna – which have no parallels in the archives of Munich or Canberra. In addition they include aerial photographs of more southern sites as well as a large number of ground shots, especially of Beersheba, Ramleh, and Samakh – the localities near which Squadron 300 had been stationed.[8] In 1990, Helmut Felmy of Bad Soden placed at my disposal photographs from the collection of his father, Hellmuth Felmy, commander of Squadron 300.[9] Dr. Ernst Schmittdiel of Erlangen allowed me to use the war diary of his father, Heinrich Schmittdiel, who served as a soldier in the same squadron. In 1992 Nanna Steiner of Munich and Knud U. K. Steiner of Espoo, Finland, gave me the collection of their father, Erich Steiner, who had served as observer and commander with Squadrons 302 and 305.[10] In 1993 I located additional material in the Public Record Office in London and in the Australian War Memorial in Canberra, and Susanne Kollmar of Munich placed at my disposal several photographs from the World War I album of her grandfather Adolf Schreiber. And in 1995 Elisabeth Rengstorf of Münster gave me the collection of her late husband, the biblical scholar Karl Heinrich Rengstorf.

Thus I was able to assemble a considerable number of World War I aerial photographs of Palestine from various sources. The problem now was to obtain their present-day counterparts. I did not want to use the pictures routinely taken by the Survey of Israel, as they are strictly vertical. An exhibition of photographs taken by American astronauts, and of LANDSAT images – that is, of pictorial representations of data on earth scenes recorded by satellite-borne sensor systems – made me wonder whether it might be feasible to place the World War I photographs, which exemplify the earliest stage of viewing the earth from above alongside some of these most advanced representations.

At the National Cartographic Information Center in Reston, Virginia, I viewed microfilm copies of the LANDSAT images. Having learned that the satellite orbits along 251 different paths running north to south, and automatically records 119 different scenes along each path, I chose Path 188 taken on 10 September 1980. I pushed a button and started speeding southward from the Arctic via the then Soviet Union to the Black Sea, gradually slowing down over Turkey and the Bay of Alexandretta, and bringing the machine to a standstill first at image 188-D-037, which centered on the area south of Haifa, then at 188-B-038, which centered on the sand dunes south of Tel Aviv, and finally at 188-D-038, which centered on the northwestern Negev.

The sight is unique. Here the country is seen – or, more accurately, sensed – from a height of 920 kilometers, with all its ridges, valleys, towns, villages, roads, fields, harbors, and jetties clearly visible. I was especially struck by the fact that on the LANDSAT images one can see large stretches of the pre-1967 armistice lines between Israel and the Arab countries, as well as much of the present-day Israeli-Syrian cease-fire line on the Golan Heights. I found a convincing explanation of this phenomenon in an article by Joseph Otterman, an environmental scientist at Tel Aviv University. Otterman was struck by a NASA image of 1972 that shows a pronounced contrast between northeastern Sinai, which appears very bright, and the northwestern Negev, which is considerably darker, with the sharp demarcation line between these two desert areas coinciding precisely with the pre-1967 Egyptian-Israeli armistice line. He made ground surveys on both sides of the divide and

22 October 1972. [NASA ERTS E-1091-07482-5]

concluded that the contrast resulted primarily from overgrazing by goats, camels, and sheep on the Egyptian (Sinai) side. On the Israeli (Negev) side, where only a few herds grazed, natural vegetation grew in relative abundance.[11] In fact, cessation of grazing in a given area of the desert can within a very short time change the way it looks like from space. A comparison of satellite images of northeastern Sinai taken in 1972 and 1980 reveals that the fencing-in of a sizable rectangle of the desert, undertaken in about 1975 in order to encompass a new military airfield, had by 1980 caused the rectangle to be about as covered by natural vegetation as the western Negev (see photos above and right).

But the LANDSAT images, even after partial enlargement, did not prove to be adequate counterparts of the World War I aerial photographs. I returned to the original idea: to oppose the old photographs with new, oblique ones to be taken from a similar height and angle. These confrontations form the main part of this book.

The zigzag journey that began with an adolescent fantasy has thus led me to pursuits and contacts that would hardly have taken place in the ordinary course. It has aided my research on a twelfth-century castle and on other medieval issues, and allowed me to experiment with a stimulating historical technique – the serial confrontation of paired aerial photographs. But there has been more to it: the excitement of seeing the country through a prism of scores of years and from an altitude of hundreds of kilometers. Above all, there remains the memory of that moment when an infant Tel Aviv, struggling in the sands just west of Jaffa's orchards, sprang to life in a Munich darkroom.[12]

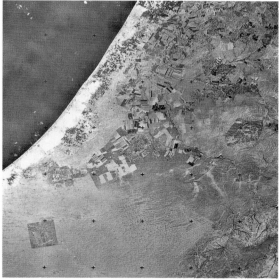

10 September 1980. [LANDSAT 188-D-038]

Observers of the 1st Squadron, Australian Flying Corps, at Ramleh, 1918. [AWM B- 02076]

A German Rumpler C-V [M 1260]
Type: *Two-seat fighter.* **Engine**: *260 hp Mercedes D.IVa.* **Dimensions**: *Span 12.66 m; length 8.4 m; height 3.25 m.* **Weight**: *Empty 1,010 kg; loaded 1,530 kg.* **Performance**: *Maximum speed 170 km/h; operational ceiling 6,500 m; endurance 3.5 to 4 hours.* **Armament**: *One fixed Spandau machine gun; one Parabellum machine gun in rear cockpit; four 25-kg bombs.*

A Turkish caravan leaves camp after the raid on El-Qatiya in the western Sinai, end of April 1916. [G 198]

World War I brought to Palestine most innovations of contemporary military technology. Both the Turkish-German force that held Palestine and initially attempted to cross the Suez Canal into Egypt, as well as the British who first defended the Canal and then advanced eastward into the Sinai and Palestine, used machine guns and artillery, telephones, telegraph, and heliographs, motor vehicles and field hospitals; and they constructed hundreds of kilometers of roads and railways to supply the many tens of thousand soldiers at the front. The British employed, in addition, armored cars, tractors, and a handful of tanks.

Both sides also used airplanes.[13] French seaplanes, which took off from a British cruiser sailing along the Sinai coast and were manned by French pilots and British observers, overflew Beersheba in the winter of 1914-15 and discovered the Turkish preparations for the drive on the Suez Canal. These seaplanes, as well as British airplanes that took off from the Canal town of Ismailia, later kept track of the advance of the Turkish expeditionary force, which had no planes at its disposal, and bombed it several times. After the Turkish attempt to cross the Canal on 3 February 1915 had been repulsed, they reported on the Turkish retreat into the Sinai.

The Turks and their German allies learnt their lesson, and the German Squadron 300 ('*Pascha*') was sent to Palestine in preparation for the next push toward the Canal. The squadron with its 14 airplanes arrived in Beersheba in April 1916 and during the following summer supported – from an airfield at El-'Arish and the Bir el-'Abd landing ground in western Sinai – the unsuccessful Turkish-German attempt to dislodge the British from northwestern Sinai. Its 160 horsepower Rumpler C-I two-seaters were qualitatively superior to the 90 horsepower B.E. 2c's of the British No. 14 Squadron and the 1st Australian Squadron, and the Germans largely retained their superiority even after the British had been equipped with more advanced aircraft.

This state of things lasted until September 1917. German pilots bombed the towns along the Suez Canal, as well as Cairo, and tried repeatedly to hamper the construction of the railroad crucial for the British advance along the northern coast of the Sinai. They also reported accurately on the British moves during the First and Second Battles of Gaza (26-29 March and 17-20 April 1917), thereby enabling the Turkish-German Command to counter them. They also attempted to prevent the British airplanes from ranging their artillery. Gerhard Felmy, the German ace on the Palestine-Sinai front, landed during the Second Battle of Gaza some 150 kilometers west of the front line and succeeded in blowing up the British pipeline

that carried water from Egypt, via the northern Sinai, to the expeditionary force south of Gaza. A month later, Felmy repeated his feat.[14] Nevertheless, the German squadron failed to prevent British and Australian reconnaissance flights over southern Palestine and the repeated bombing of Beersheba. Consequently the German squadron was forced to leave Beersheba for Ramleh at the end of February 1917. A month later, Australian airplanes began operating from a field near Rafah, on the border of Egypt and Palestine.

Already during the Sinai battles, both sides had engaged in aerial photography. It was the aerial observer's duty to place the large glass plates into the camera, expose them to light, and remove them (his other task being to operate the machine gun). At first it had not been possible to develop the plates, as the gelatin layer melted in the water because of the summer heat, but the problem was later solved. The German observers photographed the British camps along the Suez Canal and the advance of the British railhead along the Sinai coast. They also assisted the German archaeologist Theodor Wiegand, charged with the preservation of antiquities, and photographed for him the ruins of the ancient towns Sbeita (Shivta), Ruhayba (Rehovot), and other sites in the Negev Desert. When the front stabilized south of Gaza, the German aviators, in need of a detailed map for the ranging of their artillery, prepared one with the help of aerial photographs; its scale was about 1:100,000. The Australians and British, too, photographed the camps and trenches of their enemy, and their cartographical work was much more sophisticated. Aviators and surveyors cooperated in developing a new method, based on strips of consecutive, partially overlapping, vertical photographs, taken by a camera rigidly mounted on a straight-flying plane. Such strips served for the preparation of the town maps of Gaza, Beersheba, and Ramleh printed in early 1917, and of the Turkish systems of trenches along the Gaza-Beersheba road. Aerial photography for the purpose of map preparation intensified in the coming months, with most of the sorties flown by Australian crews. Between April and September 1917, 2,977 pictures were taken, resulting in the preparation of twenty 1:20,000-scale maps.

Upon assuming command of the British expeditionary force at the end of June 1917, General Allenby submitted, inter alia, requests for three additional squadrons of advanced aircraft. He was given two, Squadrons 111 and 113, and thus had by the end of October four squadrons, or 75 airplanes; six of these were Bristol Fighters, superior to the aircraft flown by the German Squadron 300. The four squadrons operated from fields in the western Negev. At Deir el-Balah, south of Gaza, there were two sections of balloons that served for stationary observation.

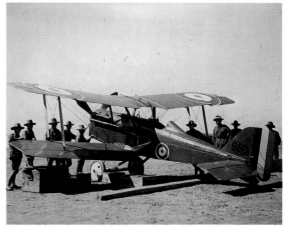

A British S.E.5a [AWM B-1656; one of Hurley's color photos]. **Type**: *Two-seat fighter.* **Engine**: *220 hp Hispano-Suiza.* **Dimensions**: *Span 8.12 m; length 6.38 m; height 3.2 m.* **Weight**: *Empty 640 kg; loaded 900 kg.* **Performance**: *Maximum speed 190 km/h; operational ceiling 5,900 m; range 480 km.* **Armament**: *One fixed Vickers machine gun; one Lewis machine gun on upper wing; four 11-kg bombs.*

Beersheba, May 1916: A reviewing party headed by Jamal Pasha at a dress parade of German Squadron 300. [G 191]

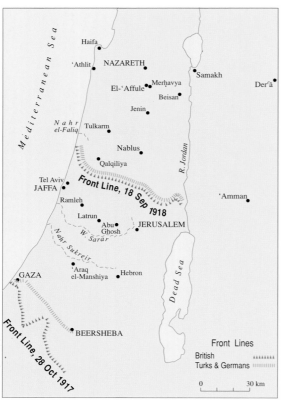

The front lines in Palestine, 1917-18

Air superiority now passed to the British, even though the Germans were reinforced in October 1917 by four squadrons – 301, 302, 303 and 304 – comprising 56 planes. At the end of that month, British and Australian pilots prevented their German counterparts from crossing the front line (see map) and observing the secret deployment of two infantry and two mounted divisions, which were to launch a crucial surprise attack on Beersheba. The one German plane that succeeded in photographing this massive deployment was shot down by a Bristol Fighter. As a result of these and other activities, the Turkish-German Command was led to believe that the main British force remained in the Gaza area and that Gaza continued to be its primary objective. At the same time, a unit of the Australian squadron improved its performance to the point where it was capable of passing on to field headquarters aerial photographs of the Turkish line just four or five hours after they had been taken. At the beginning of November 1917, with Beersheba in British hands and the Turkish Beersheba-Gaza line shattered, British aviators strafed the retreating Turkish columns and bombed railroad stations as well as the German airfields in southern Palestine. The German squadrons beat a hasty retreat northward, leaving much material behind and ceasing operational flights for about a fortnight.

At the end of 1917, as the front stabilized north of Jaffa and Jerusalem, the British squadrons moved northward to become ultimately stationed at Ramleh, Wadi es-Sarar (the present-day Nahal Soreq), Sarona, and Jerusalem, while the Germans established quarters at Jenin, El-'Affule, Merhavya, and Samakh. In February 1918, Allenby received another squadron, No. 142, and in the same month German Squadron 305 arrived in Transjordan, where it was to operate from fields near Der'a and 'Amman. In March, a German squadron of battle planes (*Jasta* 1) reinforced the German aviators at Jenin, and in June, Ottoman Squadron 14, manned mostly by Germans, arrived in 'Amman (see map on p. 29).

The rival aviators took off on reconnaissance and bombing sorties, participated in the major operations east of the River Jordan, and took aerial photographs by the thousands. For instance, during two weeks in January 1918, the Australian Squadron completely photographed a 50-kilometer-wide strip behind (that is, north of) the Turkish line; the ensuing 1,616 photographs served for mapping the area. On the German side, a surveyor detachment prepared a series of maps partially based on aerial photographs.

An interpreted photomosaic of Port Said and the northern end of the Suez Canal, prepared by German Squadron 300 from aerial photographs taken on 4 August 1917. [G 335]

A German photomontage contrived to embarrass the British and dropped at one of their airfields: The pyramids as photographed by aviators of Squadron 300 who took off from Beersheba in November 1916, and a German airplane affixed above them. [F 35; the story of the hoax is told on the back of the photo]

Above: Types of aerial cameras used by the British and the Australians in Palestine. [AWM P – 1184/26/02]

Below: A German observer's trophy - the wings of a downed Royal Flying Corps pilot. [S]

Insignia of a German aerial observer. [S]

10 April 1918, near Kafr Qasim: A British plane shot down by Hauptmann Erich Steiner. [S]

Men of the photographic section of the Australian Flying Corps engaged in trimming and drying prints at Ramleh, 1918. [AWM B-02072]

British manual for the tactical use of aerial photographs: A photograph and its interpretation [AWM]. The photo, taken by British Squadron 113 on 24 January 1918, 12:00 hours, shows Turkish trenches in the orchards of the Jewish colony of Kfar Sava. The same trenches appear on a photo taken by Bavarian Squadron 304 on 17 January 1918, 14:30 hours [M23, see below right]. The two photos exemplify the tendency of the British to photograph a small area vertically, whereas the Germans used to photograph much larger areas obliquely. (We aligned the German photo with the British one in order to facilitate comparisons; otherwise the German photo should be viewed from the right.)

Both sides compiled booklets containing instructions for the tactical use of the aerial photographs. A copy of the British handbook is deposited in the Australian War Memorial;[15] a copy of its German counterpart, captured by the British, can be consulted in the Public Record Office at Kew.[16] A confrontation of the two is illuminating. The British booklet begins with a short list of rules such as: "Much information can be gleaned by comparison of photographs of the same area taken on different dates", and then goes on to present a series of rudimentarily interpreted photographs, with the photograph on one page and the interpretation on another (see example above). The German booklet starts with a table showing various types of British tents, the purposes they serve, their surface in square meters and the number of men they can accommodate (see below left). The next table allows distances to be calculated on vertical aerial photographs according to flight altitude and the camera's focal distance. The interpreted photographs that follow are grouped methodically ("units on the march", "units in camp", "roads and vehicles", etc.) and often provide clues to the size of the enemy force in question. In short, the German manual allows for a considerably more sophisticated utilization of aerial photographs.

German manual for the tactical use of aerial photographs: Data on British tents.
[PRO Air 1/2287/209/75/55]

Engländer Zelte

Grundriss	Zweck	Bemerk.	Grösse	Fassung
gr.ovals Dachzelt	Magaz		200 qm	70 Mann
mittl.oval.Dachzelt	Lazarett Magazin		85 qm	30 Mann
Kl.oval.Dachzelt	Lazarett		55 qm	12 Mann
gr.rechteckiges Hauszelt	Lazarett		78 qm	25 Mann
mittl.rechteckiges Hauszelt	Lazarett		48 qm	15 Mann
rundes Spitzzelt	Marschzelte Lazarette Magazine Truppenlag.		12 qm	12 Mann 1 Zug + 1 Reihe Komp.: 10–11 Zelte + 1 Zugsreihe Baon: 4 Kompa-Gruppen
kl.Hüttenzelt	Marschzelt.		5 qm	3 Mann 1 Zug + 1 Reihe Komp.: 4 Zugsreih

German and British squadrons on the Palestine front, Summer 1918: Reconnaissance sectors of German squadrons as of June 1918; British forces as at Zero hour, 19 September 1918

Watercolor paintings of a German airfield (probably at Jenin) presented to Hauptmann von Heemskerck, commander of German aviators in Palestine [Collection Hilwa von Heemskerck, Munich / Joachim Raich, Stadtbergen]

*The German airfield near Merhavya. 20 January 1918, 15:00 hours, alt. 2,500 m [M 527a]. The limits of the airfield of Bavarian Squadron 304 are marked on the photo; the word **Flugpl**[atz] in the center means "airfield." Take-off and landing marks are visible mainly in the field's left section. The straight line running from the lower right corner to the middle of the left margin is the El-'Affule-Beisan railway.*

Of the squadrons stationed in Palestine during the war's final year, the Bavarian Squadron 304 is probably the best documented. This is so because of the copious material Fritz Berthold deposited in the Munich War Archives. From November 1917 onward, the squadron operated from a field near Merhavya (photo left). As at the other airfields, there were no landing strips; the pilots took off from a roughly level stretch of land, touched down on any part of it they happened to choose, and parked the planes in or between large tents. When heavy rains turned the field into a quagmire, all flights became impossible. On 28 December 1917, Berthold made the following entry in the squadron diary: "Throughout the day, occasional sunshine alternating with heavy cloudiness. Towards noon the squadron commander [Walz] attempts three times to start; as the field has not sufficiently dried up, the airplane sinks up to the axle. Same phenomenon at Squadron 302 [in El-'Affule]. The airfields of Squadrons 301 and 303 at Jenin and especially the airfield of Squadron 300 in Samakh are already serviceable, as they are situated on a slope." And on 17 February 1918, Berthold reported that his squadron's airfield was improved by harrowing that lasted for several days, followed by rolling with a cylinder pulled by several buffaloes.[17]

While the other German squadrons were allotted various sectors of the British front – which at the time ran through central Palestine – Squadron 304 was especially entrusted with long-range reconnaissance (see map above), and its planes got as far south as Beersheba and Gaza. The squadron's observers frequently photographed the outlet of Nahr Sukreir (the present-day Nahal Lakhish), because the British chose an uninhabited spot just north of it as their main disembarkation area (the same spot is now occupied by the harbor of Ashdod). One of the photo-

British disembarkation activities near the outlet of Nahr Sukreir, photographed by Bavarian aviators on 9 January 1918, 15:00 hours, alt. 1,500 m. [M 360 b, partial enlargement]

Men of the Egyptian Labour Corps unload cargoes from surf boats near the outlet of Nahr Sukreir [AWM B-1415]. This Australian picture was taken on 10 January 1918 – a day after the Bavarians photographed the area from the air.

A British train in the sands west of Isdud. 21 January 1918, 14:15 hours, alt. 4,000 m. [M 413a, partial enlargement]

graphs (see photo left) shows surf boats that carry cargoes from a transport steamer anchored offshore to a reloading camp on the sand dunes north of the outlet. A photograph of 25 May 1918 shows a train moving along the new British railway that ran parallel to the Palestinian coast (see photo left below): the train, with smoke rising from its engine, is visible on the sand dunes, with the large Arab village of Isdud (destroyed after the 1948 war) to its left. The Bavarians also photographed time and again Allenby's general headquarters at the German Spohn Farm at Bir Salim, west of Ramleh. The small British airfield south of Jerusalem, on the old road to Hebron, was also carefully watched: according to a squadron diary entry of 3 June 1918, two planes were parked there, but there were no tents or hangars; on 1 August it was noted that the field now had eight tents; on 10 August it was observed that one of the tents had been folded.

The British and Australians for their part repeatedly photographed and bombed the airfield of the Bavarian squadron. For example, on 3 January 1918 the squadron diary reports that some 15 airplanes attacked El-'Affule railroad station and the nearby airfield of Squadron 302, and threw about 30 bombs on the airfield of Squadron 304 at Merhavya.[18] One of the Bavarians photographed the attack from

the ground (see photo on next page). There were no casualties, but all the planes and tents were hit, with one tent showing 200 machine-gun holes. All the planes were repaired during the night, and four of them left in the morning for a reprisal attack on the British field at Ramleh. One of the four turned over during take off, and a second had to land because of mechanical failure, but the remaining two attacked the target despite difficult weather.[19] Yet alongside the ongoing warfare the rival aviators adhered to a rather chivalrous code, with each side informing the other about the fate of its airmen who had been brought down. For instance, on 27 May 1918 the British dropped the following message (see below):[20]

Contemporary newspaper accounts of aviator exploits bring to mind medieval narrations of the wondrous deeds of some knight errant. For instance, on 18 April 1918 *The Palestine News*, the weekly published for British troops fighting in Palestine, carried a report by 'Icarus' entitled "Our Airmen above Palestine," which included the following:

Two of our scouts engaged an enemy two-seater near El Kefr. They attacked him and drove him down almost to the ground, but in the meantime 6 enemy Scouts had arrived and commenced diving on our machine. One of our Pilots turned on the leader and after skilful manoeuvring fired 50 rounds into him from a favourable position, which caused him to go into an uncontrolled dive till he crashed into the hills. While this was happening the lower of our Scouts, after following the two-seater, being unable to see his companion, went home, but the remaining one continued the fight for 15 minutes against the 5 Scouts left. He was gradually driven down towards the ground, when he found himself under heavy fire from the Scouts above and also from troops below. As the Scouts started to climb again our Pilot also climbed, to about 100 feet, when the enemy machines attacked him simultaneously and he found himself in the centre of a cascade of bullets. It was very difficult for the Pilot to reply owing to the necessity of constant manoeuvring, but he eventually got off half a drum into one of the enemy, who went down in a spin out of control, and did not appear again. The remaining four however continued to attack with vigour until, owing to engine trouble, he got into a spin and only regained control within a few feet of the ground. On flattening out, his engine cut out and he had to land; on landing however his engine picked up and enabled him to again take off. He commenced to make for home, hopping along at a height of 5 to 20 feet and coming down at intervals when his engine failed. It was not long before the enemy Scouts saw that he was off and they kept swooping down and firing with both their guns. For about 10 miles this fight continued, the machines above keeping up a constant stream of fire, bullets were passing all round, but miraculously failed to hit the Pilot or his engine. At intervals, hostile parties on the ground were encountered who brought out machine guns and joined in the fight. Against these the Pilot was only able to reply by flying straight at the gun, which was invariably abandoned by its crew as the machine approached. He frequently had to land and taxi along the ground, and on one of these occasions he landed between 2 rows of bivouacs occupied by Germans, they were unarmed and having breakfast and were too surprised to attack him. The engine picked up again and he managed to proceed a little further, taking away a clothes-line with him. The enemy scouts did not cease to attack until after he had crossed their lines, and one of them even followed and made a final attack from a very low height. After dodging round a tree, our Pilot managed to get some parting rounds into him during a period when the engine picked up a little, and the enemy gave up the contest. So our Pilot, who was by this time more than wearied by the attentions of the enemy and his surprising adventures, was able to bring home his riddled bus in triumph.[21]

Lt. G.O. Coulson: Water color paintings of aerial combats, Palestine, 1918. [The paintings are reproduced in H.S. Gullett and C. Barrett, eds., Australia in Palestine, Sydney 1919, opposite pp. 94, 96]

A memorial stone at the Beersheba military cemetery. The inscription reveals that the monument was originally erected by Germans in commemoration of a British airman killed in action. [Photo: author]

The Australians bomb the airfield of Squadron 304 at Merhavya, 3 January 1918. [M 1255b]

Tabulation of the data contained in the weekly reports of Squadron 304 from February to September 1918 gives the following picture:[22]

	Feb.	Mar.	Apr.	May	June	July	Aug.	Sept. (1-12)
Combat flights	15	20	33	38	20	19	11	6
Hours in air	37:35	39:50	74:35	91:20	50:10	47:00	31:15	14:30
Aerial photos	161	162	460	714	537	458	279	143
Aerial combats	2	5	4	4	1	5	2	1
Bombs (in kg.)	225	500	338	750	500	550	-	-

Australians of the Imperial Camel Corps on sandhills at Rafah near the Egyptian-Palestinian border, 26 January 1918. [AWM B-1627; one of Frank Hurley's color photos]

An Australian crew loads bombs at the airfield near Julis [AWM B-1591]. The Australian squadron was stationed there from December 1917 to April 1918.

An Australian Light Horseman collecting anemones near Deir el-Balah, southwest of Gaza. [AWM B-1664; one of Frank Hurley's color photos]

The table points to the steady decrease in the squadron's activities after May 1918, a trend that starkly differs from the one emerging from the corresponding monthly reports of the Australian squadron:[23]

	Feb.	Mar.	Apr.	May	June	July	Aug.	Sept.
Reconnaissance:								
Strategical	28	48	47	29	42	37	31	53
Photographic	18	23	23	16	16	24	39	8
Hours in air	449	632	594	445	716	727	512	866
Aerial photos	507	518	609	367	365	524	959	387
Aerial combats						14	15	8
Bombing raids	6	17					1	140
Attacks on troops on ground			1	8	16	31	24	156

Below: Turkish cavalry in the Negev. [JNUL, TMA 4185, No. 85]

Bottom left: Von Heemskerck, commander of German aviators on the Palestinian front (at right), and Walz, commander of Bavarian Squadron 304. [M 1259]

Bottom right: Officers of Bavarian Squadron 304 at Merhavya. First from left, sitting: Fritz Berthold. [M 1266 h]

The decrease in activities was common to all the German squadrons, affected as they were by the growing qualitative and quantitative superiority of the British and Australian planes. On 6 June the commander of German aviators in the Palestinian theater, *Hauptmann* (Captain) Weyert, gave orders to use the remaining forces most sparingly, owing to the extremely limited number of flying personnel.[24] Squadrons 300 and 302 were constrained to cease all operational flights at the end of July, Squadron 301 at the end of August. By the beginning of September, the other squadrons had between them only 13 serviceable planes. Yet each of the two squadrons stationed west of the River Jordan, 303 and 304, had a 260 horsepower Rumpler C-IV capable of operating at an altitude of more than 5,000 meters – an altitude at which the British did not usually fly. German planes thus continued to cross the front line, but the British superiority was so overwhelming that on 3 September a senior German officer asked the commander-in-chief of the Turkish-German force in Palestine, General Liman von Sanders, to stop aerial reconnaissance above his sector of the front because the air combats, which ended repeatedly in a British victory, undermined the already low morale of his troops.[25]

As part of the preparations for the decisive British offensive scheduled for 19 September 1918, Allenby received two more squadrons, Nos. 144 and 145. In all he now had at his disposal seven squadrons totaling 105 airplanes (the Germans estimated the number at between 130 and 150). These played an important role in foiling most German attempts to cross the front line in the crucial weeks before the offensive, and the Turkish-German Command remained consequently unaware of Allenby's massive but effectively camouflaged concentration of five infantry and three cavalry divisions in the coastal sector of the front. The diary of Squadron 304 allows us to follow in detail the last activities of the Bavarian unit:

A crashed plane of Squadron 304. [M 1260g]

> 12 September 1918. *Hauptmann* Walz, the squadron commander, and *Leutnant* Kretschmann start at 06:20 for a long-range reconnaissance flight. Engine trouble south of Jaffa forces them to return. They observe an increase of camps in the coastal sector north of the Jaffa-Lydda line.
>
> 14 September 1918. An airplane flown by *Vizefeldwebel* Hoffmann and *Lt* Heidschuch starts at 10:50 for long-range reconnaissance, but is attacked already during approach near Jenin by two Bristol Fighters that force it to land. In the evening the machine flies back to base.
>
> 15 September 1918. Walz and Kretschmann succeed in carrying out the mission prevented on the previous day. They report an increased concentration of troops and material at Jerusalem, Latrun, Wadi es-Sarar, and Sarafand, and an increase in air power at Ramleh and Wadi es-Sarar. The flight has confirmed agent reports on "a partial withdrawal of cavalry in the coastal sector" [*sic*] as well as on regrouping.
>
> 16 September 1918. No long-range reconnaissance.
>
> 17 September 1918. No long-range reconnaissance.
>
> 18 September 1918. Hoffmann and Heidschuch start at 06:40 on long-range reconnaissance; the flight is cut short by a water main burst. They restart at 08:55, but strong headwind during approach prevents them from reaching the front line.
> According to intelligence agents and prisoners-of-war, the great offensive is to begin on 19 September.[26]

Turkish equipment captured by the British at Tulkarm. [AWM B-03502]

Allenby's offensive indeed started on that day. At 04:30, 385 British guns opened fire on the 24-kilometer-long coastal sector of the Turkish front, with two destroyers shelling objectives north of the mouth of Nahr el-Faliq. The fifteen-minute bombardment, the heaviest ever witnessed in the Palestinian theater, was immediately followed by the advance of some 35,000 infantry against the Turkish-German line held by some 8,000 men. The advance, faster at the coast and slower in the foothills, opened an ever-widening gap through which three cavalry divisions sped northward. At 04:30 the next day, 20 September, a British cavalry brigade attacked the Turkish-German general headquarters at Nazareth, some 70 kilometers northeast of the breached front. When another brigade seized El-'Affule about three hours later and still other cavalry units took Jenin and Beisan in the afternoon, the Turkish-German force in central Palestine was cut off from its rear. Only the difficult escape route eastward across the Jordan River fords remained open to it for the next four days or so. All of Palestine was in British hands within a week of the offensive's start, and Allenby could begin his drive on Damascus.

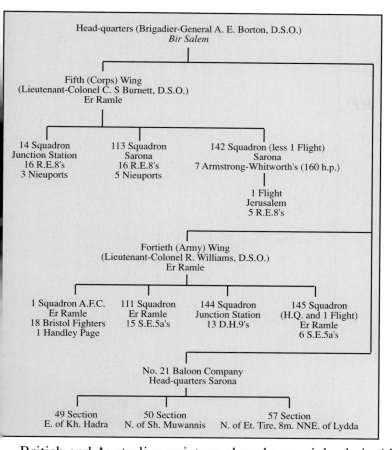

◄ *Order of battle of the Palestine Brigade, Royal Air Force, 19 September 1918* [H.A. Jones, The War in the Air, vol. 6, Oxford 1937, p. 209]

▲ *Guns and wagons of the Seventh Turkish Army along the Wadi al-Farʿah road, after British bombardment on 21 September 1918.* [YBZ: C.H. Lewton-Brain's collection]

British and Australian aviators played a crucial role in Allenby's offensive. In fact, it opened at 01:15 on 19 September, when a large two-engine Handley-Page bomber, with sixteen 112-pound bombs, attacked the central telephone exchange of the Turkish-German force at El-ʿAffule. (The pilot was Captain Ross M. Smith, an Australian who became famous a year later for making the first flight from England to Australia.) El-ʿAffule was bombed again in the morning and at noon of 19 September; also bombed that morning were the headquarters of the Seventh and Eighth Turkish Armies at Nablus and Tulkarm, as well as three secondary headquarters. As the British infantry advanced in the coastal plain, aviators of Squadron 113 on two occasions created smoke screens in front of them. Aviators of the Australian squadron, entrusted with strategic reconnaissance and bombing, reported on the advance of the British cavalry and on five different occasions that day, bombed and strafed the Turks who were attempting to escape the British infantry by taking the Tulkarm-Nablus road. Throughout the day, patrols of Squadrons 111 and 145 sat over the German airfields at Jenin and did not allow the Germans to take off. In fact, the only Germans who succeeded in flying over the battlefield on that crucial day were Hoffmann and Heidschuch of the Bavarian Squadron 304. The first time they took off at 09:05 and landed at 10:40, reporting two torpedo ships off ʿAthlit, "halfway between Jaffa and Haifa." The second time they took off at 11:50, got as far as Jaffa, and landed at 14:30 to report the "general impression" that the British were moving forward from their reserve positions...[27]

Perhaps still more outstanding was the role British aviators played two days later, on 21 September, when columns of the Seventh Turkish Army were attempting to retreat from Nablus by the Wadi el-Farʿa road, which descends to the Jordan Valley. An Australian dawn reconnaissance patrol spotted the troops and transport advancing along the road and alerted headquarters by wireless. A general bombing was ordered immediately, with two bombing planes to arrive over the target every three minutes and a bombing formation of six every half-hour. All seven squadrons serving under Allenby took part in the attack. The head of the column was bombed first, and soon the road became completely impassable for transport, with panic spreading and lorries, guns and wagons piling into one another (see photo top right). As H. A. Jones, author of the history of the Royal Air Force during World War I put it, thereafter "the attacks degenerated into a slaughter which made many pilots sick who took part."[28] Unbeknown to them, they were ushering in that twentieth-century scourge, the *Blitzkrieg*.

The line broken in September 1918 disappeared long ago and became forgotten; later wars and more recent fronts have taken its place in our minds. Almost all of those who took part in the fighting – Turks, British, Germans, Australians, Indians, Arabs, New Zealanders, Jews, Armenians, Austrians, French, Italians – are dead, their armaments long turned to junk. But the glass plates that some 200 observers had exposed to light enable us today to see the country as it was then.

Pilot, observer, and Bristol Fighter F.2B plane of the No. 1 Squadron, Australian Flying Corps. The pilot is Lt. Ross-Smith.
[AWM B-1633; one of Frank Hurley's color photos]

The Pictorial Confrontations

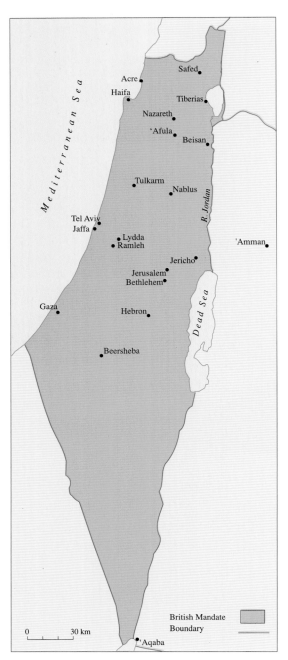

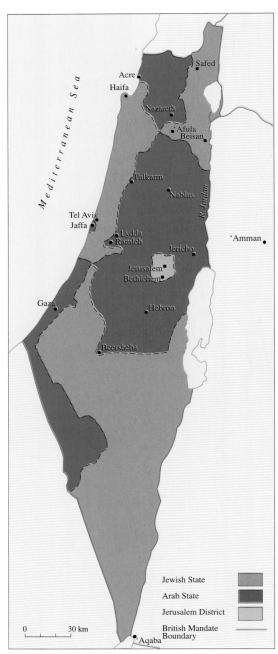

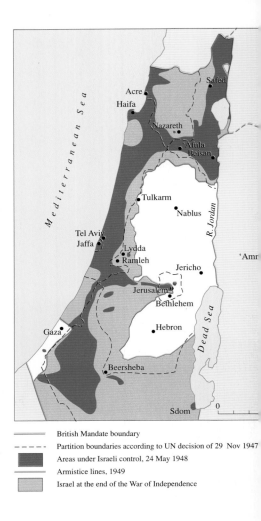

Israel's War of Independence, 1948-1949

British Mandate boundary
Partition boundaries according to UN decision of 29 Nov 1947
Areas under Israeli control, 24 May 1948
Armistice lines, 1949
Israel at the end of the War of Independence

Jewish State
Arab State
Jerusalem District
British Mandate Boundary

Palestine under the British Mandate, 1920-1948

*The United Nations partition plan,
29 November 1947*

Of the several thousand World War I photographs preserved in German, Australian, Israeli, and British collections, only about seventy are confronted here with their present-day counterparts. I believe that I owe my readers an explanation as to why I chose to focus on these seventy sites.

My principal consideration was to display the main types of contrast between 1917-18 views and present-day ones: an Arab village or town of 1917-18 representing the nucleus of a much larger present-day Arab village or town, whether in Israel, the Gaza Strip, or on the West Bank; a Jewish village that is now a town, with erstwhile paths and tracks transformed into streets and roads, and with only a few of the old buildings still to be seen; an Arab village, town, or quarter of 1917-18 transformed or obliterated by a Jewish village, town, or quarter now standing either in its place or nearby; an ancient site largely covered by houses in 1917-18 but now excavated; an ancient site still discernible in 1917-18 but now buried under houses; a town of 1917-18 virtually erased and replaced by modern buildings; a town standing largely unchanged but now surrounded by modern suburbs; well-nigh naked hills and mountains of 1917-18 now covered with trees; patches of desert, swamp, and uncultivated land now occupied by villages, fields or orchards; sand dunes of 1917-18 now covered by towns. I do not pretend to know the exact frequency or proportion in which these different types of past-to-present relations occurred, but I do believe that all of them are represented in this book. And they all attest to the immense transformation of the country between the end of World War I and the present – a transformation due mainly to Jewish, but also to Arab and British, activities. Indeed, when S. D. Goitein, the great historian and wit, was shown some of the old photographs, he quipped: "No land is more man-made than the land promised by God."

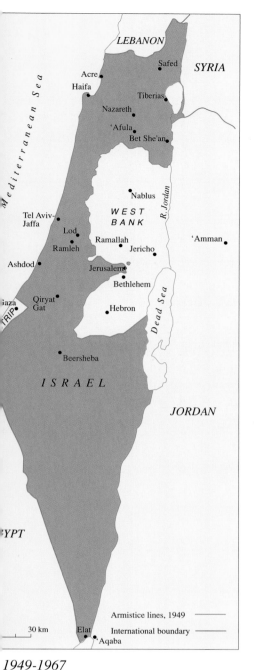

1949-1967

The Six-Day War, 5-10 June 1967

Armistice lines, 1949 ——————
International boundary ——————

Armistice lines, 1949 ——————
Cease-fire line, 1967 ——————
Jerusalem new municipal ——————
boundary, 1967

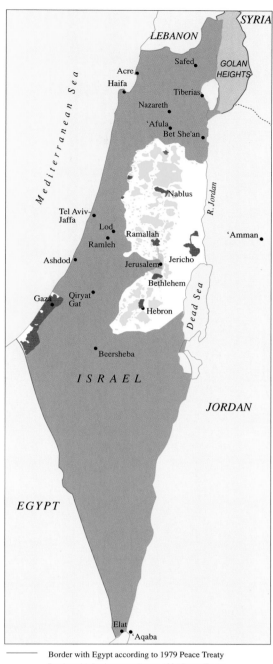

—————— Border with Egypt according to 1979 Peace Treaty
—————— Border with Jordan according to 1994 Peace Treaty

Palestinian Interim Self-Government Authority
(according to the 1994 and 1995 agreements between
Israel and the Palestine Liberation Organization)

Palestinian responsibility for internal security
and public order

Palestinian responsibility for public order for Palestinians;
Israeli overriding responsibility for security

The situation in mid-1998

My second objective in selecting the seventy pairs of photographs was to include examples from the country's various regions. This consideration led me to choose some old photographs of relatively low quality when they would extend the selection's geographical coverage. Of course, the inventories of the World War I photographic collections constituted a rigid constraint: the Galilee panhandle, most of western Galilee and the central and southern Negev, as well as several other sub-regions, are represented either not at all, or by single, low-quality photographs that cannot profitably be reproduced. I should add that the quest for broad coverage resulted in a selection whose geographical breakdown is quite different from that of the original collections, where photographs of the areas close to the 1918 Turkish-British front in central Palestine massively preponderate.

Whenever possible, I chose old photographs which include a natural or man-made feature that did not change much between 1917-18 and the present. These constants provide a convenient starting point for the do-it-yourself exercises in visual history here proposed, especially for readers unfamiliar with aerial photographs. I decided to refrain from interpreting the photographs by printing symbols or words on them, as I believe that this procedure harms and flattens the view. Aerial photographs constitute the main text of this book – and a text, visual or otherwise, should not be tampered with. Data on the provenance of each old photograph; the date, time and height of the shot; a brief identification of the main objects visible on it – all these are given outside the photograph itself. [A list of abbreviations representing the various collections appears on p. 204]. There is also information on the British conquest in 1917-18, which is intended to clarify whether the photograph was taken – from the photographer's viewpoint – over friendly or enemy territory, during a battle or not. For greater clarity, the sites are presented

Kluger's pilot: Emanuel Zurr, chief aviator of Aviron Co., with a signpost near the Dead Sea that carries a warning in Hebrew, English, Arabic and in a pictorial language designed for the illiterate.
[Dr. Miriam Zurr's album]

Zalman Leef, 1900-1950
[Nimrod Leef's album]

roughly according to the chronological order in which the British conquered them. Demographic data on the localities visible on the photographs – old and new – are also given, so as to allow the reader to make additional comparisons of his own.

Descriptions of several sites, written during World War I by members of various nationalities then living and fighting in the country, allow us to confront the visual texts of the aerial photographs with far more subjective, verbal ones. Ground photographs taken at the time provide a further comparative dimension. I chose to lay emphasis upon the years 1914-18, in the belief that this crucial period remains largely unknown.

When the time came to take the new aerial photographs, I had to decide whether they should be black and white or in color. Strict correspondence to the old photographs called for black and white. Yet the photographers of 1917-18 had employed the most advanced methods then available, and I felt that the new photographs, too, should be taken with the more advanced techniques of the present. I realize that this was a problematic decision, since the juxtaposition of an old black and white photo with a recent one in color may mislead an inexperienced observer into overestimating the increase in cultivation. But a closer study of such photos leads quite readily to a more accurate appraisal of such a change. I should also mention here that, owing to technical constraints, most of the new photographs are more oblique than the old ones. Most were taken from a height of 2,000 meters or less – and yet haze has impaired their sharpness much more than that of the old photographs, taken from altitudes more than twice as great! And while the World War I aviators had been able to photograph throughout the year, the denser haze of today well-nigh precluded photography during the summer months.

To allow for still more revealing exercises I have, in most instances, inserted roughly comparable aerial photographs from the 1930s, 1940s, 1950s, 1960s or 1970s, alongside the ones taken during World War I and very recently. Those from the 1930s were taken by Zoltán Kluger, a Jewish photographer who, having served as an aerial observer in the Austro-Hungarian air force during World War I, worked first in his native Hungary and then in Berlin, and after Hitler's rise to power came to Palestine and specialized in ground and aerial photography of recently established Jewish settlements.[29] The photos from the 1940s are from one of four sources: (a) the 1944-45 survey by the Royal Air Force, the first to cover all of Palestine from the air;[30] (b) a collection of photographs taken by the fledgling Jewish air force during Israel's War of Independence in 1948;[31] (c) the 1949 aerial survey of large parts of Israel, made by an Israeli-Dutch team headed by Zalman Leef;[32] and (d) photographs from Kluger's collection. All photographs from the 1950s, 1960s and 1970s were taken by the Survey of Israel. Since all these photos are black and white, they allow the observer to gauge the increase in cultivation by comparing them one to another, and thus they reduce still further the danger that the recent color photos might lead to an overestimate of that increase.

On the whole I chose to concentrate, on the one hand, on photos from the years 1944-49, so as to present the situation at the close of the British Mandate. This is why, whenever I had at my disposal a reproducible photo from 1948, I chose to print it; whenever I had the choice between a RAF or Leef photo, I preferred the latter on account of its decidedly superior quality. On the other hand, I decided to concentrate on the year 1967 and reproduce photos taken by the Survey of Israel immediately following Israel's victory in the Six-Day War of 5-10 June. This was the earliest date for which aerial photos of the West Bank and the Gaza Strip, conquered by Israel in that war, were available to me – and such photos show the situation at the conclusion of Jordanian or Egyptian rule over these areas. For consistency's sake, I chose 1967 photos for Israeli localities as well. Whenever I could not find a reproducible photo from that year, I selected one of a slightly later date for West Bank or Gaza Strip localities (or of a slightly earlier or later date for localities within Israel). And I confess that whenever there were suitable photographs by Kluger, I could not resist publishing them, even though they are not always easily alignable with those from World War I.

I believe that the inclusion of photographs from years between the end of World War I and the present facilitates perception of the changes that took place during this period. Yet I have decided to refrain from attempting to explain how and why these changes occurred. In other words, I do not intend to retell here in detail the story of Jewish efforts to establish a National Home under British auspices and of the Arab attempts to thwart them in order to retain the country's Arab character. Neither do I propose to relate here once again how and why the United Nations General Assembly voted on 29 November 1947 to establish in Palestine a Jewish and an Arab state as well as an internationalized Jerusalem; how Palestine's Arabs took up arms to foil this partition plan; how, upon the proclamation of the Jewish state on 14 May 1948,

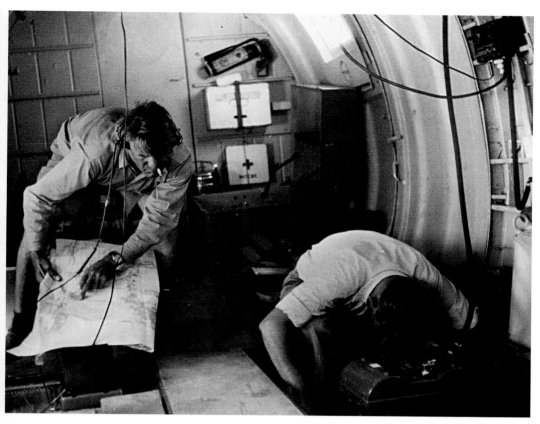

Arab armies invaded Palestine in an attempt to help the country's Arabs and nip the new state – Israel – in the bud; how Israel emerged victorious both from the struggle with Palestine's Arabs and from the war with the neighboring Arab states, and how some 700,000 Palestinian Arabs fled or were expelled during these hostilities. Nor do I propose to present an abbreviated version of the subsequent Middle Eastern conflict and of the more recent peace agreements, or of social and economic developments throughout the period. All this has been told and retold time and again, from many different points of view and with varying degrees of commitment to objectivity, and I trust that my readers are fairly familiar with the story's general outline. Obviously, were I to offer my own version of it, I would have had to use documentation of a kind quite different from that presented here, and a quite different book would have been the upshot.

My aim, I reiterate, is to allow the reader to confront, through the visual texts proffered by aerial photography, some of the physical changes that took place during this stormy century in a number of localities throughout the country. Yet in order to appreciate these changes one must have at least a rudimentary knowledge of the political fortunes of these localities. For instance, to comprehend the changes that occurred in the originally Arab quarters of Katamon or Baq'ah in Western Jerusalem, or in the Jewish quarter of Jerusalem's Old City, one must be aware of what happened in the city during Israel's War of Independence in 1948 and after the Six-Day War of 1967. Similarly, when confronting a sequence of aerial photographs of an Arab town or village, it is essential to know whether that town or village was, between 1948 and 1967, under Israeli, Jordanian, or Egyptian rule. I have resolved therefore to include maps that show basic political changes, and to supply some verbal information about the localities whose aerial photographs I chose to reproduce. Like the biblical Shunammite, "I dwell among mine own people," and I am therefore well aware that in some cases such information may be decried as fragmentary or tendentious; certainly some of it – especially that regarding the Palestinian exodus of 1948 – is based on incomplete documentation, allowing for conflicting interpretation of what happened. Such differing views, often rooted in preconceptions, exist of course with regard to many other issues as well.

Precisely the existence of such varying views and interpretations has prompted me to present the qualitatively different data – limited, yes, but more objective than other – that I believe aerial photography proffers. In these days of incipient Israeli-Palestinian reconciliation, I would like to hope that these data may help us better confront, comprehend and come to terms with our recent history, now so befogged by selective, self-righteous and often inflammatory "narratives." Perhaps they may also help men and women on each side to evolve some empathy with, or at least a more fair understanding of, the other side in the conflict, now hopefully waning, that has for so long troubled the land lying between the River Jordan and the Mediterranean Sea.

'Aqaba, Elat

This hitherto unknown oblique photograph of the head of the Gulf of 'Aqaba, taken from the east on 26 Aug 1918, forms part of the private collection of Erich Steiner, acting commander of German Squadron 305. Made during a bombing and strafing raid on the British, it shows the village of 'Aqaba with its two short jetties at the eastern (near) side of the head of the gulf. British tents can be seen on the sands north of the gulf. A triangle of vegetation adjoins the gulf's northwestern corner, and mountains rise abruptly from the gulf's far shore. The line that runs along the northern shore and then ascends the ridge and turns left is the *Darb el-Hajj*, the pilgrims' road from Egypt to Mecca.

The Arab Hejaz Army with Captain T.E. Lawrence ('Lawrence of Arabia') wrested 'Aqaba from the Turks on 6 Jul 17. It soon became the base of the Arab Northern Army under Emir Faysal, and two months later a few British planes known as 'X Flight' were stationed there in permanent attachment to the Arab forces.

1918

1945

At the time the RAF shot its vertical photograph on 17 May 1945, the area was about equally divided between Trans-Jordan and Palestine, both of which were, though in varying degrees, under British tutelage. The border between the two coincided roughly with the eastern limit of the vegetation triangle. A comparison with the photograph from 1918 shows that an anchorage was constructed just north of 'Aqaba's northern jetty. The straight dark line on the sands northeast of the harbor is a road that runs in the direction of Ma'an.

In the final act of the War of Independence, Israel's Negev and Golani brigades on 10 Mar 49 reached the gulf's northwestern corner. The photograph taken by the Survey of Israel in Nov 1956 shows the new Israeli town, anchorage, and landing ground of Elat near the gulf's northwestern corner, and the considerably larger Jordanian 'Aqaba, expanding mainly north of its original nucleus. The armistice line between Israel and Jordan corresponds to the former border between Palestine and Trans-Jordan.

1995

1956

Our taking of the color photograph of the area on 26 Feb 1995 was made possible by the Israeli-Jordanian peace treaty, signed a few months earlier, and by the goodwill of various Israeli and Jordanian officials; ours was the first Israeli plane permitted to cross the border and, from a spot above the mountains east of 'Aqaba, to take a shot that would correspond to the one Erich Steiner had taken 77 years earlier.

The photograph shows that 'Aqaba has vastly expanded since 1956. The old, densely built part of the town – which, in its turn, constitutes an extension of the village seen on the older photographs – differs markedly from the planned, rectangular quarters that now cover most of the sands extending along the Jordanian part of the gulf's northern shore. The fortress (or fortified khan), originally erected by the Mamluks in the early 16th century, stands out near the western end of the erstwhile village, and the large, new harbor extends south of it. The Israeli town of Elat (pop. 38,600 in 1995) looms at the far end of the gulf. Artificial lagoons, one of them surrounded by hotels, extend landward from Israel's part of the gulf's northern shore. Regularly laid out groves and saltpans occupy much of the triangular area that appeared in the 1918 photograph as covered by vegetation. Some groves are visible on the Jordanian side of the border (near the middle of the photograph's right-hand margin).

A German air raid on ʿAqaba, 26 August 1918

▶ *Steiner's route: Derʿa-ʿAqaba-ʿUneyzeh-Derʿa. Numbers 1-5 on the map show locations of sites whose aerial photographs appear on this and the following page.*

One of the most daring exploits of the air war that took place in the Near Eastern theater in the years 1916-18 has been almost entirely forgotten; it can now be reconstructed through some photographs from Erich Steiner's private collection and through some of his personal documents.

Steiner (1883-1943) was a man of varied interests and a checkered career. He served in the German infantry from 1904 onward, and in the years 1911-12 undertook study trips in Germany's African colonies. Upon the outbreak of World War I he fought with a rifle battalion on the French front and was promoted to Hauptmann *(captain) at the end of 1915. In July 1917 he received training as an aerial observer and subsequently served in this capacity on the Romanian front. In March 1918 he was transferred to Squadron 302, which was stationed at that time near El-ʿAffule. On 10 Apr 18 Steiner shot down a British airplane near Kafr Qasim; a photograph of its wreckage figures in his collection (see p. 25, bottom). On 27 July he was transferred to Derʿa and appointed acting commander of Squadron 305, with which he served (with one short interruption) until the end of the war and of which he became commander on 2 Oct 18. After the war he was active as officer, farmer, author, and aviator. He intended to publish a book about his Levantine experiences and prepared a portfolio of aerial and ground photographs that were to illustrate it, but the book's draft has not survived. In the wake of a serious brush with the law, Steiner went traveling and in 1938 settled down in Danzig, then a free city under League of Nations protection. His fate under the subsequent German occupation is not known. He died in the city's police prison on 29 Aug 43, the official cause of death being* Herzmuskelschädigung *(impairment of the heart muscle).*[33]

Little was known until now about the activities of Squadron 305, the only all-German air unit active east of the Jordan River. Its base was at Derʿa, near the junction of the Hejaz railway with the Samakh-El-ʿAffule-Haifa line. From February 1918 onward, the squadron strafed and bombed concentrations of Arab rebels,

▼ *The town of Derʿa (now in southern Syria, a few km north of the Jordanian border). The photograph was taken by Squadron 305 on 4 Mar 18 from an altitude of 2,000 m.*

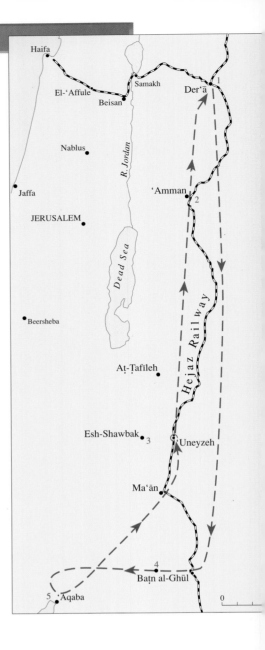

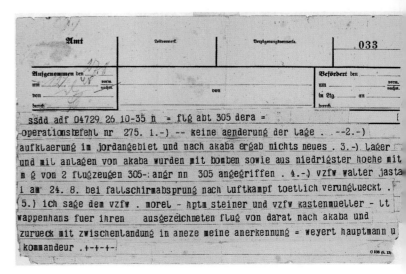

H ans-Erich von Tzschirner-Tzschirne, governor of Turkish ʿAqaba in the early months of World War I, relates that the place consisted of about one hundred mud huts, with gardens lying between them and the sea. Of the more than ten wells, only two provided sweet water. According to T. E. Lawrence, at the time of its conquest on 6 Jul 17, ʿAqaba was in ruins. "Repeated bombardments by French and English warships had degraded the place to its original rubbish. The poor houses stood about in a litter, dirty and contemptible, lacking entirely the dignity which the durability of their time-challenging bones conferred on ancient remains. We wandered into the shadowed grove of palms, at the very break of the splashing waves....Green dates loaded the palms overhead. Their taste, raw, was nearly as nasty as the want they were to allay. Cooking left them still deplorable."[35]

moving at one point to ʿAmman so as to be closer to its operational theater. On 1 July it undertook a reconnaissance flight to ʿAqaba. These activities continued after Steiner's arrival. Three of his photographs document aerial attacks of encampments near Esh-Shawbak, at At-Tafileh, and west of Maʿan. Years later, in the margins of his copy (in German translation) of T.E. Lawrence's description of a German plane that had circled over Lawrence and his men near El-Azraq on the morning of 9 Sep 18, Steiner was to scribble: *"Ich selbst mit Aufnahmen, Führer Morel"* (Myself taking photographs; pilot, Morel).[34]

The culmination of Steiner's activities was the bombing and strafing raid of ʿAqaba on 26 Aug 18, which he led in person and which was to earn him German, Ottoman and Austro-Hungarian decorations. The distance from Derʿa to ʿAqaba is some 360 km as the crow flies, but both of the planes that took part in the raid returned to Derʿa safely.

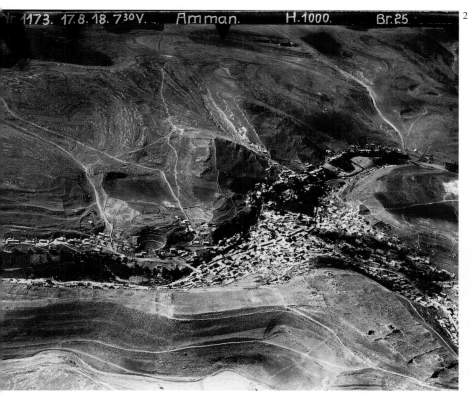

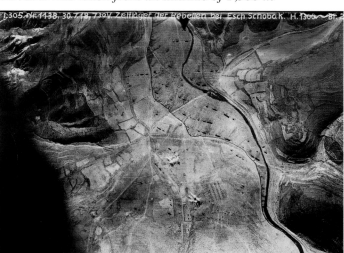

◀ The town of 'Amman (now capital of the Hashemite Kingdom of Jordan), with remains of the Roman theater just left of center. This photograph was taken by Squadron 305 on 17 Aug 18 from an altitude of 1,000 m.

▼ A camp of the Arab Northern Army near Esh-Shawbak, bombed by Squadron 305 at 7:30 a.m. on 30 Jul 18. This appears to be the only aerial photograph of an Arab camp during the 'Desert Revolt' against the Turks. It was taken from an altitude of 1,300 m

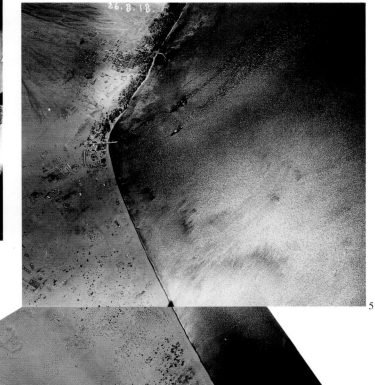

▲ A stretch of the desert photographed by Steiner on his way to 'Aqaba on 26 Aug 18; the second plane participating in the raid is visible left of center. The location of this picture is given as "Mountainous region west of Batn el-Ghul." It was taken from an altitude of 2,500 m.

▶ To present a fuller view of the gulf's north-eastern corner, we combined two of the photographs Steiner took during his raid. The upper photo shows the village of 'Aqaba and its two jetties. Two British ships are steaming toward the northern jetty. The large quadrangle flanked by round towers, on the southern edge of the village, is the originally Mamluk fortress. The lower photo shows three concentrations of tents on the sands adjoining the northern shore of the Gulf of 'Aqaba: two near the left margin and the third – which served the British 'X Flight' – near the center. Note the configuration near the upper left corner, which may conceal some ruins.

◀ 26 Aug 18, 10:35 p.m. Weyert, the commander of German aviators in the Palestinian theater, reports that two planes of Squadron 305 attacked camps and military installations at 'Aqaba with bombs and machine guns "from the lowest altitude"; he expresses his appreciation of the "outstanding flight" of Steiner and his men from Der'a to 'Aqaba and back, with an intermediate landing at Aneze [= 'Uneyzeh].

Beersheba

In 1900 the Turks erected Beersheba as their administrative center in the Negev Desert. The undated oblique photograph from Fritz Groll's private collection, which shows the town from the northeast, was probably taken in 1917 by German Squadron 300. Beersheba's Turkish railway station is in the foreground. (The railway reached the town in 1915, in preparation for the Turkish advance on the Suez Canal). The mosque, three large public buildings, and a garden are right of center. The town with its planned, straight streets is surrounded by military camps.

On 31 Oct 17 the British took the Turks and Germans completely by surprise when they attacked Beersheba with four divisions that had succeeded in reaching the town's immediate vicinity without being detected. The day-long battle ended with the 4th Australian Light Horse Brigade galloping over fences and trenches and, despite machine-gun and rifle fire, on into Beersheba. The town's conquest signaled the collapse of the Turks' Gaza-Beersheba front.[36]

1917

1949

The vertical photograph taken by Zalman Leef's team on 24 Sep 1949 shows that Arab Beersheba expanded, mainly on a northeast-southwest axis, in continuation of the original Turkish gridiron. The Turkish railway track is still visible in the foreground, though no longer in use. The British military cemetery, in which soldiers who fell during the battles of 1917-18 are buried, is the rectangle near the photograph's right-hand margin.

On 21 Oct 48, mounting a surprise attack from the north, three battalions of Israel's Negev and Eighth brigades succeeded in wresting Beersheba from an Egyptian battalion whose headquarters were in the old Turkish railway station. The capture of Beersheba lifted the five-months-long siege of two Israeli settlements east of the town and isolated the Egyptian forces in the Hebron area. Most of Beersheba's inhabitants fled to Hebron or Gaza; the rest were expelled to Gaza a few days after the conquest.[37]

1994

1968

Beersheba became a large Jewish city, situated mostly north of the original gridiron – the 'Old Town' – which appears in the upper right corner of the photograph taken by the Survey of Israel on 19 Jul 1968. The line once drawn by the Turkish railway is largely followed by the main road leading to the southern Negev. The new Israeli railway can be seen in the lower left corner.

The photograph we took on 26 Feb 1994 shows the 'Old Town' with some of the new quarters surrounding it.

Population:

1915	**c.3,000**	(mostly Arabs)
1945	**5,570**	(Arabs)
1968	**72,000**	(Jews)
1995	**152,600**	(Jews)

47

▶ *Combining two photos from Fritz Groll's album, both taken from the mosque's minaret, we get a panoramic view of Turkish Beersheba. The governor's residence is at left; the garden is at right.*

▲ *Our color photo, taken from the minaret, shows the governor's residence – now a part of the local museum – and one of the Old Town's high-rises.*

Contemporary appreciations of Turkish Beersheba differed widely.

Jamal Pasha, the Turkish commander of Syria and Palestine, wrote in memoirs published in 1920: "Especially noteworthy are the buildings which I ordered erected in Bir Seba [Beersheba] on the edge of the desert, as well as the public gardens, the small forests, the mills, the agricultural experimental stations I created there. I introduced electric light to Bir Seba, and the bases' workshops were operated by electricity. At each place like Hafir, Kuseime, and elsewhere were built pretty stone structures, and kitchen- and pleasure-gardens were created, also tree nurseries for afforestation. A professor of the agricultural school 'Rischon le Zion' [mistake for: 'Miqve Israel'] near Jaffa, who served as agricultural adviser, and a number of graduates of this school who were working under this agricultural adviser, went to the greatest trouble on that score."[38]

◀ *The airfield of German Squadron 300.*

The first Turkish military train arrives in Beersheba, 1915.

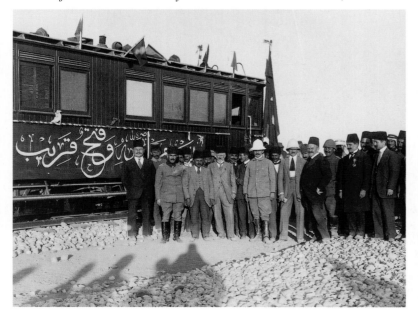

Captured British aviators, with remains of their plane, surrounded by officers and men of Squadron 300.

Sven Hedin, the noted Swedish explorer of Central Asia, arrived in Beersheba in August 1916 as Jamal Pasha's guest. He wrote: Until the war broke out, Bir es-Seba – or 'The Seven Wells' – was a miserable hole; now it has suddenly become an important base....When the worst heat was over, the [Turkish] colonel and the government surveyor, Dr. Schumacher, took me on a tour of the town, which is springing forth out of the desert at an American pace. We visited the various buildings on the base, the electric stations, the factories and workshops, the printing office, the bazaar, the hotel, the parks and gardens – which of course have not yet grown much – and the ice factory - the most beneficial establishment in this heat. Then we visited the agricultural school, the motor-driven pumping plants, and the immense reservoirs, at which water is distributed to camels, horses, asses, and mules. Finally we visited the hospital, in which 400 sick were lying at the time, cared for by Austrian physicians and nurses.

Bir es-Seba's climate, while not exactly unhealthy, is very unpleasant. The region is very windy, the desert sandy, the soil broken up because of the heavy traffic, and no vegetation offers protection from the suffocating dust clouds that roll from all sides into the burning hot streets."[39]

Quite different were the impressions of Lt.-Col. Preston, who took part in the town's conquest: "The house of the enemy commander....was one of the fine stone buildings, of which there were a number, surrounding a large public garden, and which had been built by the Germans during the war. The whole of this modern portion of the town appeared to have been built for propaganda purposes, or like the cities of lath and plaster which are run up in a few days for cinematograph productions. From time to time articles on the war in the East appeared in the German papers, generally synchronising with some reverse on the Western Front. In these articles, which were lavishly illustrated, Beersheba figured under headings such as 'the Queen City of the Prairies.' Apparently, in order to supply the necessary pictures, the Germans had laid out a large public garden, and built around it a series of imposing public buildings, including a Governor's house, Government offices, hospital, barracks, mosque, and even an hotel. The surrounding country abounds in a species of hard white limestone admirably suited for building, and all the houses were built of this and roofed with red tiles. They were ranged round the square, like four rows of stiff white soldiers with red helmets, and were so sited that any number of photographs could be taken from various positions, each showing a different view, and each hiding the real town behind the brand new German architecture. But once behind these houses, a shocking contrast met the eye. Here was the real Beersheba, a miserable collection of filthy mud hovels, huddled shrinkingly as though trying to hide their shabbiness from their gorgeous neighbours. The place in the centre was conspicuously labelled 'Bier Garten,' and was laid out with a number of little paths in an exact, geometrical pattern. The flower-beds supported a few dusty shrubs and a quantity of those hideous 'everlastings' so dear to the Teuton heart. All the buildings were laid out exactly facing the four points of the compass, except the mosque, which, in deference to Moslem prejudices, had been built with its *mihrab* turned towards Mecca, and consequently was lamentably askew. The Huns [=Germans] had taken their revenge, however, by garnishing the windows with German stained glass of an ugliness so startling that the Australians vowed their horses shied at it!"[40]

Morning routine at the base of Squadron 300; Fritz Groll at center.

Bedouin women selling oranges and an aviator of German Squadron 300.

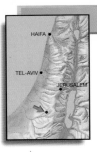

Edh-Dhahiriya

The road from Hebron to Beersheba, constructed in 1915 by the Turks in preparation for their advance on the Suez Canal, is the bright strip that runs upward from the bottom margin of the Bavarian photo (this is how photographs of Bavarian Squadron 304 will henceforth be referred to) of 13 Jul 1918. Almost all houses of the Arab village of Edh-Dhahiriya are to the right of the road, most of them on a hill that appears in the photo's upper part. The bright circles of the village's threshing floors stand out to the left of the road. One orchard can be discerned to the right of the village's center, and another in the *wadi* (dry river bed) near the photo's lower left corner. Three elongated buildings, apparently Turkish barracks, stand to the left (east) of the road.

1918

▼ *Some villagers and houses of Edh-Dhahiriya, 1918.*

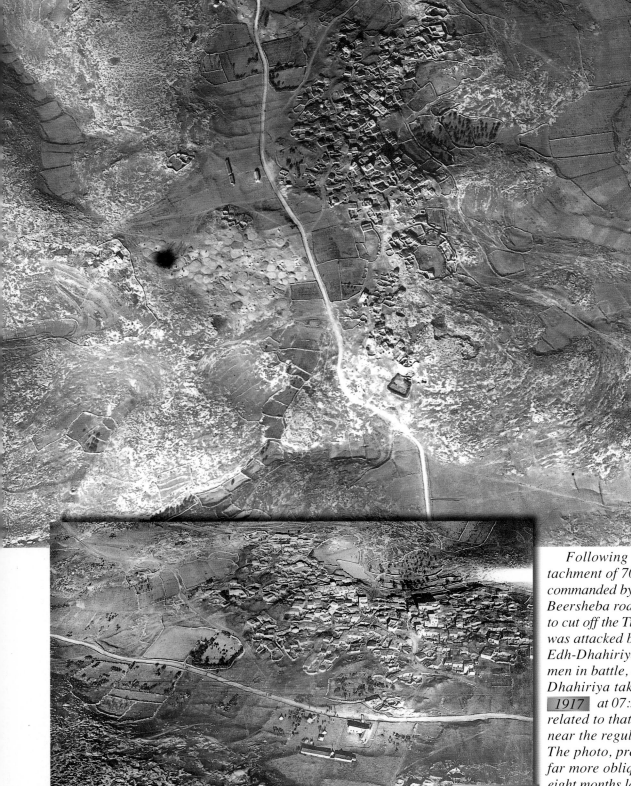

1917

Following the British capture of Beersheba, a detachment of 70 British camelry and some Arab scouts commanded by Lt.-Col. Newcombe blocked the Hebron-Beersheba road north of Edh-Dhahiriya in an attempt to cut off the Turks' retreat. On 2 Nov 17 the detachment was attacked by Germans from Hebron and Turks from Edh-Dhahiriya, and Newcombe, having lost 20 of his men in battle, decided to surrender. The photo of Edh-Dhahiriya taken by German Squadron 303 on 2 Nov 1917 at 07:30 hours may document Turkish activities related to that attack: it shows a large number of men near the regularly laid out buildings east of the road. The photo, preserved in Rengstorf's collection, being far more oblique than the one taken by the Bavarian eight months later, reveals the dimensions of the houses, some of them two-storied.

1994

The RAF photo of 16 Jan 1945 shows the large police station constructed by the British on the northern outskirts of the village. The rectangular building, topped by a small dome, that stands in the area where the threshing floors used to be, is Edh-Dhahiriya's mosque. There are some houses to the left of the Hebron-Beersheba road.

Our oblique color photo of 26 Feb 1994 shows the further expansion of Edh-Dhahiriya. It also accentuates the difference between the low brownish houses in the original, densely crowded part of the village and the taller houses in the newer parts, many of which are built of bright stone. A minaret stands to the left of the mosque.

Population:	
1922	2,266
1945	3,760
1967	4,875
1996	14,643

1945

1967

The photo of 18 Jun 1967, taken a few days after the Israeli conquest of the area in the Six-Day War, shows Edh-Dhahiriya on both sides of the Hebron-Beersheba road, with extensions branching out in several directions. Several clumps of trees can be seen.

The Abu-Hureira redoubt – Tidhar

The large river bed at the center of this undated German photograph, probably taken by Squadron 300 in   1917,   is Wadi esh-Sheri'a. The Gaza-Beersheba road runs across the middle of the picture from left to right and crosses the wadi near Tell Abu-Hureira, the ancient mound that served as a main Turkish redoubt along the Gaza-Beersheba front. The long, straight diagonal close to the right margin is a Turkish field railway; Turkish trenches can be seen left of center and also elsewhere. Several fields that appear to have been worked with threshing machines – by local Bedouins or by Arabs from Gaza – are visible in the lower half of the photo as well as near its left margin.

The British conquered the redoubt on 7 Nov 17. The Bedouins of the region believed that the Turks lost the battle as punishment for having cut down a tree of the holy place atop the mound.[41]

1917

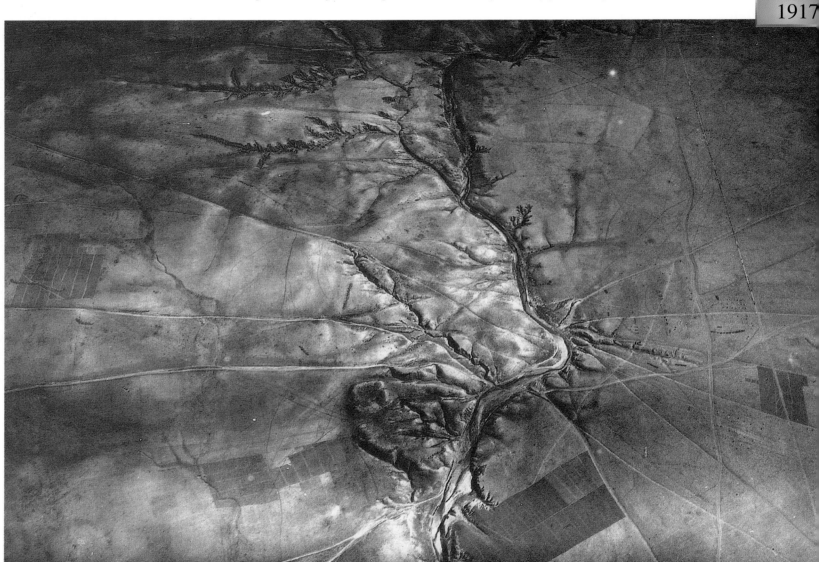

1945

C apt. John More, of the 53rd (Welsh) Division, took part in the fighting in this area in November 1917. In his memoirs he wrote: "In spite of the barren appearance of the country around Beersheba a considerable quantity of corn was grown – as also around Gaza. It seems a pity that the waters of the Jordan are not utilised to irrigate this tract of country as well as other parts; a vast undertaking no doubt, but not impossible."[42]

The RAF photo of 14 Mar   1945   shows most of the area under cultivation. Hangars of a British World War II landing ground appear in the upper right corner. The photo reveals that many more Turkish trenches were dug after the German aviators had taken their picture and before the British captured the redoubt. It discloses also that the first British paving of the Turkish Gaza-Beersheba road included a sharp bend near the wadi but that later they built a new stretch that crossed the wadi in a straight line.

Zalman Leef's photograph of 26 Oct   1949   shows almost the entire area uniformly ploughed by Israeli tractors.

1994

1949

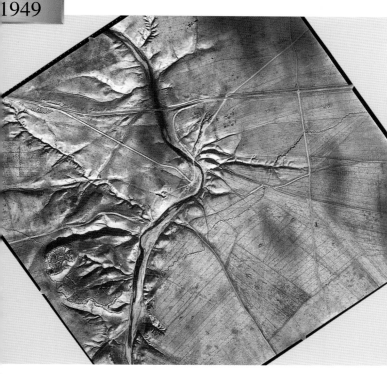

Our photograph of 26 Feb 1994 shows a further expansion of cultivation. Only a few remnants of the Turkish trenches can now be seen along the edges of the ancient mound. The tiny bright rectangle at its summit is the tomb of Abu Hureira, a companion of the Prophet Muhammad.

1966

The Survey of Israel photo of 23 Jul 1966 shows the change that took place in the area after the foundation, in the early 1950s, of several Jewish villages. One of them, Tidhar, is partially seen near the upper margin; its fields differ markedly in layout from the ones they superseded. The Gaza-Beersheba road is lined with trees. The ancient mound, now renamed Tel Haror, forms part of an area that is being afforested.

Tidhar and the neighboring villages of Brosh and Te'ashur are named after Isaiah 41:19: "I will plant the pine [in Hebrew, brosh] on the barren heath, side by side with fir [tidhar] and box [te'ashur]." The wadi is called now Nahal Grar. Since the completion of the National Water Carrier in 1965, the area is irrigated by water channeled from the River Jordan.

Population:		
Tidhar	1966	**373**
	1995	**198**

▲ A present-day photo show
Bedouin tents and remains of
Turkish World War I trenches
east of Tidhar.

▲ Turkish soldiers in trenches of
the Abu-Hureira redoubt.

▶ An anti-aircraft gun and its
Turkish crew near Tell Esh-Sheri'a,
east of the Abu-Hureira redoubt.

▶ A Turkish field
kitchen at the move
near Tell Esh-
Sheri'a.

▼ Distributing
food to Turkish
soldiers in the
Negev.

▼ Turkish
soldiers eating from
a common bowl
placed on an
improvised sand
table.

▲ *One of Frank Hurley's color photographs shows squadrons of the 4th Australian Light Horse Brigade among the ruins of Gaza; the tall structure in the upper right corner is the Great Mosque's destroyed minaret.*

Edwin Blackwell and Edwin C. Axe, NCOs with an artillery battery of the 54th (East Anglian) Infantry Division, passed through Gaza soon after its conquest on 7 Nov 17. In their memoirs they wrote: "The town, from which all the civilian population had been evacuated long since, was found to be in a deplorable condition. The greater part of the woodwork of the houses had been removed for use in the trenches or for firewood. Immense damage was effected by explosions of Turkish ammunition dumps collected in the mosques and public buildings, and detonated by British gunfire."[43]

▲ *An Austro-Hungarian howitzer in firing position near Gaza.*

▲ *A British field kitchen. (The Germans found this photo among the possessions of a British officer who had been killed in action).*

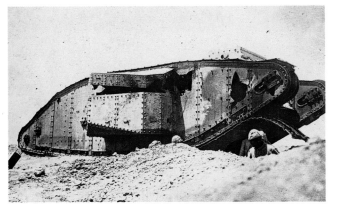

◀ *A knocked-out British tank above a forward Turkish trench southeast of Gaza.*

Gaza

One of the largest towns of Palestine at the beginning of the century, Gaza suffered heavy destruction during World War I. The British attacked the town twice, in March and April 1917, but failed to conquer it. In the April attack they made use of eight Mark I tanks; these were the first armored vehicles to appear on Palestinian soil, but their impact was slight and one of them, knocked out by a direct hit, remained standing above a forward Turkish trench southeast of the town (see photo on p. 55, bottom). Following the conquest of Beersheba, and after bombardment from land and sea, the Gaza defenses were assailed for a third time, and when the British finally entered the town on 7 Nov 17, many houses were mere shells.

The Bavarian photo of 25 May 1918 shows Gaza from the southwest. Of the two lines that run closely parallel in the right half of the photo and seem to converge at midpoint, the right, grayish one is the new British railroad leading from Egypt to Lydda; the left, brighter line is the main coastal road. The older, and larger, part of Gaza lies to the left (i.e., west) of this road. The town's Great Mosque – originally a twelfth-century crusader parish church – is the large building just below and to the left of the photo's center; its northern part forms a diagonal with the surrounding buildings. The mosque was severely damaged during the fighting (see photo on p. 55, top).

The RAF photo of 10 Jan 1945 indicates that Gaza's built-up area grew only moderately under the British Mandate, the main additions occurring in the center, southeast of the Great Mosque. The straight wide street that in 1918 led northwestward from the Great Mosque now runs also southeastward and links with the main coastal road. It has become the town's main street.

1993

1967

Our photo of 11 Dec 1993 shows the original nucleus of Gaza. A second photo shows a part of the Shati refugee camp.

Gaza, where the Palestinian uprising, or Intifada, started in December 1987, became the seat of the Palestinian Self-Government Authority in the wake of the Gaza-Jericho agreement of 4 May 1994 between Israel and the Palestine Liberation Organization.

photo of 10 Jul 1967, taken by the Survey of Israel one after the conclusion of the Six-Day War which brought Gaza Israeli control, shows the immense expansion of the town since an expansion resulting mainly from the influx of Arab refugees reas that became Israel in 1948. There are blocks of houses on ide of the main thoroughfare – 'Omar el-Mukhtar Street – almost way to the sea. The small, regularly laid out dwellings near the constitute the Shati refugee camp.

1993

Population:	
1922	**17,480**
1945	**34,170**
1967	**118,272**
1996	**282,894**

Deir Suneid – Yad Mordekhay

1918

1945

The mosaic we prepared from two Bavarian photos of 15 Apr 1918 shows an area about 12 km northeast of Gaza. Two lines run roughly parallel to each other in the upper photo: the lower is the main coastal road, the upper is the new railway that the British, after the capture of Gaza, laid beside the line that the Turks had previously constructed in order to supply their troops on the Gaza front. The British standard-gauge railway reached this area on 27 Nov 17, and a reloading station was set up to transfer supplies to the narrower Turkish line, soon reactivated all the way to Lydda. The dark area between the road and the railway near the picture's right margin is the Arab village of Deir Suneid, with some of its fields enclosed by hedges. A major British supply depot can be seen just north of the village, with several tent camps around it. A train stands on a siding that turns southeastward. The bright areas near the lower right corner of the picture form part of the coastal sand dunes; the river bed that snakes along their edge is that of Wadi el-Hesi, a tributary of which, Wadi 'Abd, can be seen in the center.

The RAF photo of 1945 shows, on a hill north of Deir Suneid, the *kibbutz* (communal settlement) Yad Mordekhay, founded in 1943 and named after Mordekhay Aniliewicz, commander of the Warsaw Ghetto Uprising against the Nazis. Zoltán Kluger's oblique photo of 1947 shows the young kibbutz from the south, dominated by its water tower.

On 19 May 48 the Egyptians, advancing from Gaza in the direction of Tel Aviv, attacked Yad Mordekhay, defended by 130 men and women. The battle, in which the Egyptians employed two infantry battalions, Bren gun carriers, armored cars, and airplanes, lasted for five days. With 23 of their number killed and 34 wounded, and with an Egyptian force having prevented the major part of a reinforcement from reaching the kibbutz, the remaining defenders retreated in the early hours of 24 May; three were captured and apparently murdered. When the area was retaken by the Israeli army on 6 Nov 48, the kibbutz was largely in ruins; some of its possessions and tools were found in neighboring Arab villages. The inhabitants of those villages left with the retreating Egyptian troops or were expelled by the advancing Israeli ones.[45]

1994

The vertical Survey of Israel photograph taken on 10 Jul 1967 and our color photograph of 26 Feb 1994 show the rebuilt kibbutz as well as the site of Deir Suneid, which ceased to exist in 1948.

1947

1967

Population:				
	1922	1945	1948	1995
Deir Suneid	356	730		
Yad Mordekhay			298	654

59

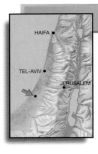

Julis – Hodiyya

The Arab village of Julis, about 27 km northeast of Gaza, appears at the center of this photo from Erich Steiner's collection, taken by aviators of German Squadron 302 on 23 Nov 1917 – that is, a fortnight after the advancing British had conquered the area. The line that connects the points marked A and B on the margins is the railway the Turks had laid to supply their troops on the Gaza front; the line connecting points C and D is a stretch of the Latrun-Gaza road constructed in 1915, on the initiative of the Turkish authorities, by several Jewish contractors (among them the future mayor of Tel Aviv, Meir Dizengoff).

1917

1918

A Bavarian photo of 21 Jan 1918 shows, wes of Julis, the airfield of the 1st Squadron of the Austra lian Flying Corps. According to the squadron's wa diary for January 1918, "This aerodrome is undulating and is situated in a small ridge of hills which stanc higher than the surrounding country, consequently i drains well and on no occasion when weather was oth erwise favourable was it impossible to carry out the work owing to having wet ground. The aerodrome anc site is sandy - the surrounding flat country is a dark clay soil and very sticky."[46]

The RAF photo of 27 Jan 1945 shows that, ir the immediate vicinity of Julis, the new British roac follows the line of the dismantled Turkish railway, thus by-passing the village from the north. The ways leading north and south from the village are paved. Althougł the population of Julis more than doubled since 1945 (see data below), there has been no marked increase ir the village's built-up area. (The same observation ap plies also to other Arab villages).

1994

1966

When the 3rd Battalion of Israel's Giv'ati Brigade advanced on Julis during the night of 10/11 Jun 48 and seized the junction to its west, the villagers fled. The Israeli move formed part of attempts at improving positions a few hours before the first Arab-Israeli truce was to take effect. About the same time the Egyptians seized another junction 4 km south of Julis, seeking to cut Israel's link to the Negev. Gamal Abdul Nasser – staff officer of the Egyptian 6th Battalion at the time, and Egypt's future president – decries in his memoirs the Egyptians' poorly coordinated attempt to conquer Julis on 6 Jul 48.[47]

1945

In 1949 the Jewish village of Hodiyya was founded just west of the erstwhile Arab one. The photo of 23 Jul 1966 shows the houses of Hodiyya spread out regularly on either side of the village street; radiating outward, there is a shed beyond each house and a rectangular field beyond each shed. The rest of the area shown on the photo is also under cultivation, but the parcelling differs in most cases from the pre-1948 one. The one stretch of land that is not cultivated is the site of Julis and its immediate vicinity.

Our photo of 26 Feb 1994 shows the growth of Hodiyya. What was formerly Julis is now covered by a grove.

Population				
	1922	1945	1966	1995
Julis	481	1,030		
Hodiyya			398	419

Sawafir – Shafir

On this Bavarian photo from 21 Jan the narrow line connecting the points marked A and B on the margins is the Turkish railway leading to the Gaza front; the ribbon of lines linking points C and D represents the irregular tracks of the Latrun-Gaza road. The road passes two Arab villages, Sawafir el-Gharbiya (western Sawafir) at center and Sawafir esh-Sharqiya (eastern Sawafir) to the left of it. A third village, Sawafir esh-Shamaliya (northern Sawafir), appears at lower left. The bright area between eastern and western Sawafir served in October 1917 as an airfield for German Squadron 302.[48]

The 2nd Australian Light Horse Brigade took the Sawafir villages on 9 Nov 17, during the great northward drive of Allenby's forces that followed the collapse of the Turkish Gaza-Beersheba front. On 21 Nov 17, during the British offensive aimed at Jerusalem, General Allenby positioned his forward headquarters at western Sawafir.

1918

Zalman Leef's photo of 23 Oct 1949 attests to the considerable growth of eastern and western Sawafir under British rule. Along this stretch, the British Latrun-Ascalon road follows closely the line of the Turkish road. At the time the photo was taken, all three Sawafir villages had been deserted for more than a year, the inhabitants having fled on 18 May 48 when the 1st Battalion of the Giv'ati Brigade conquered the villages in an attempt to secure the road to the Negev. In 1949 three Jewish villages were founded in the area. Upon their release from Jordanian captivity, members of the two kibbutzim 'Eyn Zurim and Masu'ot Yitzhaq – originally situated southwest of Bethlehem and conquered by Trans-Jordan's Arab Legion on 14 May 48 – reestablished their communal villages here. The third new village was the *moshav* (co-operative village) Shafir. In the 1949 photo, the temporary camp of 'Masu'ot Yitzhaq appears to the south of eastern Sawafir.

1949

1994

1966

H| enry S. Gullett, author of the official Australian account of the Palestinian campaign, describes what happened in the immedi- ate aftermath of the British conquest on 9 Nov 17: "All night the crooked little streets of the mud-built, straw-thatched villages were packed with restless, thirsty horses, and gaunt, dusty, unshaven [Australian] men, careless of their exhaustion in their desire to relieve their animals, and in the buoyancy of the indescribable sense of sweeping victory. Where ropes were missing they were replaced with bridle-reins and telephone wire, and cattle and horses, thus attached to the buckets and walking out in a straight line, hauled the water from depths as great as 200 feet. Mingled with the troops and their horses were crowds of dirty, ragged, picturesque natives, who had been denied their supply during the fight and now, very thirsty, were clamorously fighting for their share. Telephone wires saved the bri- gade. All night, and until late on the following day, the water was raised bucket by bucket, and the work went on until all the parched horses had been relieved. In the areas where prisoners were assem- bled the horror of war was seen at its worst. Hundreds of hapless Turks, fighters for a cause for which they knew no enthusiasm and which was even beyond the understanding of men so simple and ignorant, moaned and cried in their sickness and thirst. 'Moya! Moya!' (water! water!) sounded all through that hideous night; and the light horsemen, deeply moved by pity for a foe whom they always regarded with respect and even kindliness, shared their own scanty supply with the afflicted prisoners, and worked the night through to bring them a little ease."[49]

The Survey of Israel photo of 18 Jun 1966 shows the straight, single street of Shafir at left, 'Eyn Zurim and Merkaz Shapira at center, and Masu'ot Yitzhaq at right. The course of the two main streams and their right-angled confluence near the lower margin's midpoint remain unchanged. The site of western Sawafir is not cultivated.

Our photo of 26 Feb 1994 shows the new four-lane road running, near Merkaz Shapira, slightly to the south of the British (and Turkish) road. The differences in hue in the fields at center mark secondary streams that are no longer in existence.[50]

Population				
	1922	1945	1966	1995
W. Sawafir	572	1,030		
E. Sawafir	588	970		
N. Sawafir	334	680		
Masu'ot Yitzhaq			400	546
Merkaz Shapira				1,040
'Eyn Zurim			320	525
Shafir			293	333

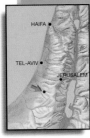
'Araq el-Manshiya – Qiryat Gat

The large oval tell, or ancient mound, close to the lower margin's midpoint in the Bavarian photo of 16 Jun 1918, is named after Shaykh Ahmad el-'Areini. To the left of it is the Arab village of 'Araq el-Manshiya, surrounded by fields. The line running from right to left, which passes west of the village, is the Turkish railway from Wadi es-Sarar to Beersheba.

Bavarian Squadron 304 arrived at 'Araq el-Manshiya in mid-October 1917 and soon began operational flights from a field west of the village. On 7 Nov, with the British drawing closer, Squadron Commander Walz ordered the evacuation of equipment to Wadi es-Sarar to the north, and preparation there of a new airfield. On 8 Nov, British planes bombed the airfield at 'Araq el-Manshiya at noon and again at 16:40. As the bombs had cut the telephone lines, a plane took off for Jerusalem and dropped at the Turkish-German headquarters on the Mount of Olives a report containing information about a reconnaissance flight over the northern Negev that had taken place that morning (a part of the report appears on p. 13 above). Early in the morning of 9 Nov, the Turkish commander informed the Germans that the British would arrive within the hour. The six serviceable planes immediately took off for the north. Equipment impossible to evacuate was burned, and at 08:30 the last soldiers set off northward on foot, their equipment loaded onto wagons pulled by oxen. In the meantime the Turks destroyed the railway station near the village. Walz, the squadron's commander, was the last to leave the place; his plane took off at 09:00.

The withdrawal was unduly hasty. Not until midnight did troopers of the 3rd Australian Light Horse Brigade reach the village's railway station, and only the next morning did they enter the village. As they rode through the deserted German airfield they saw destroyed hangars, many corpses, and the skeletons of seven burnt-out planes.[51]

'Araq el-Man[...] German plan[...] the Turkish railroad stat[...] photographe[...] the advancin[...] Australians, 9 Nov 17.

Machines damaged by bombs and burnt by enemy and station buildings and R.S. damaged by bombs.

1994

1945

In 1954 Qiryat Gat was founded as the urban center of the new Jewish villages of the Lakhish area. The Survey of Israel photo of 23 Jul 1966 shows a part of Qiryat Gat on the far side of the new Israeli railway to Beersheba (running from point A to point B on the margins), which coincides here with the old Turkish track. Qiryat Gat's industrial zone is on the railway's near side. Most of the houses of 'Iraq el-Manshiya no longer exist, but the village's general layout can still be traced.

Our picture of 26 Feb 1994 shows, in the lower left corner, the oval mound – now renamed Tel 'Erani – and, in the upper half, all of Qiryat Gat. The vestiges of 'Iraq el-Manshiya have by now been largely obliterated by the expanding industrial zone.

When the RAF took their photo on 5 Jan 1945, 'Iraq el-Manshiya (this being how the Arabic name was now transcribed) was considerably larger than in 1918. The British road by-passed the village to the north; the Turkish railway track was out of use.

In November 1948, 'Iraq el-Manshiya formed part of the small, Egyptian-held "Faluja Pocket" created by the Israeli victories in the area the month before. (Gamal Abdul Nasser, Egypt's future president, was one of the officers commanding the troops in the enclave.) Upon the signing of the Israeli-Egyptian armistice agreement on 24 Feb 49, the Egyptian troops were allowed to leave, and some villagers departed with them; during the ensuing weeks, Israeli forces intimidated the remaining inhabitants into leaving for the Jordanian-occupied Hebron area.

1966

Population				
	1922	1945	1965	1995
'Iraq el-Manshiya	1,132	2,010		
Qiryat Gat			15,600	45,200

Nahr Sukreir - Ashdod

In the upper right corner of this Bavarian photo taken on 29 Jan 1918, Nahr Sukreir flows into the Mediterranean. The stream, 27 m wide and 3 m deep close to its mouth, provided a plentiful supply of water to the troopers and horses of the 1st Australian Light Horse Brigade, which occupied the area on 12 Nov 17. Five days later, with the front already much farther to the north, the British began sending ships to a point northwest of the outlet and despatching their cargoes to shore by boat. As a result, Allenby was able to send two additional infantry divisions northward.

▲ *A unit of the Egyptian Labour Corps at Nahr Sukreir, Christmas 1917.*

1918

1917

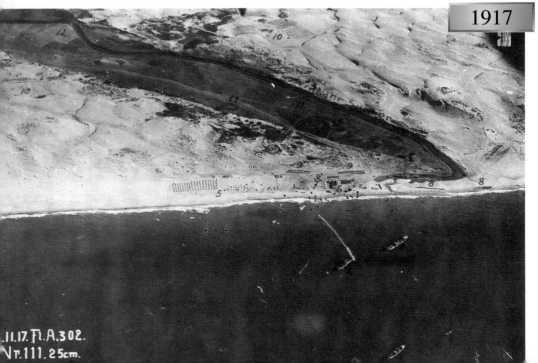

11.17. Fl.A.302.
Nr.111. 25cm.

German aviators repeatedly photographed the British unloading operations. The 1918 photograph shows the loading camps situated on the sand dunes south of the outlet as well as the camp to the north of it. In the second range of dunes south of the stream, at the top of a hill whose broad foot casts a shadow northward, one can discern the tomb of Nebi Yunis, the Prophet Jonah of Muslim tradition. Hill and tomb stand out on a more oblique photo taken by Squadron 302 on 30 Nov 1917; an interpreted version of this picture (see left) appears in the German manual for the tactical use of aerial photographs that was later captured by the British.

Leef's photo of 19 Oct 1949 shows the hill and the tomb in the foreground. Few vestiges of the British activities in 1917-18 are discernible north of the stream now called Nahal Lakhish. The location of its mouth has changed slightly.

1994

The photos of 12 Jul 1966 and 26 Feb 1994 document the growth of the town of Ashdod, founded in 1955. Nahal
Lakhish flows into the Mediterranean just south of the harbor, part
of which appears in the upper right corner.

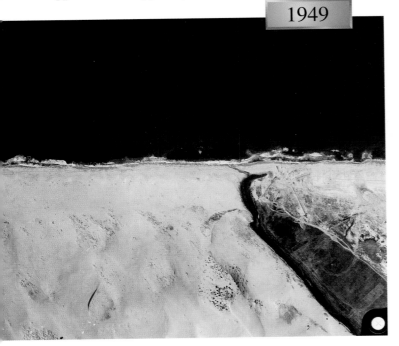

1949

1966

Population	
1966	27,000
1995	128,400

A team of Australian-bred draught horses on the sand dunes near Isdud, 11 Jan 18. (Color photo by Frank Hurley).

The camp of a squadron of the Australian Light Horse Regiment among fruit trees of the Arab village of Isdud, 2 Jan 18. (Another of Hurley's color photos).

Frank Hurley examining shells left by the Turks near Qatra, 4 Jan 18.

The activities of the Egyptian Labour Corps at Nahr Sukreir and elsewhere were described on 11 Jul 18 in *The Palestine News*, the weekly published for the British soldiers fighting in Palestine: "There are few units that are better known in the Force, and of which less has been seen in print, than the Egyptian Labour Corps....At Deir El Belah, which was then the advanced base, a strong detachment was continuously at work unloading ships in the offing, and bringing the supplies ashore in our surf boats manned by E.L.C. boatmen specially recruited for the purpose. Similar work was performed at Sukerier [=Sukreir], near Jaffa, as soon as our command of the coast had been thus far extended....After [the conquest of] Gaza, there came another great forward movement of the Egyptian Labour Force into Palestine. Railways and roads were the chief objects towards which labour was directed. No time was lost in setting about the extension of the main line of railway towards Jaffa. With thousands of labourers at work the new track made its way rapidly up the coast, while in the meantime a network of roads had been prepared and was being maintained by the Egyptian Labour Corps in order to facilitate the adequate provision of supplies and ammunition to the troops operating at so great a distance from the base.... Many miles of quagmire that harassed the progress of our troops in the winter advance have been converted into motor roads that not a few rural councils at home might envy. And the work still goes on."

◀ *An Australian Light Horse Field Ambulance wagon. (One of Hurley's color photos).*

Qatra, Gedera

The Bavarian photograph of 25 Nov 1917 shows an area captured by the British just 12 days earlier. An ancient mound – perhaps of biblical Gedera – appears close to the left margin's midpoint, crowned with a ribbon of dark vegetation. To the right of it is the Arab village of Qatra. The four-sided area standing out at lower right is the Jewish village of Gedera, founded in 1884 by pioneers from Russia. Houses spaced at regular intervals line a wide street, while the stables and cowsheds form stripes parallel to the street on either side, creating a defended compound. The elongated strips of Gedera's fields and orchards contrast with Qatra's hedged, irregular enclosures. The line running diagonally across the photo's lower third is one of the roads linking Ramleh with Gaza.

The official Australian history of the Palestinian campaign of 1917-18, records that "slightly north [should be: 'south'] of the native mud-built village [of Qatra] is a trim little Jewish settlement which, with its well-kept orchards and white, red-tiled houses, afforded the first glimpse of Western civilisation seen by the British troops during the campaign."[52]

By 29 Dec 1944 the road had been paved by the British. A large rectangular police fortress, built by the British, stands near it, across from Qatra. Since 1917, the Arab village has grown somewhat, southward; Jewish Gedera has expanded much more, mainly eastward. Qatra's inhabitants fled after the 3rd Battalion of the Giv'ati Brigade had begun on 6 May 48 to disarm the village and the foreign volunteers who were in it; or were expelled when, three weeks later, the Egyptian army reached nearby Isdud.

1944

◄ A World War I machine gun, now in the Gedera museum.

1990

The color photo of 8 Apr ▢1990▢ shows Gedera's expansion
northward and eastward; just a few vestiges of Qatra are discernible. The ancient mound with its flat and gray top, surrounded by
Gedera's northernmost streets, stands out above the midpoint of the
photo's left margin. The village's original street, and the quadrangle
formed by stables and cowsheds, are slightly right of center.

Population			
	1922	1945	1995
Qatra	**640**	**1,210**	
Gedera	**140**	**970**	**9,600**

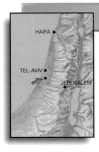

Rehovot

This undated, low-altitude Australian photograph, probably taken in 1918, shows the Jewish colony of Rehovot, founded in 1890. The main road, seen running parallel to the photo's lower margin, leads northward to Rishon le-Zion and Jaffa; the village's two main streets are at right angles to this road. The large two-storied building at the head of the shorter of the two streets is the village synagogue.

▶ *Men of the 2nd Australian Light Horse Brigade passing through the Arab village of Zarnuqa, southwest of Rehovot, 17 Jan 18.*

1918

A

▶ *A crashed airplane in a vineyard near Rehovot.*

1990

1949

Leef's photograph of 16 Nov **1949** documents the growth of Rehovot under the British Mandate. The main road to Rishon le-Zion and Tel Aviv-Jaffa, which at the end of World War I had been on the outskirts of the village, is now Herzl Street, Rehovot's main thoroughfare.

Our photo of 8 Apr **1990** shows the further expansion of Rehovot (accorded the status of a town in 1950). The central bus station stands out near the center of the lower margin. The Weizmann Institute for Science is seen in part near the upper left margin. A comparison of the photographs reveals the extent to which the layout of the village's fields dictated the location of the town's streets. Very few of the houses appearing in the Australian photo are still standing.

Population	
1918	**1,190**
1948	**12,542**
1995	**86,700**

Troopers of the 1st Australian Light Horse Brigade entered Rehovot on 14 Nov 17. C. Guy Powles, author of an account of the New Zealand part in the Palestinian campaign, writes that the Light Horsemen "were astonished to see in front of them, nestling in the hollow, a modern village with red-tiled houses so different to the flat-topped oriental architecture our men had become accustomed to. It was a sight to make one rub one's eyes and fear that it were a dream...[They] were met by an enthusiastic crowd of Zionists – men, women and children."[53]

Dr. R. N. Salaman, the noted Anglo-Jewish geneticist, who served as medical officer with the 2nd Jewish Battalion (the 39th Royal Fusiliers), visited Rehovot on 11 Aug 18. A day later he reported to his wife in England: "It is a most picturesque village, and we were given a most cordial welcome and a delightful supper....The Jewish colonies are very refreshing – an extremely nice type of people, hospitable, free, and of good physique. I notice an interesting thing, viz. a great preponderance of pseudo-Gentile types amongst both old and young, and this bears out an idea which has often floated through my mind: that whilst the Hittite type is linked with *Rahamonus* more or less, the pseudo-Gentile is more adventurous and independent. In the colonies are also a goodly number of Yemenites. Some are picturesque and a few of the women are beautiful; but the more I see them the less fascinated I am, and I am glad to say that white Jews do not marry with them."[54]

Arab and Jewish villages were contrasted by other combatants as well. For instance, Major W.S. Kent Hughes of the 3rd Australian Light Horse Brigade wrote: "These Arab villages [of Palestine's southern coastal plain] were composed of the usual collection of mud-huts and filth that is so characteristic of the native, while a few stunted trees and prickly-pear hedges often grew in the vicinity....[The Jewish] colonies were usually very picturesque with their houses of stone or wood and plaster, with red-tiled roofs and whitewashed walls, which were surrounded by vegetation – a pleasing contrast to the mud and filth of the Arab villages. The streets were wide and regular, while trees and vegetation were plentiful. Orchards and vineyards often surrounded the settlement on every side; but Arabs appeared to do most of the labour, and the villagers did not seem to enjoy work....Even though the villages always looked nice and clean, and the houses were as a rule well-kept, yet the sanitation of these villages was beyond description. In this respect they were certainly not more than a stage above the Arab villages, which was a strange state of affairs considering the extent to which they were above the Arabs in every other way."[55]

Turks, too, drew comparisons between the Jewish and Arab villages of Palestine. Falih Rifki, private secretary to Jamal Pasha, wrote: "I toured Jewish Palestine several times, from Jaffa to Jerusalem. The new towns and villages of Palestine are the work of the Jews. This is not just a new Palestine but a staggeringly new Palestine. In the village, the headman is an English Jew who puts on a dinner jacket in the evening. Rosy-cheeked German Jewish girls ride home to the village from the vineyard in carriages, singing. The Muslim Arab serves these masters; the Arab laborer squeezes the grapes and the plump Jew drinks the wine. In the old Palestine, the Arab village is a heap of earth, the gardens ruined, the people naked, the eyes diseased. In Jewish Palestine the towns are filled with the scent of oranges, and the well-maintained roads are lined with prickly pears. Women in low-cut dresses in February are waiting for the end of the war in rich hotel lounges decorated with strongly-perfumed roses and ripe oranges."[56]

▲　*A swamp northwest of Rehovot is surrounded by British camps. The straight line to the left of the swamp is the new British railroad leading from Egypt to Lydda. The dark areas in the corners are some of Rehovot's groves. The photo was taken by Bavarian Squadron 304 on 19 Mar 18.*

▶　*Camels of the Australian Light Horse at Rehovot loaded ready for the march.*

Rehovot, 14 Jan 18: Arab drivers attached to the transport section of the Imperial Camel Corps. (color photo by Frank Hurley).

▼ The caption of this color photo taken by Hurley in 1918 reads: "A typical Jewish cottage in the village of Khurbet Deiran [that is, Rehovot], in Palestine."

▼ An Australian officer looks at Rehovot. The small houses in the photo's lower half belong to Jews from Yemen. The large building on the horizon is Rehovot's synagogue.·

Rishon le-Zion

This undated photograph from Fritz Groll's collection, probably taken by aviators of German Squadron 300 in ▐ 1917, ▌ shows Rishon le-Zion ('The First to Zion'), one of the earliest Jewish colonies, founded in 1882. The wide road at lower right leads from Jaffa to Rehovot. The one at right angles to it leads into the village and ends in front of the synagogue. The dark rectangle to the right of this road is the village orchard; the large building to the right of it, topped by parallel roofs, is the winery. The outer boundary of the village's fields, and the uncultivated terrain beyond it, appear along the photo's upper margin.

Menashe Meirowitz of Rishon le-Zion described in his Hebrew-written diary the village's transition from Turkish to British rule: "On the 12th [of November] there came suddenly a Turkish officer with a group of soldiers and set out to arrange for a telephone [link] between Ramleh and Rishon le-Zion. It appears that they wanted to set up in the colony a temporary center for soldiers of the army. And on the fourteenth, early in the morning, we learned that the Turkish officer with his soldiers disappeared. We felt that serious and important moments are ahead of us. At first light we felt that the English come closer to us. And on Thursday morning, 14 [should be: 15] November, the English vanguard entered the colony with four New Zealand horsemen. The appearance was so sudden that we could not believe our eyes. The horsemen passed the colony's streets warily; they looked with much care at every house, at every passer-by. They have no idea of the joy and happiness their appearance caused the colony."[57]

1994

1949

Leef's photo of 6 Oct 1949 shows that many field paths have turned into streets. The main road from Tel Aviv-Jaffa to Rehovot now passes along the edge of the orchard and the winery.

Our photo of 26 Feb 1994 shows only a part of Rishon le-Zion, a town since 1950. What was the boundary of the village's fields on the German photo now marks the end of the main built-up area of the town; and only a few of the structures appearing in that picture are still standing, one of them being the synagogue, partially hidden by a high-rise building.

Population	
1917	1,459
1948	10,445
1995	165,300

◀◀ *Unloading grape-baskets at the winery, c. 1918*

Ramleh

This photo from the Steiner collection, taken by German Squadron 302 on 3 Dec 1917, shows the Arab town of Ramleh less than three weeks after its capture by the British on 15 Nov. The Jaffa-Jerusalem road is the bright line running between points A and B. The curvy gray line between points C and D is the Jaffa-Lydda-Jerusalem railway of 1892, the first in the country. The main mosque in the center of town – originally a 12th-century crusader church – appears as an elongated rectangle parallel to the Jaffa-Jerusalem road; the road from Lydda runs from point E on the left margin to the mosque's eastern extremity. The large complex at the northern end of the town, to the right (west) of the Jaffa-Jerusalem road, is the Franciscan monastery.

1917

3.12.17. Fl.A.302.
Nr.116. 21km.
H.3500. B.
Ramleh.

1918

The rapid pace of British construction activities is attested to b a Bavarian photo of Ramleh taken from the opposite direction 6 Mar 1918. A new stretch of road to Lydda runs to point E the right margin. The Jaffa-Lydda-Jerusalem railway is connecte to the new British coastal railway by the bright line leading to poi G. The White Tower, erected by the Mamluks in 1318, casts i shadow left-and upward just below point H. British camps stan out in the photo's lower half.

The RAF photo of 10 Dec 1944 shows a significantly e panded Ramleh. The large rectangle left of the Jaffa-Jerusale road is the British police fortress.

In July 1948 Ramleh was held by local and semiregular fighter reinforced by a detachment of Trans-Jordan's Arab Legion. Ope ation Dani, in which four Israeli brigades were to seize control the main road from Tel Aviv to Jerusalem and eliminate Arab bas in Tel Aviv's immediate vicinity, aimed inter alia at the conquest Ramleh. The Qiryati Brigade's attack on Ramleh during the nig of 10/11 Jul failed; but after the fall of nearby Ludd and the retre of the Arab Legion detachment, Ramleh surrendered on 12 Jul 4 and most of its remaining inhabitants were expelled. Soon thereaft Ramleh became a largely Jewish town.

1997

1944

Our photo of 7 Feb 1997 documents the growth of Israeli Ramleh. The White Tower, formerly outside the town, now stands near the center of the built-up area. The gray rectangle of the main mosque, and its minaret, stand out in old Ramleh. The main streets and the railroad follow the same lines as in 1918; the four-lane road that has by-passed Ramleh since the early 1970s appears in the left-hand third of the photo.

Population		
1922	**7,312**	(5,837 M, 1,440 C)
1945	**15,160**	(11,900 M, 3,260 C)
1995	**58,600**	(incl. 10,100 Arabs and others)

▶ *The roofs of Ramleh, 1917.*

▲ *Ramleh from the top of the 14th-century White Tower: (a) above, Hurley's color photo of 1918; (b) next page, top – the view today.*

◀ *German officers sitting on a Muslim grave at Ramleh.*

▲ *A Christian Arab couple, neighbors of German Squadron 300 in Ramleh.*

◀ *Aviators of German Squadron 300 in a Ramleh coffee-house.*

Joseph Klausner, the Jewish historian and publicist, visited Ramleh in 1912. Shortly afterwards he wrote: "I toured the ancient tower of this town (an important remnant from the time of the crusades), its main, more or less European, street, and its bazaar, which is so similar to other bazaars of the Orient, and I wandered about in its dark narrow alleys until I reached the gardens and olive orchards in its vicinity, which are unmatched in beauty and abundance. Fertile, multibranched fig trees were also seen here and there, and a few date palms. In some places I saw pools hewn of marble, and stone buildings with beautiful domes."[58]

The 1912 edition of Baedeker's guide to Palestine and Syria includes the following piece of information: "Chief mosque, once a church of the crusaders (12th century). Unbelievers are not always permitted to visit it, but the effect of the all-powerful bakshish may be tried (5 piastres; shoes must be taken off)."[59]

A squadron of the 1st Australian Light Horse Brigade entered Ramleh on the morning of 15 Nov 17. The author of the official Australian history of the campaign later wrote: "Both Arabs and Christians seized the stirrups of the Australians, kissed their dusty boots, and hailed them with a tumultuous show of feeling which, if insincere in the Arabs, was a very convincing act of mob acting."[60] Richard Meinertzhagen, in charge of Allenby's Intelligence Section, made the following entry in his diary on 2 Dec, 17: "The Arabs of Ramleh gave us an amusing incident yesterday which accurately reflects their attitude towards us. A large batch of Turkish prisoners was being marched through the village but they were not preceded by their British Guard. The Arabs, thinking it was the return of the Turkish Army, turned out in force, yelling with delight and waving Turkish flags: it was not till the end of the column appeared and they saw British soldiers with fixed bayonets that they realized their mistake and great was their confusion. Their faces fell with a bump and they slank disconsolate to their hovels."[61]

◀ *Ramleh: the market, 1917.*

▼ *The original caption of this Australian photo reads: "A native market at Ludd, Palestine, in 1918."*

Lydda (Hebrew Lod, Arabic Ludd)

The Arab town of Ludd is the densely built-up triangle in the upper right portion of this Bavarian photo of 24 Jul 1918. Near the triangle's lower (southern) side one can discern a large, bright, rectangular building – the Greek Orthodox Church of St. George, standing on the ruins of the 12th-century crusader cathedral. Ludd's mosque stands to the left of it. The town is surrounded by tracks, olive orchards and fields. The bright circles of threshing floors are seen south of the town.

At the time this photo was taken, Ludd was rapidly becoming the hub of the Palestinian railway system. The Jaffa-Jerusalem railroad, completed in 1892, by-passed the town to the west; in the summer of 1915, a Turkish military railroad reached Ludd from the north, linking it with Damascus and, somewhat later, with Beersheba; early in 1918, the British coastal railroad from Egypt reached Ludd as well. All these lines are clearly visible on the photo. British camps appear in the photo's lower half.

1918

Leef's photo of 6 Oct 1949 documents the considerable expansion of Ludd under the British Mandate, mainly along a north-south axis west of the original nucleus.

Like Ramleh, Ludd was a main target of Operation Dani. On 11 Jul 48 Battalion 89 under Moshe Dayan broke into Ludd from Ben Shemen, east of the town: the column, headed by a captured Arab Legion armored car, made its way through Ludd to the eastern end of Ramleh and then returned to Ben Shemen. Later that day elements of the Palmah[62] Yiftah Brigade entered Ludd from the southeast and occupied the town's center. On the following day, encouraged by an Arab Legion armored patrol which briefly penetrated the town, some local inhabitants opened fire on Israeli soldiers, who retaliated massively, killing many and wounding others; subsequently, the operations officer of Operation Dani, Yitzhak Rabin, issued the order to expel Ludd's inhabitants.

1997

Our photo of 7 Feb 1997 shows the northern part of the Is-raeli town of Lod, most of whose inhabitants are Jewish. Much of Ludd's original nucleus is an open space bounded by three-storied buildings; to the south of it one may discern the Church of St. George and the mosque's minaret. The layout of the roads and railroads is the chief remainder of World War I Ludd. The quarters built under the British Mandate form a small part of the present-day town. The road that by-passes Lod to the east stands out at right.

Ludd, 26 Jan 18 (a mosaic of two Australian photos). The minaret is at left.

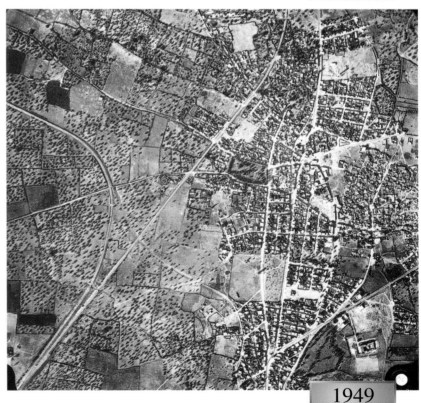

1949

Population		
1922	**8,103**	(7,466 M, 926 C)
1945	**16,780**	(14,910 M, 1,840 C)
1948	**1,056**	
1995	**52,600**	(incl. 11,200 Arabs and others)

Ben-Shemen

Ben-Shemen, located about 3 km east of Lydda, appears right of center on this Bavarian photo of 14 Feb 1918. Established in 1906 as a Jewish agricultural school, Ben-Shemen became the experimental farm of the Zionist Organization in 1909. The rectangular courtyard that accommodated the farmhands was built in 1913. A few hundred meters to the east (to the left, on the photo), a row of six houses was erected in 1911 for Jewish silversmiths from Yemen, who were expected to earn their living from their craft as well as from agriculture. One can see some British tents near these houses.

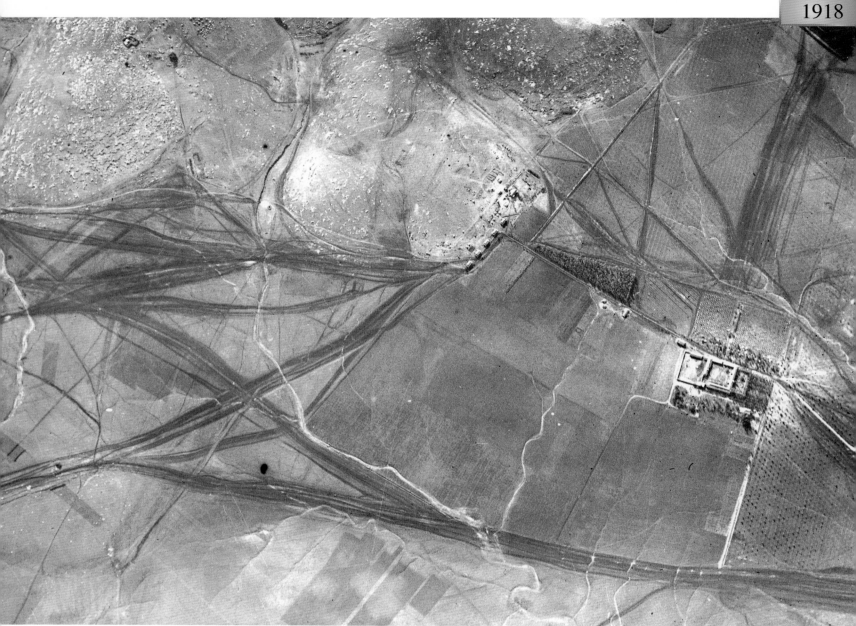

Chaim Weizmann – the Zionist leader destined to become Israel's first president – arrived in Palestine on 3 Apr 18 at the head of the Zionist Commission, which was to form a link between the British authorities and the Jewish population, deal with relief work among the latter, and foster friendly relations with the Arabs. On 30 Apr 18 Weizmann wrote from Tel Aviv to his wife, Vera, in London: "Yesterday I went to Ben-Shemen (*Herzlwald*) and looked over our farm. It's the first Zionist farm established by the N[ational] F[und]. You must certainly remember how many arguments there were about those farms at the [Zionist] Congress, and there's no doubt that many mistakes were made, but looking at the final results, they've performed miracles on this farm in eight years. It is a model farming unit, with the latest things in science being put into practice. Olives have taken a back seat and now, besides 6,000 olive trees, of which the British destroyed some 2,000 for firewood, there's a model dairy and cattle farm, there are bees, almond trees, wheat – the best in Palestine – and wonderful vegetables. There are about 70 Jewish farmhands working on the farm and, they assured me yesterday, it's beginning to pay its way. When one considers that 8 years ago this was bare rock, one must admit that much can be achieved by Jewish hands on Palestinian soil."[63]

1997

The youth village's courtyard, with its rectangular buildings topped by pink-gray roofs, stands out at the center of our photo of 7 Feb 1997. The Tel Aviv-Jerusalem highway, opened to traffic in 1978, and a new north-south highway under construction, dominate the left side of the photo. The Tel Aviv-Jerusalem highway passes just east of the 1929 wall.

In 1927 Ben-Shemen became a youth village. From the late *oring* of 1948 it was isolated and besieged by Arab forces, until *s* relief during Operation Dani. Lt.-Gen. Glubb, the commander *f Trans-Jordan's Arab Legion, writes in his memoirs that he *roposed to capture Ben-Shemen while it was isolated, but the *ayor of Arab Ludd, mindful of his good relations with the youth *llage and afraid of Israeli retaliation, dissuaded him from doing *.*[64]

Leef's photo of 26 Oct 1949 shows the eastern part of the *outh village at right. The houses originally occupied by the sil-*rsmiths, which in 1922 became the nucleus of a moshav, also *amed Ben-Shemen, are at left; the defensive wall erected at the *me of the Riots of 1929 is to their left.

The Survey of Israel photo of 10 Jun 1969 shows the youth *llage in its entirety; the new moshav Ben-Shemen, founded in *952, appears in the upper right corner.

1969

Miqveh Israel

The bright, straight diagonal in the upper left corner of this Bavarian photo of 12 Dec 1917 is the road linking Jaffa with Jerusalem. Between the road and the sand dunes are the buildings and fields of Miqveh Israel, the first Jewish agricultural school, founded in 1870 about 4 km southeast of Jaffa. At lower left are Arab houses and orchards.

▶ *The cypress-lined lane leading to Miqveh Israel's main building, 1917.*

Eliyahu Krause, director of Miqveh Israel during World War developed a friendly relationship with Jamal Pasha, the Turkis commander of Syria and Palestine. Miqveh pupils planted palm tree in Jaffa along the boulevard that was initiated by Jamal and bore h name. In 1915, Krause presented a memorandum to Jamal suggestir that he establish experimental agricultural stations in Beersheba ar points west in the desert. Jamal accepted the plan and entruste Krause with its execution. When in March 1917 the Turks ordered th evacuation of Jaffa, Miqveh was not affected, and some Jews fro Jaffa and Tel Aviv found refuge there.

Leef's photo of 14 Oct 1949 shows a considerably large Miqveh and, on the sand dunes, parts of the Jewish quarter c Holon, named after the sand (Hebrew, *hol*) on which it was founde in 1933.

◀ *Miqveh's main building, 1913.*

1994

1949

The Survey of Israel photo of 12 Jul 1968, and ours of 26 Feb 1994, show the growth of Holon – a town since 1950 – which now envelops Miqveh on three sides. A stretch of the Tel Aviv-Jerusalem highway appears at upper left.

1968

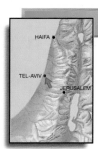

Jaffa, Tel Aviv and surroundings

In this Bavarian photo of 10 Jan 1918, Arab Jaffa's Old City dominates the small bay. A ship is at anchor outside the harbor, and three small vessels lie close to it. Jaffa's new Arab and Jewish suburbs are visible south, east and north of the original nucleus. Tel Aviv – Jaffa's newest Jewish suburb, founded in 1909 on the dunes northeast of the Old City – stands out by its straight streets, the more substantial size of its houses and the larger spaces separating them. The trapezoid enclosure in the sand dunes, close to the photo's lower left corner, is Tel Aviv's cemetery. The stream that meanders between the points marked A and B on the margins is Wadi el-Musrara. The land on either side of it is cultivated, but the higher ground to the east of it is not. The railroad from Jaffa to Jerusalem passes along the outskirts of Tel Aviv, bends eastward, then runs along the western bank of Wadi el-Musrara and finally continues in a straight line to point C on the upper margin. The road to Jerusalem starts at the northeastern corner of Old Jaffa then leads southeastward, passing north of Miqve Israel to point D.

On 28 Mar 17, with the British within reach of Gaza, the Turks ordered the evacuation of Jaffa and its suburbs. Only orange grove proprietors were to be allowed to remain. On 15 Nov 17 the Turkish commander of Jaffa was notified that the British would attack the town in a day or two. He was ordered to expel the remaining civilians and burn the police barracks and the city hall. After setting fire only to the barracks, the commander and his soldiers set off for Nablus. When a British plane bombed them along the way, the soldiers fled back to Jaffa without their commander. Troopers of the Wellington Regiment of the New Zealand Mounted Rifles Brigade, "plucking oranges from the trees as they passed through the groves," entered the town the following morning without encountering significant resistance. The remaining civilians welcomed them warmly. A few days later, the town's inhabitants began returning to their homes.[65]

1918

1997

policing of the area during the Arab Revolt. (According to an official British report compiled shortly afterward, the operation provides a good illustration of a means of reducing a recalcitrant urban area by the most human means.")[73]

Leef's vertical photo of 14 Oct 1949 shows the full extent of the British demolition operation, as well as Jaffa's further growth.

By the time this photo was taken the town had however assumed distinctly different character. A few days after the United Nations Partition resolution of 29 Nov 47 (which envisaged Jaffa as an Arab enclave within the future Jewish state), Jaffa's Arabs began sniping at adjacent Jewish quarters, and soon exchanges of fire became common along the line dividing Jaffa from Tel Aviv. On 25 Apr 48 the Irgun Zeva'i Leumi (IZL), the dissident Jewish organization, attacked Manshiya, Jaffa's northernmost quarter, and two days later succeeded in cutting it off from the rest of the town. IZL mortar fire wrought havoc on the center of Jaffa and triggered mass flight. The British intervention on 28 Apr did little to reassure them, for at the same time the Haganah – the main Jewish militia conquered the area east of the town and completed its isolation, while local Arab militiamen looted and intimidated the population. The Arab exodus continued. On 13 May, upon the final British departure, representatives of the remaining four or five thousand Arabs surrendered to the Haganah. Jaffa was soon repopulated by Jewish immigrants and in 1950 was municipally united with Tel Aviv.

New Jaffa's main artery – originally Jamal Pasha Avenue, King George Avenue under the British, and renamed Jerusalem Avenue after the establishment of Israel – is the green diagonal in the left-hand half of our photo of 8 Feb 1997. A large part of Jaffa's Old Town has become the "Summit Garden."

1949

Population				
1922	**32,524**	(20,621 M,	5,807 J,	6,808 C)
1945	**94,310**	(50,880 M,	28,000 J,	15,400 C)

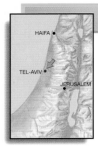

Summeil – Northern Tel Aviv

The Arab village of Summeil, some 4 km north of Jaffa, is visible near the right margin of this Bavarian photo taken on 27 Nov 1917, ten days after the British conquered the area. The road that passes through the village, parallel to the coast, leads from Jaffa northward. The road leading from the village to the coast has fields on either side; at the coastal end, above the cliffs, is a small rectangular building – the tomb of Sheikh 'Abd an-Nabi. Trench systems that start in the sand dunes at the cliffs extend some 200 m eastward.

1917

The RAF photograph of 11 Dec 1944 documents Tel Aviv's northward expansion along the coast. The small harbor near the city's northern limit was built in 1938. The main north-south axes are Ben Yehuda Street (at left) and Dizengoff Street (at right).

The villagers of Summeil fled on 25 Dec 47; they were among the first to do so.

1944

1997

By 1956 most of the area had been built up. Only a few mains of Arab Summeil can be seen. The road that ran northward om Jaffa and passed through Summeil has become Ibn Gevirol treet, one of Tel Aviv's main thoroughfares.

On our photo of 8 Feb 1997, Ibn Gevirol Street is the raight diagonal extending from the middle of the right margin to e middle of the upper margin. On it are located the Tel Aviv Iunicipality building and the expansive Kings of Israel Square, enamed Yitzhak Rabin Square after the prime minister who was ssassinated there on 4 Nov 95. A few houses of erstwhile Summeil an be discerned near the black-brown "Sheqem" high-rise close the upper margin; they are eclipsed on all sides by Tel Aviv's ouses. In the west, the Marina and the artificial breakwaters stand ut. North of the Marina, along Independence Garden, the natural oast line has been preserved, but a comparison with the older hotos shows that it has been considerably eroded since 1917. The arden is dominated by the Tel Aviv Hilton; the small white rectan- le at the southern end of the garden is the tomb of 'Abd an-Nabi.

1956

99

Ramat Gan

This Bavarian photo of 3 Mar 1918 shows a largely uninhabited area about 6 km northeast of Jaffa. The stream flowing leftward from point A to point B is Wadi el-Musrara. The wide bright ribbon running from point C to point D is the 'Auja (Hebrew: Yarqon) River; no trees are visible along its banks. The confluence of stream and river takes place somewhat beyond the left margin (compare pp. 146-147 below). The small Arab village of Jarisha is on the southern bank of the 'Auja, near point D. The bridge over which the Jaffa-Tulkarm-Nablus road crosses the Musrara, and the stretch of road leading from it northeastward, stand out in their brightness. Four quadrangles of British tent encampments can be discerned to the right of the bridge – that is, in the uncultivated area on the high ground above the stream. Another quadrangle of tents is visible south of Jarisha, at the foot of the oval-shaped Napoleon Hill.

◀ The lower course of the Yarqon on a postcard of 1921. The original caption reads: "The River Auja near Jaffa and the place of allied victories in Palestine."

A part of the town of Ramat Gan, founded in 1921, occupies the right half of Leef's photo of 14 Oct 1949. The Jaffa-Tulkarm-Nablus road has given way to the highway that links Tel Aviv with Ramat Gan and Petah Tiqva. In the lower right corner is one of Tel Aviv's residential areas, adjoining a soccer stadium; at lower left is the Arab village of Jammasin. The inhabitants of Jammasin fled in January-March 1948.

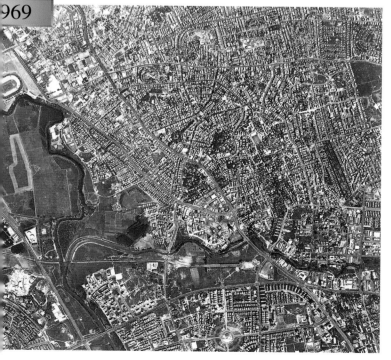

1969

The Survey of Israel photo of 21 Apr 1969 documents the growth of Ramat Gan and Tel Aviv. The soccer stadium gave way, in the mid-1950s, to Tel Aviv's central railway station. Nahal Ayalon (Wadi el-Musrara) is now a regulated water channel; the erstwhile large loop near Napoleon Hill has been straightened out.

Our photo of 8 Feb 1997 shows Nahal Ayalon at the center of the Ayalon Freeway, Greater Tel Aviv's main traffic artery. The area of the stream's former loop is covered by a grove. The undulating course of the River Yarqon at upper left is indicated by the trees along its banks.

Population					
	1922	1945	1948	1966	1995
Jammasin	200	1,810			
Jarisha	57	190			
Ramat Gan		10,200	17,182	105,000	121,700

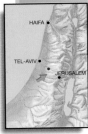

Beit Sira, Makkabim-Re'ut and Modi'in

After their conquest of the coastal plain up to the river 'Auja (Yarqon), the British began their push eastward to Jerusalem. On 19 Nov 17 they entered the Arab village of Beit Sira, in the foothills about 21 km northwest of Jerusalem. The village appears at the center of the Bavarian photo taken on 16 Dec 1917; the road running from right to left leads to Latrun, on the main Jaffa-Jerusalem road.

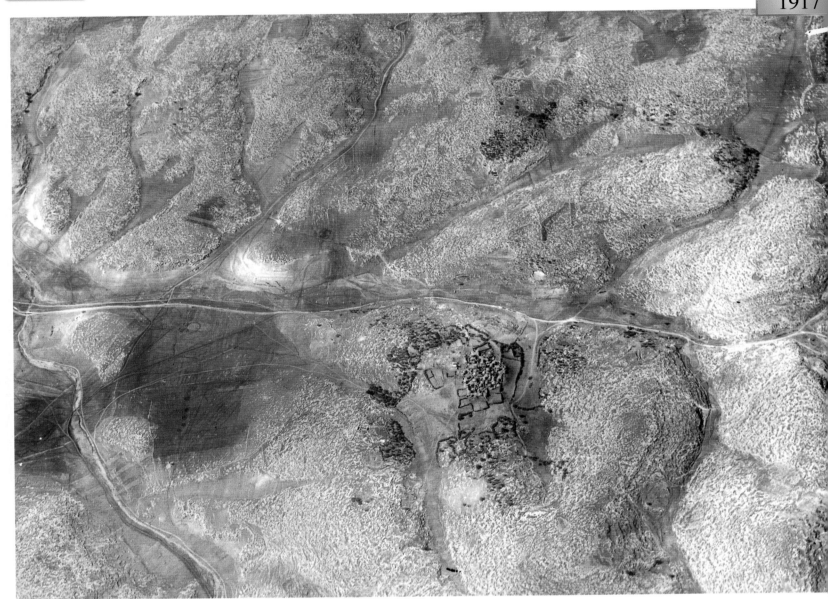

R. Skilbeck Smith, a subaltern in the 10th (Irish) Infantry Division, wrote in his memoir: "We....pushed again in the rain to a rocky and depressing *khud*-side possessing the name of Beit Sira. Fortunately we managed to find a cave, dirty but dry, which we at once monopolised as a mess....Nowhere either in Egypt or in India, have I seen such awful dwelling-places as the unspeakably filthy huts of these peasants. And the inhabitants reproduced in face and figure the squalor of their abodes. Nine out of ten were obviously suffering from some form of sickness or other, and chronic eye diseases seemed to be the common lot. Only in certain parts of Oman, along the infrequent maritime villages, have I seen negroes and Arabs living under conditions as bad, perhaps slightly worse than those prevailing under the oppressive rule of the Turk."[74]

◀ *The Third Australian Light Horse Regiment machine gun in action northwest of Beit Sira, 31 Dec 17. (Frank Hurley's color photo)*

1997

The RAF photo of 3 Jan 1945 shows a track leading to the village's center, some expansion of the village to the east and south, and a different parcelling of its fields. After the 1948 war, the village became part of the Kingdom of Jordan's West Bank; in the Six-Day War of 1967 it came under Israeli rule. The Survey of Israel photo of 2 Sep 1969, and ours of 7 Feb 1997, document the village's further, more substantial growth. Our photo shows also, on the ridge west of Beit Sira, the Jewish rural center of Makkabim-Re'ut, founded in 1986; parts of the new town of Modi'in, founded in 1996; and, near the right margin, a stretch of the road linking Ben-Shemen with the northern suburbs of Jerusalem. In the distance, Tel Aviv and the Mediterranean Sea.

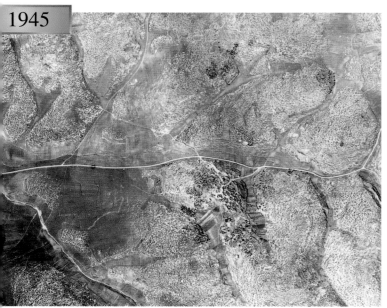

1945

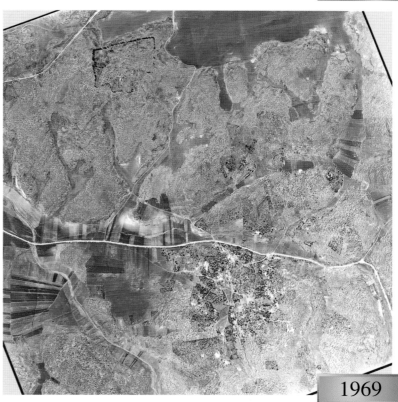

1969

Population					
Beit Sira	1922	**381**	**Makkabim-Re'ut**	1989	**1,100**
	1945	**540**		1995	**10,300**
	1967	**680**			
	1996	**1,195**			

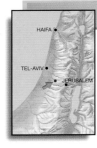

Bab el-Wad – Sha'ar Ha-Gay

The point where the broad, white ribbon of the Jaffa-Jerusalem road – on which some moving vehicles can be seen – leaves the Judean Mountains, is known in Arabic as Bab el-Wad (Gate of the Valley). Left (south) of it stands a khan, or travelers' inn. There are a few trees on the mountain north of the road; the slope south of it is partly covered by vegetation. A British camp lies alongside the narrow road leading southward to Arab 'Artuf and Jewish Hartuv. A small Turkish watchtower tops a hill northwest of the turn to 'Artuf/Hartuv. This Bavarian photo was taken on 29 Nov 1917, ten days after infantrymen of the British 75th Division reached Bab el-Wad.

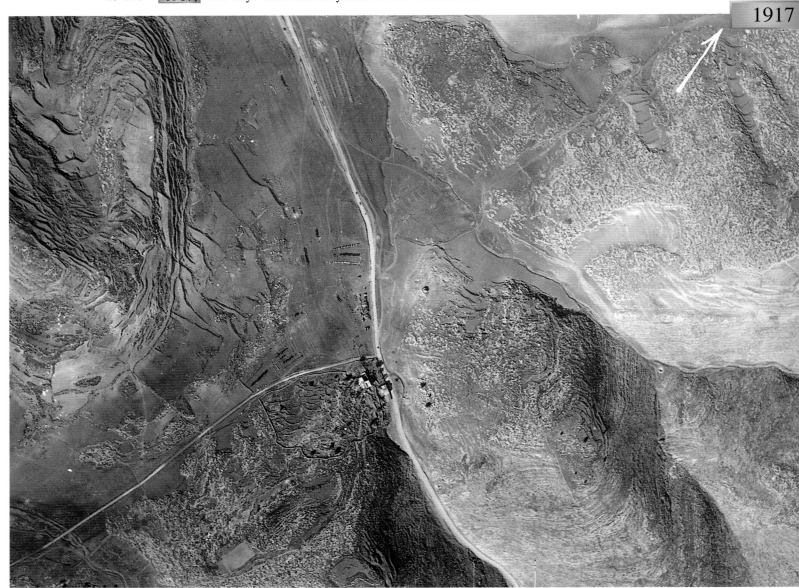

1917

The British photo of 29 Dec 1944 shows few changes in this area.

1944

In the early stages of Israel's War of Independence, when Arab attacks on Jewish vehicles compelled the Haganah to organize convoys, the narrow ravine east of Bab el-Wad was repeatedly the scene of assaults on convoys trying to reach Jerusalem. On 8-12 May 48 two battalions of the Palmah Har'el Brigade, under the command of Yitzhak Rabin, secured control of the stretch extending from Bab el-Wad (Sha'ar ha-Gay, in Hebrew) eastward upto Jerusalem. A 10-km stretch of the road west of Bab el-Wad/Sha'ar ha-Gay, around Latrun, became – according to the 1949 armistice agreement between Israel and Jordan – part of a no-man's-land. Traffic from Jerusalem to the coast had therefore to turn left at Sha'ar ha-Gay and then, after 4 km, take a new road that ran parallel to the original, now unusable one. To facilitate traffic at Sha'ar ha-Gay, a detour was cut through the hills south of it.

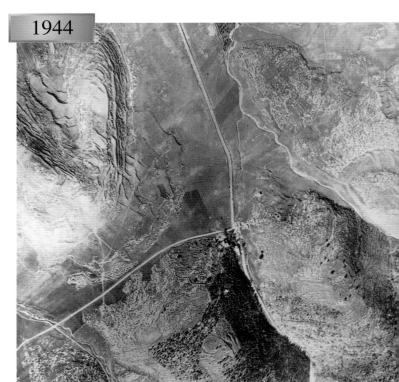

1997

1967

1995

To show the progress of afforestation in the area as well as the recently constructed Sha'ar ha-Gay interchange, the photo of 6 Apr 1995, was taken from a point considerably more to the east of that from which the Bavarians had shot theirs in 1917. Remains of the khan are visible to the left of the four-lane Tel Aviv-Jerusalem highway, opened to traffic in 1978. The now rather superfluous detour is in the lower left corner. Our photo of 7 Feb 1997 shows the effects of the great fire of 2 Jul 95.

This new road stands out starkly on the Survey of Israel photo 18 Jun 1967; it was taken a few days after the Israeli victory the Six-Day War that, inter alia, abolished the no-man's-land and ce again allowed the use of the original main road, via Latrun, m Jerusalem to the coast. The photo also testifies to the affores-ion efforts of the Jewish National Fund.

The ascent to Jerusalem

The Bavarian photo of 4 Dec 1917 shows a 5-km stretch of the road ascending from Bab el-Wad to Jerusalem. Indian troops of the 75th Division wrested most of this stretch from the Turks on 19 Nov 17. No trees are seen on the mountains north of the road, but some are scattered in the depressions to the south of it. The Muslim prayer place of the Imam 'Ali is marked by a clump of trees at the bend of the road in the center of the photo.[75] The ground photo of a stretch near the prayer place (see right) shows a British officer, leaning on his car, who observes Arab villagers ascending the road.

1917

L andscape of this kind spurred the American archaeologist Elihu Grant to observe in about 1907: "One thought that may occur to an American or European as he looks at the numerous hills and mountains up and down the middle and back of Palestine is that never before has he had such a fine opportunity to see the shapes of hills and valleys. For at home he seldom sees the whole, real shape of a hill or a mountain, so covered is it with trees or smaller growth. But here there is very little clothing on the hills. Their knobs and shoulders, cliffs and ribs, are almost as naked of trees as the blue skies above them. The rock layers stand out at the worn edges very plainly. Some hills are banded round and round horizontally with successive layers of rock. Others are made up of layers slightly inclined, and some look like giant clamshells set down on the land....Ordinarily the tops of the hills assume a long, sloping, rounded shape because of the soft nature of the rock and the wearing power of the deluging rains."[76]

1968

1997

By 1968 afforestation, started by the British and now carried out by the Jewish National Fund, has advanced considerably. The road linking Jerusalem with Tel Aviv and the coastal plain is being expanded to a four-lane highway, with the prayer place of the ham 'Ali and the trees around it lying between the northern and southern lanes.

By 1990 forests and increased natural vegetation have blurred to a considerable extent the original outlines of the mountains and valleys. North of the highway, trails give access to parts of the afforested area.

Our photo of 7 Feb 1997 shows the effects of the fire of 2 Jul 95.

1990

Abu Ghosh

The Bavarian photo of 15 May 1918 shows a stretch of the road ascending to Jerusalem as it makes a wide bend north of the Arab village of Abu Ghosh, conquered by the British on 20 Nov 17. The large rectangular building to the right (west) of the narrow road going up to the village is a 12th-century crusader church that forms part of a Benedictine monastery established in 1901. On the hill close to the photo's lower margin is the modern church of Notre Dame de l'Arche de l'Alliance, with the remains of a Byzantine church close by.[77]

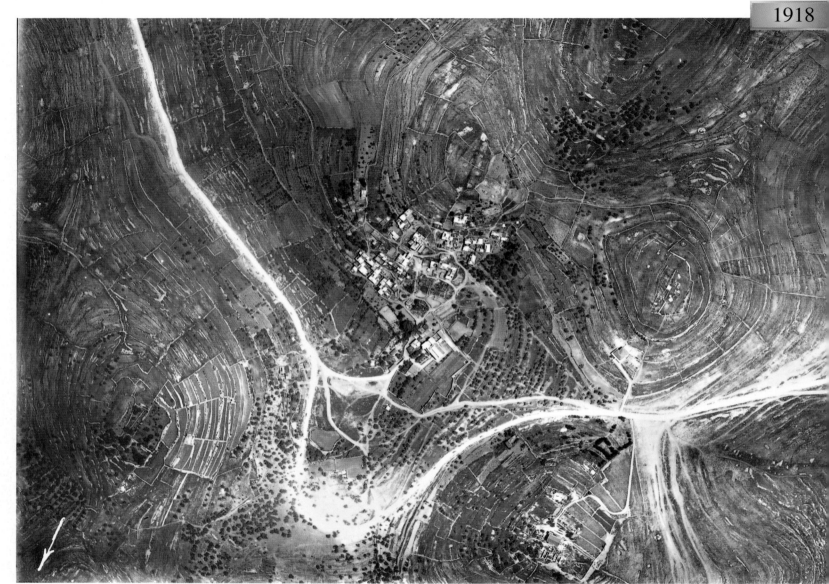

Turkish soldiers killed in combat, 1917.

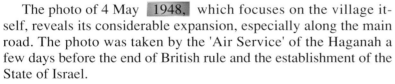

1994

The photo of 4 May **1948,** which focuses on the village itself, reveals its considerable expansion, especially along the main
road. The photo was taken by the 'Air Service' of the Haganah a
few days before the end of British rule and the establishment of the
State of Israel.

*Most villagers of Abu Ghosh maintained friendly relations with
the Haganah and therefore stayed put while other Arab villagers
in the area fled during the early stages of Israel's War of Independence. Nevertheless, most of Abu Ghosh's inhabitants left early in
July 1948, prompted by the advice of Israeli officers. Israeli commanders, apprehensive of intelligence leaks to near-by Arab forces,
urged evacuation of the remaining villagers but were overruled by
the Government, and in the ensuing weeks most of those who had
left were allowed to return.*[78]

The diagonal in the upper third of our photo of 2 Aug **1994**
is the four-lane highway leading to Jerusalem, which cuts through
two hills and passes an expanded Abu Ghosh on the south side.
The road paved by the Turks now serves as a secondary road, with
the houses of Abu Ghosh on either side of its wide bend. Qiryat
Ye'arim (Telshe-Stone), a Jewish residential quarter founded in
1975, stands on the round hill west of Abu Ghosh, close to the
highway.

Population			
	1922	1945	1995
Abu Ghosh	**475**	**860**	**4,160**
Qiryat Ye`arim			**2,130**

The British photo of 28 Nov 1917 was taken while a fierce battle for the possession of the summit of An-Nabi Samwil, which dominates the area northwest of Jerusalem, was under way. The large building on the summit – seen near the middle of the right margin – is a mosque (originally a 12th-century crusader church) that Jewish, Christian and Muslim traditions alike regard as the resting place of the Prophet Samuel. The road from Jerusalem, seen in the upper right corner, passes the small Arab village of An-Nabi Samwil before reaching the mosque.

The outcome of the battle for An-Nabi Samwil sealed the fate of Turkish Jerusalem. Two British infantry regiments of the 75th Division captured the summit on 21 Nov 17. The following day the Turks shelled An-Nabi Samwil and launched three attacks, the last of which was repulsed with great difficulty. The Turks attacked again on 27 and 29 Nov; their shells destroyed large parts of the mosque and smashed its minaret, but the British succeeded in holding their position.

▲ *British soldiers burying Turks killed in combat, 1917.*

▼ *British soldiers in ruined An-Nabi Samwil, 1917.*

K halil al-Sakakini, a Christian-Arab innovative educator, followed the batt from his Jerusalem home. He wrote in his diary:

"Saturday, 24 Nov 17. Yesterday the guns resumed their shelling and did not sto all night; it was as if the shells were fired near my ears. The shelling intensified sunrise and we went up to the upper chamber and saw with our own eyes wha we have often heard of, or seen, in war newspapers. We saw the bombs fallin near the village of An-Nabi Samwil, their smoke rising like clouds, their spark flashing. Some of them fell behind the mountains, and we saw only the smok here and there, but the guns' noise at the firing was powerful. Later an airplan appeared and started to circle above the mountains, as if it were a reconnaissanc plane. The guns began to shell it and we saw the bombs' smoke above, unde neath or near it.

"There can be no doubt that he who hears the noise of the guns from a distanc does think that Jerusalem has been reduced to dust and her inhabitants to ashe: If all the guns we have been hearing for days would have hit their targets – th war would have come to an end, but it seems that the hits are very few, and the continue to shoot all this time, as if saying, 'Perhaps among those that go astra one arrow shall hit.'

"Tuesday, 27 Nov 17.... Heavy shelling continued until the morning hours fro various directions. At 3 p.m. the shelling reached an unprecedented intensity. Th shells fell like drops of rain on the mosque of An-Nabi Samwil and its surrounding and at 4 p.m. the minaret fell down, after having withstood so remarkably. Lat shells started coming down on the mountain from its beginning to its end, on i sides, at its feet, and in the wadis around it, until it resembled an erupting volcan At sunset the shells exploded with blinding flashes. Later the shooting of the gu subsided, then stopped entirely and it became silent. God knows the number dead and wounded on both sides. Undoubtedly it is enormous."[79]

1995

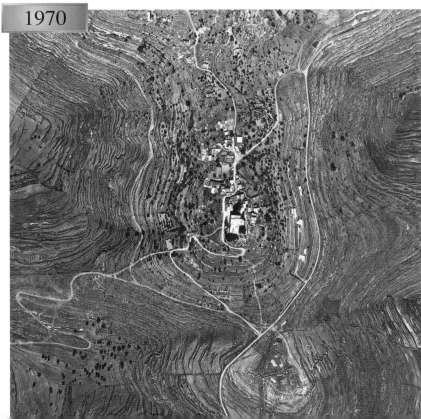

1970

The mosque and the minaret were repaired during the years of British rule. On 22/23 Apr 48 the 4th Battalion of the Palmah Har'el Brigade attacked An-Nabi Samwil, in an attempt to relieve Neve Ya'aqov and 'Atarot, two isolated Jewish settlements north of Jerusalem, but were repulsed after suffering heavy losses. An-Nabi Samwil subsequently became part of the Kingdom of Jordan's West Bank. One of the villagers headed a band that repeatedly crossed the armistice line, killed Israelis and stole cattle, triggering an Israeli retaliatory raid on the night of 11/12 Jul 53. During the Six-Day War of 1967, the inhabitants of An-Nabi Samwil fled; their houses (with one exception) were destroyed on the orders of Israeli commanders who remembered the costly setback in 1948.[80]

The Survey of Israel photo of 8 Jun 1970 shows the area three years later. Our photo of 10 Feb 1995 shows recent excavations which prove that the crusader church stood at the center of a fortified monastery. One can also see the spread of afforestation and the road that links Jerusalem with Giv'at Ze'ev.

Population			
1922	1945	1967	1996
121	**200**	**66**	**96**

Hebron

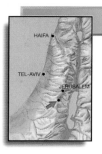

The Bavarian photo of 4 Sep 1918 shows Hebron as consisting of dense clusters of houses built along the valley and on the slopes above it. Adjacent to the rightmost cluster is a large gray rectangle with bright edges. This is the building that Herod the Great erected above the Cave of Machpelah, which, according to tradition, is the burial place of the patriarchs Abraham, Isaac and Jacob. Under the Byzantines the sanctuary became a church; and under the Muslims, the Mosque of Abraham. In the 12th century the crusaders erected the sloping-roofed cathedral church of Saint Abraham, which occupies the southeastern two-fifths of the Herodian precinct. The dark rhombus close to the lower margin is Birket es-Sultan (the Sultan's Pool). The Jewish quarter is located close to

▲ *The Cave of Machpelah / the Mosque of Abraham and its surroundings on a 1921 postcard*

1918

the left edge of Hebron's largest cluster of houses, above and to the left of this pool. Larger, more widely spaced houses are seen near the photo's center, along the roads leading to Jerusalem and Beersheba. Biblical Hebron is said to have been situated on the round tree-covered hill at lower left.

The British entered Hebron on 5 Dec 17, more than a month after they had conquered Beersheba. Franz von Papen, operations officer of the Turkish-German force in the Palestinian theater (who was to become Germany's chancellor and later served as Hitler's ambassador to Austria and Turkey), wrote in his memoirs that he was never able to understand why after the conquest of Beersheba the British did not attempt to advance directly to Hebron and thence to Jerusalem.[81] Allenby preferred to advance along the coastal plain and threaten Jerusalem from the west, thereby forcing the Turks in the Hebron area to withdraw northward. His plan succeeded: when Maj.-Gen. Mott's Detachment eventually advanced on Hebron from the south, it encountered no Turkish forces.

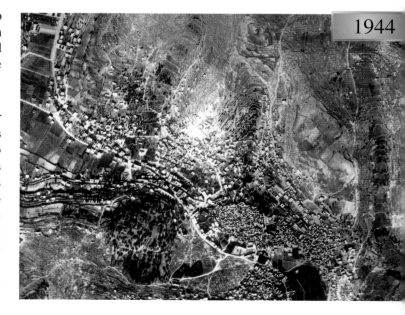

1944

1994

By the time the RAF took its photo on 16 Dec 1944, Hebron ad no Jewish inhabitants. After the massacre of 59 Jews during e Riots of 1929, the small Jewish community dispersed; an tempt to renew it was cut short in 1936, at the outbreak of the rab Revolt. The photo of 1945 shows some sprawl of the town to the hills above the densely built old clusters, as well as the rge British police station northwest of them. The photo of 18 Jun 1967 – taken by the Survey of Israel shortly after Hebron was ccupied by Israel during the Six-Day War – indicates that, under rdanian rule (1948-67), the town had continued to expand. The yout of the old clusters remained unchanged, with one notable ception, that the area south of the Cave of Machpelah – the uslim Mosque of Abraham – has been razed to facilitate access the sanctuary. The large, flat-roofed buildings of the wholesale arket stand out to the left of the Sultan's Pool. Our photo of 26 b 1994 shows that under Israeli rule Hebron has expanded ill more. The small bright block of the renovated Jewish quarter ands out above and to the left of the Sultan's Pool, to the right of

the wholesale market. We took the photo one day after a Jewish fanatic had murdered 29 Muslims who were praying in the mosque; some of the blood-soaked carpets can be seen being washed on the building's roof (see photo left).

The Israeli army evacuated most of Hebron on 17 Jan 97.

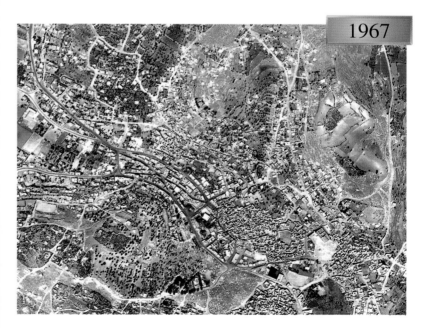

1967

Population	
1922	**16,577** (incl. 430 J)
1945	**24,560**
1967	**38,309**
1996	**94,758** (plus 5,220 J in Qiryat Arba')

Bethlehem

The photo taken by German Squadron 302 on 23 Nov 1917 and preserved in the Steiner collection shows Bethlehem from the southeast. The large complex on the high ground at the southeastern end of the town is that of the 6th-century Byzantine Church of the Holy Nativity. The old part of Bethlehem is the densely built cluster on the hilltop left (west) of the church. The diagonal linking points A and B is a stretch of the road from Jerusalem to Hebron. The Tomb of Rachel is the small domed building within a bright area left (west) of this road, close to point A. The large enclosure with a round building in its center that occupies a hilltop left of the densely built cluster is the Carmelite monastery.

Mott's Detachment entered Bethlehem on 9 Dec 17 without encountering any resistance from the Turks and immediately continued northward to Jerusalem.

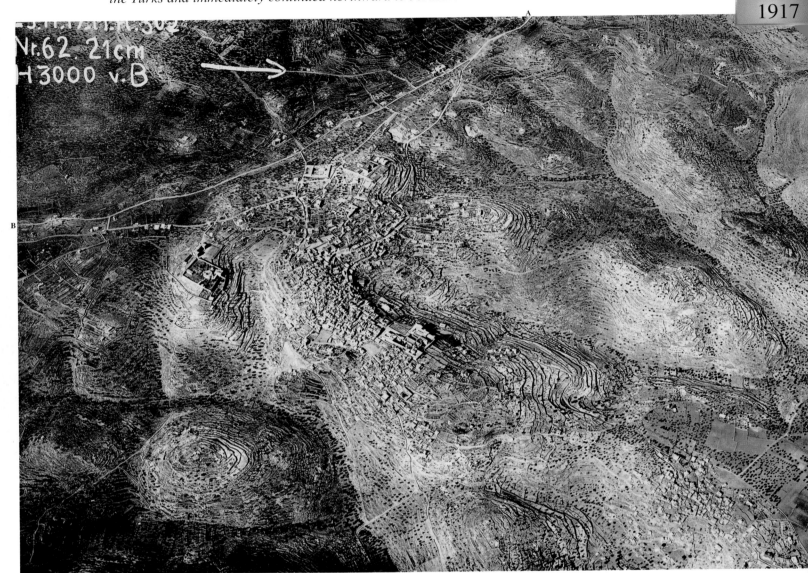

Zoltán Kluger's photo of 1939 shows a slight expanded town. The village of Beit Jala occupies th slope in the photo's upper left corner. The Survey Israel photo of 18 Jun 1967, taken a few days aft the Israeli conquest of the area, shows the town's furth growth; it also shows that a part of the old cluster houses to the west of the Church of the Holy Nativit was razed to make room for an enlarged Mange Square. The densely built blocks near the Tomb Rachel are the 'A'ida and Ghazza refugee camps esta lished in 1948 for refugees from Lydda, Ramleh, Be Jubrin and other localities.

1993

Our photo of 5 Dec 1993 documents the further growth of ethlehem under Israeli rule.

The Israeli army evacuated Bethlehem on 21 Dec 95.

1967

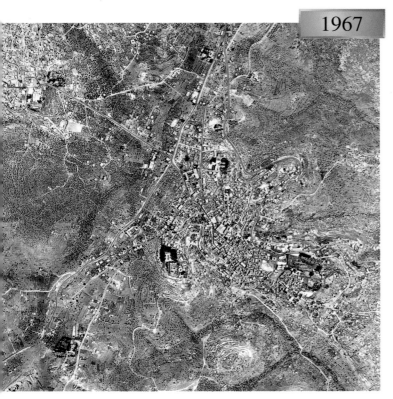

C. Guy Powles, author of the account on the activities of the New Zealand Brigade in Sinai and Palestine during World War I, wrote: "Bethlehem is a Christian city and the people are open, frank and vivacious, very different from the Moslem Arabs. It was a pleasure to ride through the streets. The people were always pleased to see our men, and took no pains to disguise their feelings, as the gloomy Mahomedans do. And it was a clean city, free from the appalling 'Eastern smell' one had found everywhere....The people declare that they are not Arabs, but that they are descendants of the Crusaders. They certainly are not generally so dark and swarthy as the Arabs. All the women have colour in their cheeks and many have blue eyes, and their dress is interesting and picturesque. Apart from its attractive colouring – a sky-blue robe with red girdle and embroidered jacket – they wear a head-dress extraordinarily like that of the ladies of the Crusaders of old. The Crusader's lady wore a head-dress not unlike a giant extinguisher, from which flowed white drapery. The women of Bethlehem wear a snowy white cloth covering the head and borne aloft upon an erection closely resembling that of the crusader's lady, and from which it flows down the back."[82]

Population	
1922	**6,658** (5,838 C, 818 M)
1945	**8,820** (6,430 C, 2,370 M)
1967	**16,313** (6,405 C)
1996	**21,697**

Jerusalem - western entrance

The broad line that traverses the Bavarian photo of 18 Jul 1918 from right to left is a stretch of the main road from Jaffa as it reaches the western outskirts of Jerusalem. The large buildings of a Jewish home for the aged and a Jewish hospital, built between 1901 and 1910, are at the center. Houses of the Arab village of Sheikh Badr are seen near the photo's left margin; a part of the Arab village of Lifta appears in the lower right corner. The straight lines in the upper right corner are the streets of the Jewish quarter of Giv'at Shaul, founded in 1910. The bright line running from the large buildings in the center to the upper margin is the road leading to the Arab village of 'Ein Karim. The narrow dark line that intersects with the roads to Jaffa and 'Ein Karim, just to the right of the large buildings, is the field railway that the British constructed in the summer of 1918 in order to supply their troops at the front, north of Jerusalem.

The ceremony surrendering Jerusalem to the British took place on 9 Dec 17 near the large buildings seen in the photo's center.

▲ *9 Dec 17: The mayor of Jerusalem, the whi flag of surrender, and Sgts. F. G. Hurcomb and . Sedgewick of the 60th (London) Division.*

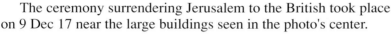

◄ *The surrender flag made from a bedsheet, now in the Imperial War Museum, London. The Arabic note reads: "The mayor of Jerusalem the Noble, Hussein Hashem al-Husseini, 9 December 1917."*

The main new features on the RAF photo of 7 Dec 194 are the Jewish quarter Qiryat Moshe, to the right of the road to 'E Karim, and the trapezoid garage of Jewish Jerusalem's bus comp ny, Ha-Meqasher, left of that road. The dot in the oval plaza in t photo's lower left corner is the monument commemorating Jerus lem's surrender on 9 Dec 17.

In Jerusalem, too, Arab sniping began in the wake of the U partition resolution of 29 Nov 47. In January 48 the Jewish militi emerged victorious from the struggle for the control of the city western entrance; the inhabitants of Lifta were intimidated ar fled and those of Sheikh Badr were expelled.

1995

The Survey of Israel photo of 16 Jun **1967** shows, left of e garage, the trapezium of Jerusalem's Conference Center. To the ft of it is the complex of single-storied buildings that houses rael's Ministry for Foreign Affairs.

Our photo of 10 Feb **1995** shows a widened entrance into rusalem that by-passes the original Turkish road from the south. rusalem's central bus station stands out in the lower left corner. e Holiday Inn (formerly Hilton) hotel soars behind the red-ofed Conference Center. The Bank of Israel building and the ime Minister's Office appear in the upper left corner.

1967

944

117

The large building near the right margin of this Bavarian photo of 4 Jun 1918 is the Greek Orthodox Monastery of the Cross, originally founded by Georgian Christians. The stretch linking points A and B forms part of a road that leads to the Old City's Jaffa Gate (which is beyond point A). The large building in the lower left corner, with two crosses painted on its flat roof, is the Ratisbonne Monastery, built in the 1880s; during World War I it served first as an Austrian and later as a British hospital.

The Bezalel Art School, founded in 1906, is situat about halfway between the Ratisbonne Monastery a the lower margin. In the center of the sparsely wood vale that runs from the Monastery of the Cross to lower margin, one may distinguish a narrow black li this is the British pipeline that carried water from Hebron mountains to Jerusalem. The regularly laid complexes near the center of the lower margin are t Jewish quarters Sha'arey Hesed and Nahalat Zede founded in 1908.

Advertisements in The Palestine News *of 28 Mar*

1994

1944

The Survey of Israel photo of 16 Jun 1967 shows, in the lower right corner, the large rectangular building of the Knesset (Parliament).

Our photo of 2 Aug 1994 shows the progress of afforestation and, on the vale's eastern slope, the high rises of the Wolfson residential quarter.

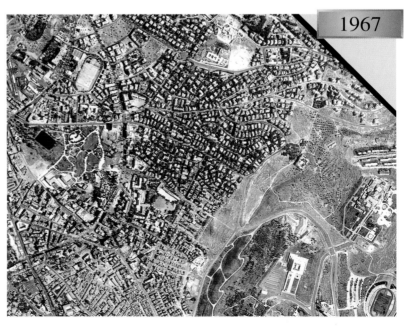

1967

The RAF photo of 7 Dec 1944 shows, on the plateau left (east) of the vale, the Jewish quarter of Rehavyah. The Arab quarter of Talbiyeh and the YMCA building with its oval stadium to its right appear in the upper left corner.

The Arab inhabitants of Talbiyeh fled during the early stages of the War of 1948. The northern part of the Vale of the Cross served as a small airfield while Jewish Jerusalem was under siege.

The Bavarian photo of 29 Apr 1918 shows, in the lower right corner, the Old City's Jaffa Gate and, immediately to the left of it, the Citadel ('the Tower of David'). The bright broad ribbon leading leftward from Jaffa Gate is Hebron Road; it runs roughly parallel to the Old City's western wall (and to the photo's lower margin), then crosses the Valley of Hinnom at right angles, and continues to point A in the bottom left corner. The regularly laid out area on the valley's far side is Yemin Moshe, a Jewish quarter founded in 1891. The elongated bright-roofed building left of Yemin Moshe is Mishkenot Sha'ananim, the first Jewish complex to be built outside the Old City, in 1860. Jaffa Road leads from Jaffa Gate to point B on the right margin; the Old City's north-western wall is the straight dark line immediately to the right of the row of houses on Jaffa Road's right side. The large building near point B is the convent of the Daughters of Charity of St. Vincent de Paul; the triangular building adjacent to it is the German Hotel Fast. Many British tents are visible among the trees in the photo's upper half.

1918

"The Last Days of Jerusalem under the Turks," an account published on 7 Mar 18 in *The Palestine News*, the weekly issued for the British soldiers in the country, says inter alia: "As the Turkish flood finally ebbed away into the shadowy depths of the Valley of Jehoshaphat, hastening down to the Jordan, the townsfolk roused themselves from the lethargy into which starvation and the Turkish police had plunged them. They fell upon a variety of buildings, official or requsitioned for official purposes, and looted them, even stripping the roofs, doors and floors of the Ottoman barracks next to the Tower of David for firewood. It must be admitted that, as the Government had furnished and maintained itself almost entirely by uncompensated requisitions, the mob was only trying to indemnify itself. But this disorder ceased as suddenly as it had arisen at the appearance of the British infantry."

▲ *An advertisement that appeared in* The Palestine News *on 2: Mar 18.*

1995

1945

The photo of 16 Jun 1967 shows the state of this strip a few days after Israel's victory in the Six-Day War: the stretch of Hebron Road from Jaffa Gate to the perpendicular crossing of the Valley of Hinnom shows signs of long disuse; many of the houses that had stood close to the outer side of the northwestern corner of the wall and were damaged in 1948, had just been razed. The road between the YMCA building and the King David Hotel is now called King David Street.

The Mamilla project, under construction outside the northwestern wall, stands out in our photo of 10 Feb 1995: it occupies a considerable part of the former no-man's-land.

The RAF photo of 15 Mar 1945 attests to the considerable evelopment of this part of Jerusalem under British rule. The most rominent additions are the YMCA building with its oval stadium nd, on the near side of broad Julian's Way, the King David Hotel.

During the War of Independence of 1948 the area saw fierce ghting that ended in a stalemate, with the Arab Legion on the Old ity walls and the Israelis dug in opposite, at Yemin Moshe. Fol-wing the Israeli-Jordanian armistice agreement of 1949, a strip land between the two became a no-man's-land.

1967

THE OLD CITY

The southwestern corner of the Old City, Mount Zion and Yemin Moshe appear in the lower right corner of this Bavarian photo of 3 Jun 1918. Above and left of Yemin Moshe, Jerusalem's railway station stands out, with several wagons on its tracks; the tracks run all the way to the photo's upper left corner. The dark triangle above the railway station is the German Colony, founded in 1873 by members of the "Temple Society;" the colony's streets are lined with trees. The regularly laid out streets to the left and above the photo's center, with houses widely spaced along them, constitute the Greek Colony. A road meandering from the right end of this colony leads to the Greek Orthodox Monastery of St. Simeon, built in 1890, which is visible at the middle of the upper margin. The narrow black line linking points A and B is the British water pipeline; it crosses a second narrow line in the photo's upper right quarter, which is the British field railway leading to the front north of Jerusalem. The broad bright line leading to point C is Hebron Road; in the photo's lower left quarter, it passes between the convent of the Sisters of St. Claire – its extensive grounds surrounded by a stone fence – and the houses of the Arab suburb of Baq'ah. Between St. Claire's and Mount Zion can be seen the houses of the Arab suburb of Abu Tor.

▼ British milita[ry] signpost in Jerusalem, now i[n] the Imperial War Museum, London

1918

1945

The RAF photo of 20 Feb 1945 corresponds to the le[ft] half of the Bavarian photo. It shows a substantially expande[d] Baq'ah and Greek Colony, as well as the new Arab quarter [of] Katamon, which extends all the way to the Monastery of St. Sim[e]on, visible in the grove in the photo's upper right corner. The sma[ll] single-street Jewish suburb of Meqor Hayyim is in the upper le[ft] corner, its houses surrounded by vegetation; the regularly laid o[ut] Allenby Barracks of the British army are in the lower left corne[r].

During World War II, with most of its inhabitants interned [or] deported by the British, the German Colony dwindled; in 1948 [it] ceased to exist. On 29/30 Apr 48 the St. Simeon Monastery was th[e] scene of fierce fighting between the 4th Battalion of the Palma[ch] Har'el Brigade and local and Iraqi irregulars of the Arab Libera[tion Army; the battle ended with a Jewish victory that put an en[d]

1995

Arab sniping on nearby Jewish quarters and to the isolation of *Meqor Hayyim and other Jewish suburbs in southern Jerusalem. The battle was followed by the flight of the remaining Arabs of Katamon and Baqʻah. The armistice agreement of 1949 gave the upper (western) part of Abu Tor to Israel and the lower part to Jordan.*

The Survey of Israel photograph of 16 Jun 1967 shows a considerably expanded Katamon (officially called Gonen) and Baqʻah (Geʻulim), both inhabited by Jews. The photo's upper right corner, with no counterpart on the RAF photo of 1945, shows the quarters of Qomemiyyut (up to 1948, Talbiyeh), Rehavyah and Qiryat Shmuel.

Our photo of 10 Feb 1995 shows the various quarters merged into a continuously built up area. The Liberty Bell Garden stands out above and to the right of the railway station. The large white building dominating the photo's upper right quarter is the Jerusalem Theatre complex; the President's residence, the Van Leer Institute, and the Israel Academy of Sciences and Humanities are to the right of it.

1967

123

The area south of the southernmost suburbs of World War I Jerusalem appears on this Bavarian photo of 11 Jul 1918. The broad bright diagonal linking points A and B is Hebron Road; the gray, narrower one linking C and D is Bethlehem Road; the partially obliterated diagonal linking E and F is the old, no longer used road to Hebron. The tent encampment along this road, with four airplanes near its largest tents, is that of the contact patrol flight (Flight C) of British Squadron 142. There are several British encampments east and west of Hebron Road. The beginning of the sharp descent to the Judean Desert is visible in the upper right and lower left corners.

1918

The RAF photo of 20 Feb 1945 shows, in the area where Flight C had encamped, the Jewish suburb of Talpiyyot, its houses surrounded by vegetation. To the north of it are the Allenby Barracks and the Arab suburb of Baq'ah. A Jewish training farm is in the lower right quarter. The few houses to the left of point N, on the rim of the descent to the Judean Desert, are those of North Talpiyyot.

On 21-25 May 48 Kibbutz Ramat Rachel, about 1 km south of Talpiyyot, came under attack by irregular Egyptian units. The kibbutz fell twice, but ultimately the Arabs were repulsed. According to the 1949 armistice agreement, the training farm fell within the Israeli part of a demilitarized zone bounded on the west by the easternmost street of Talpiyyot.

1945

The Survey of Israel photo of 16 Jun 1967 shows some orchards of Kibbutz Ramat Rachel planted in the area between the training farm and Talpiyyot. The line dividing the Israeli part of the demilitarized zone from the Jordanian one is easily discernible, as the Israeli part is considerably darker (for an explanation, see pp. 18-19). Large blocks of housing are visible south of Baqʻah (Geʼulim), and there is a cluster of log cabins – temporary dwellings for new immigrants – near North Talpiyyot. The large building in the woods in the lower right corner is the local United Nations headquarters, originally the residence of the British High Commissioner for Palestine.

On our photo of 2 Aug 1994, Talpiyyot and Baqʻah form part of a continuously built-up area. East Talpiyyot is the new quarter east of Ramat Rachel's fields. The Haas and Sherover promenades extend along the verge of the descent toward the Judean Desert; the Peace Forest covers the western part of the slope, and an Arab suburb the eastern one.

Population of Jerusalem	
1922	**62,578** [33,971 J, 14,699 M, 13,413 C]
1945	**157,080** [97,000 J, 30,630 M, 29,350 C]
1968	**275,000** [203,200 J, 71,800 Arabs and others]
1995	**591,400** [417,000 J, 174,400 Arabs and others]

Jerusalem - the New City's center

The Bavarian photo of 15 Sep 1918 shows the center of the New City, its houses markedly larger and its streets broader than those of the Old City, the northwestern part of which appears in the lower right corner. Two main thoroughfares start at the Old City's Damascus Gate: one of them, Nablus Road, leads northward to point A on the margin; the other, Prophets' Street, runs northwestward to point B. The round, dark-domed building north of this street is the Abyssinian church, consecrated in 1893. The many grayish houses of the Jewish quarter of Meah She'arim, founded in 1874, stand out in the photo's upper left quarter. Jaffa Road is the bright line linking

points C and D. The two large quadrangles to the right of Jaffa Road are pilgrim hospices belonging to the Russian Compound, which arose in the late 1850s; the two hospices flank Jerusalem's Russian cathedral. Left of Jaffa Road is the Jewish quarter of Nahalat Shiv'ah, founded in 1869. In the lower left corner is the Muslim Mamilla Cemetery, with the rectangular Mamilla Pool in its midst. The large E-shaped building adjacent to the Old City's northwestern corner is the Monastery of Notre Dame de France.

T he following proclamation was published by the British authorities in Jerusalem, probably in the summer of 1919:
"Notice is hereby given to all concerned that the speed limit of Motor driven Vehicles within the radius of one and a half miles Damascus Gate is not to exceed 8 Miles per hour.
"Any person contravening this notice is liable on conviction to a fi from one to fifteen Egyptian Pounds or from twenty four hours to or month's imprisonment and may be tried by a Civil Magistrate."[83]

The RAF photograph of 15 Mar 1945 shows the are more densely built up, some of the main additions being alor Jaffa Road and along the new Princess Mary Street that connec Jaffa Road with point E on the margin.

1995

1945

E

Our photo of 10 Feb **1995** shows the new Peace Road – which serves in this area as a divide between the Jewish and Arab parts of Jerusalem – running along the western sides of the two triangles. There are several rows of palm trees between this road and Damascus Gate. Jerusalem's new City Hall, fronted by the checkered Safra Plaza, stands out near the lower quadrangle of the Russian Compound.

1967

On 23 May 48, an armored column of the Arab Legion was *pulsed at Notre Dame de France. The 1949 armistice agreement* *tablished in the area a no-man's-land strip between Israel in the* *est and Jordan in the east.*

On the Survey of Israel photograph of 16 Jun **1967** this strip sumes the form of two dark-hued triangles, the lower of the two arting at the Old City wall. The Mandelbaum Gate, the transition int for neutrals traveling from Jordan to Israel, is near the north-n extremity of the upper triangle. (On 19 May 48, and on several casions between 9 and 19 July, other Arab Legion thrusts were iven back here.) Princess Mary Street is now called Queen Shlo-zion Street.

E

This Bavarian photo of 15 Sep 1918 partially overlaps with the previous one and was shot at the same time. Nablus Road leads from the Old City's Damascus Gate to point A on the margin. The cluster of buildings near point A, to the right of Nablus Road, is the American Colony. The next cluster to the right of Nablus Road, closer to the Old City, contains the Anglican cathedral of St. George, consecrated in 1898. Between this cluster and the Old City, also to the right of Nablus Road, the Dominican monastery of St. Etienne stands out; its church, whose flying buttresses are clearly visible, was consecrated in 1900. The broad bright way that parallels the Old City's northern wall and then turns right is a stretch of the Jerusalem-Jericho road. The small bright quadrangle that forms part of the northern wall marks Herod's Gate (in Arabic, Bab ez-Zahra). Two ways fan out northward from this gate: the one on the left – the future Saladin Street – joins Nablus road near St. George's Cathedral, while the one on the right leads to the Arab suburb of Bab ez-Zahra, founded in the early 1890s. To the right of it is the still smaller Arab suburb of Wadi el-Joz, founded about the same time.

1918

1945

The RAF photo of 15 Mar 1945 documents the considerable growth of Bab ez-Zahra and Wadi el-Joz under the British Mandate. The large complex north of the Old City's northeastern corner is the Rockefeller Museum.

The Survey of Israel photo of 16 Jun 1967 shows that, under Jordanian rule, Bab ez-Zahra and Wadi el-Joz continued to develop and eventually merged to form the center of the Arab New City. A garden can be seen east of Damascus Gate, along the northern wall of the Old City. Our photo of 2 Aug 1994 discloses no significant changes.

1967

Maj.-Gen. A. W. Money, Chi[ef]
Enemy Territory (South),
'Notice' that included the follo[wing]
"Whereas it is desirable to
Criminal Code concerning
IT IS HEREBY ORDERED
1. The penalty of whipp[ing]
boy who is over seven
The whipping shall be
not exceed six strokes
age and under, or tw
over fourteen years
strokes is ordered, th
between which there
and the offender sha
2. The whipping shall t
in charge of the prison
practitioner must be p[resent]
are given."[84]

n 20 Nov 18, Maj.-Gen. Money issued the following 'Notice': "1. Except with the consent in writing of a Military Governor or eputy Military Governor, no Olive Tree that is not either dead or past earing may be cut down for any purpose whatsoever.

2. It shall not be a defence to a charge made under this Notice that he tree or trees were cut down in order to fulfil a contract for the upply of wood to the Military Authorities.

3. An offence against this notice constitutes a misdemeanour punish-ble by imprisonment not exceeding 6 months or fine not exceeding Eg[yptian] 50 or both and may be tried by a Civil Magistrate."[87]

Our photo of 10 Feb 1995 attests to an immense growth of At-Tur and 'Isawiya; between the two is the Mount Scopus campus of the Hebrew University of Jerusalem.

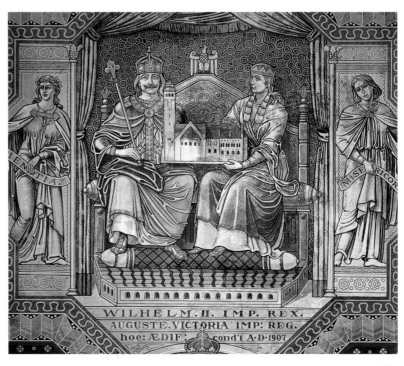

A view of the Arab village f At-Tur from the top of the ussian Tower on the Mount of lives. The round, domed uilding surrounded by a high one wall, which stands out in e village's center, is the 12th-entury crusader Church of the scension. The Old City is in the ackground.

Our color photo was taken om the same spot in July 1997.

▶ *Kaiser Wilhelm II and his wife, as they appear in a painting on the roof of the church of the Auguste Viktoria complex.*

THE OLD CITY

The Bavarian photo taken early in the morning of 22 Jun **1918** shows, at center, the estate of Sir John Gray-Hill of Liverpool, surrounded by a stone wall; Gray-Hill's residence stands left of the way leading to Auguste Viktoria (which is beyond the photo's upper margin). There are trenches beyond the southeastern part of the stone wall. The Arab village of 'Isawiya appears in the photo's lower left corner.

On 7 Feb 18 the Zionist Organization purchased the Gray-Hill estate in order to establish on it the Hebrew University of Jerusalem, and on 24 Jul 18 Chaim Weizmann presided over a ceremony in which the foundation stones of the future university were laid.

1918

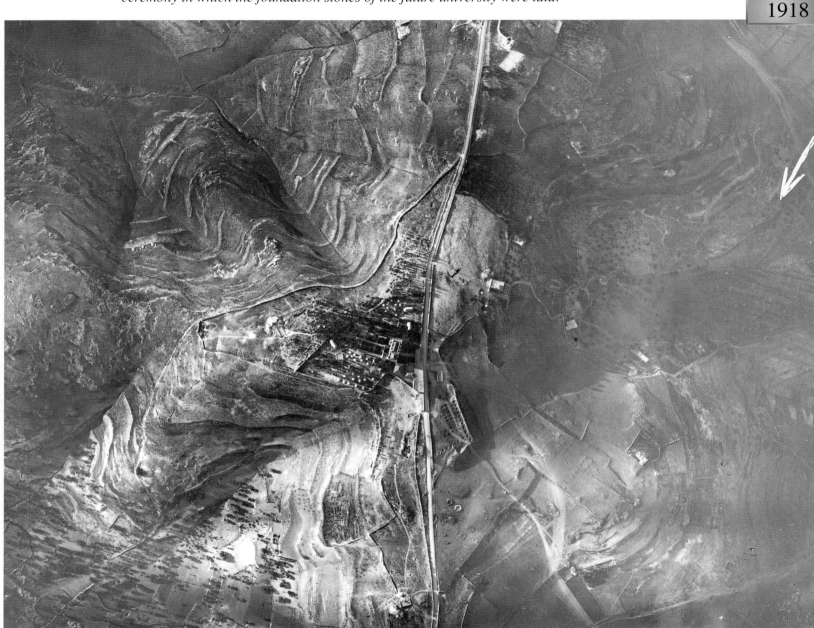

In his speech at the ceremony on Mount Scopus, Dr. Weizmann said, inter alia: "Many....will have had their attention rivetted on the apparent contrast between to-day's ceremony and the scenes of warfare within a few miles of us. For only a brief moment we are allowing ourselves to indulge in a mental armistice, and in laying aside all thoughts of strife we try to pierce the veil of war and glance into the future. A week ago we were keeping the Fast of Ab, reminding us that the Temple had been utterly destroyed and the Jewish national political existence extinguished apparently for ever. But throughout the long centuries, we, the stiff-necked people, have refused to acknowledge defeat and 'Judea capta' is once more on the eve of triumph. Here, out of the miseries and the desolation of war, is being created the first germ of a new life.... It is fitting that Great Britain, aided by her great Allies, in the midst of tribulation and sorrow, should stand sponsor to this University. Great Britain has understood that it is just because these are times of stress, just because we tend to become lost in the events of the day, that there is a need to transcend these details by this bold appeal to the world's imagination. Here what seemed but a dream a few years ago is now becoming a reality."[88]

1995

Zoltán Kluger's photo of [1937] shows the He-brew University from the east. The building with the small dome atop its northern part is the Jewish National and University Library.

During the War of 1948 Mount Scopus held out as a Jewish exclave deep within Arab Jerusalem. On 13 Apr 48, four days after units of the Jewish IZL and LHI organizations massacred more than 100 inhabitants of Deir Yassin, an Arab village west of Jerusalem, Arabs attacked a convoy that was on its way to Mount Scopus, and massacred 78 of its passengers, mostly staff mem-bers of the Hebrew University and of Hadassah Hospi-tal. In May Mount Scopus repulsed a number of Arab forays. After the war Israel maintained in the exclave a garrison – ostensibly composed of policemen – that was relieved by convoys that passed under Arab Legion escort through Jordanian Jerusalem. Meanwhile, the Hebrew University resumed its activities in buildings scattered throughout Israeli Jerusalem; in the late 1950s a new campus was established in Giv'at Ram, west of the Vale of the Cross. After Israel's victory in the Six-Day War, the Mount Scopus campus was reacti-vated and substantially enlarged, and constitutes now the university's main campus.

24 Jul 18: Chaim Weizmann and Maj.-Gen. Money arrive at the foundation ceremony of the Hebrew University.

On our photo of 10 Feb [1995,] the small dome of the old library build-ing – now the Faculty of Law – is dwarfed by the University Tower to its left. The long rectangle to the left of the summit is the old botanical garden (a new one has been set up on the Giv'at Ram campus). The Jerusalem branch of Brigham Young University is visible near the photo's upper right corner.

1937

Jerusalem - Shu'afat

The Arab village of Shu'afat, situated 3.5 km north of Jerusalem's Old City, appears on the Bavarian photo of 15 Aug 1918 to the right (west) of the Jerusalem-Nablus road. The dark narrow line between the village and the road is the British field railway that ran from Jerusalem's railway station northward to the front. A train is visible on the tracks southeast of the village.
The British occupied Shu'afat on 9 Dec 17, the day on which Jerusalem surrendered.

The RAF photo of 29 Dec 1944 shows that under the British Mandate the village extended along the route that links it to the Jerusalem-Nablus highway, and on both sides of that highway. The original nucleus of Shu'afat changed but little. The line of the disused field railway can still be traced in part.

D r. Steuber, chief medical officer of the German-Turkish forces o the Palestinian front, described the Turkish retreat from Jerusa lem northward, in which he took part in December 1917: "The Jerusa lem-Nablus road is good, but is today congested with troops an columns of the beaten and disintegrating 8th Turkish Army....Here tw brown Anatolians drag with them a mortally wounded comrade; th bloody, torn limbs hang loosely from the ripped rags. There lies a ma behind a boulder, his head covered with a kaffiyeh, and rings wi death. In between, Turkish officers on jaded, skeleton-like nags, stoli and outwardly untouched by the limitless misery all around. Sudden the motor-car stops: three camels lie down across the road, Turkis harem-women are on the camels' backs, their heads veiled, the naked legs dangling down. Only the driver's shrill siren makes ther clear the road with a wild leap. A column of rickety carts is overtaken a Red Crescent and a penetrating iodoform smell mark them a remnants of a field infirmary. Suddenly, loud shouts: a Turkish fiel battery blocks the road, and the horses, buffaloes and mules canno go on. A herd pushes into it all, and soon the car crushes a long-eare goat.... The uninterrupted, piercing sound of the motor-car sirens, th shouts of men and animals, all this preys hypnotizingly on one thinking and feeling, and deadens one so dreadfully, that in luci intervals one asks oneself whether one still is a civilized being at all."

◄ *The Sixth Australian Light Horse Regiment at camp near the road ascending to Mount Scopus.*

1995

On the night of 22/23 Apr 48, the 5th Battalion of the Palmah *…r'el Brigade captured most of Shu'afat in an attempt to open the* *…ad from Jerusalem to Neve Ya'aqov and 'Atarot, but after the* *…pulse at An-Nabi Samwil it was compelled to withdraw. After the* *…r of 1948, Jordanian Jerusalem expanded northward along the* *…ad to Nablus.*

1944

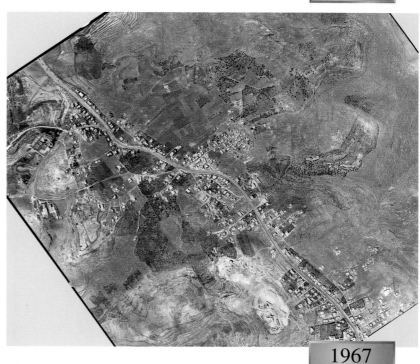

1967

The Survey of Israel photo of 16 Jun 1967, taken shortly
…er the Six-Day War, attests to the extent of this expansion in the
…u'afat area, and our photo of 10 Feb 1995 shows the sub-
…ntial continuation of this trend under Israeli rule. The complex
…der construction near the photo's upper margin is the Jewish
…burb of Ramat Shelomo.

Population	
1922	422
1945	760
1967	2,732
1996	14,923

The German "Temple Society," which established colonies in Haifa, Jaffa, Sarona and Jerusalem in the years 1869-73, founded in 1902 a further colony about 15 km east of Jaffa; it was named Wilhelma in honor of the German Kaiser Wilhelm II. During World War I, a German military hospital operated in the village (one of its patients was Rudolf Höss, who was to become the infamous *Kommandant* of Auschwitz). The Bavarian photo of 17 Dec 1917 shows the regular layout of Wilhelma about a month after its capture by the British, who on 27 Nov 17 had repulsed a major Turkish counterattack in the area.

◄ *Wilhelma peasants after divine service, c.1914.*

1990

1949

The British deported the German villagers to Egypt, but allowed their return after the war. During World War II the British interned the villagers and deported many of them. In 1948 Wilhelma had ceased to exist. On 10 Jul 48, at the start of Operation Dani, it was captured by the Alexandroni Brigade; somewhat later, Jews evacuated from ʿAtarot, a settlement north of Jerusalem, reestablished their village here, renaming the locality Bene ʿAtarot (Sons of ʿAtarot).

Leef's photo of 6 Oct 1949 shows a slight increase in the number of houses and, near the lower margin, stretches of the roads that the British paved northward from Lydda and westward from Wilhelma.

Our photo of 4 Feb 1990 shows a more densely settled Bene ʿAtarot and heavier traffic on the roads nearby it; a new road just south of the village leads to a highway that by-passes Ben-Gurion Airport from the east. The basic layout of Wilhelma is still clearly discernible.

Population				
	1922	1945	1948	1995
Wilhelma	**222**	**240**		
Bene ʿAtarot			**215**	**389**

143

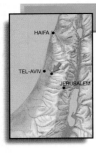

At-Tira – Bareqet

After the conquest of Jerusalem, the British decided to advance their lines northward both on the coastal plain and in the mountains, in order to remove Jaffa and Jerusalem from the range of Turkish artillery. Within this framework the British 54th Division on 15 Dec 17 captured the small Arab village of At-Tira, about 18 km southeast of Jaffa. A month later, on 15 Jan 1918, a plane of Bavarian Squadron 304, flying at the low altitude of 2,000 m, photographed the village from the northwest. The photo shows At-Tira situated along the westernmost line of foothills, at the very edge of the coastal plain. A broad track that by-passes the village from the north leads from the hills onto the plain. Many fields between track and village are enclosed by stone walls and hedges.

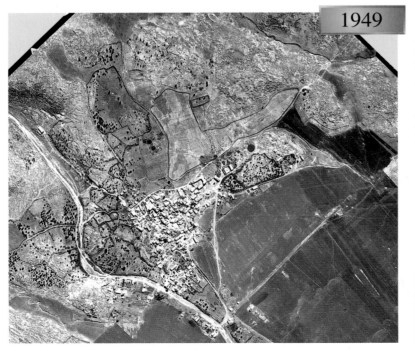

1949

Leef's photo of 26 Oct 1949 documents the considerab physical expansion of At-Tira in the years of the British Manda By the time the photo was taken, however, the village was deserte its inhabitants having fled upon the advance of Israeli forces on Jul 48, in the opening stage of Operation Dani. In 1952 the villa was resettled by Jews from Habban, in the southern part of t Arabian peninsula, and renamed Bareqet. The Survey of Isra photo from August 1956 shows the ovaloid street of Bareqe with houses on either side of it, to the north of the erstwhile Ar village, which bears some marks of destruction. East of the oval street are two rows of new houses.

Population				
	1922	1945	1966	1995
At-Tira	705	1,290		
Bareqet			660	626

1994

1956

Our photo of 2 Aug 1994 shows the further expansion of Bareqet, with some of At-Tira's houses near a street that is parallel to and south of the ovaloid one.

1966

The Survey of Israel photo of 30 Jul 1966 shows between ese rows a street that extends to the ovaloid one. By now there e sheds behind all of Bareqet's houses. The lower (southern) part `At-Tira has been razed, and only few trees remain. But several ouses of the Arab village's upper (northern) part, adjoining areqet, are standing.

145

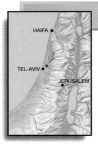

The River Yarqon (Nahr el-'Auja)

The Nahr el-'Auja – the biblical Yarqon – is the most abounding of the country's rivers that flow into the Mediterranean. In December 1917 the northern bank of its lower course – only some 6 km north of Jaffa – was in Turkish hands. During the night of 20/21 Dec 17 the British 52nd Division, commanded by Maj.-Gen. Hill, forced a sur-
prise crossing at three different points. At daybreak pontoon bridges were thrown over the 'Auja, and a barrel bridge, previously assembled in the Wadi el-Musrara, was floated into the 'Auja and completed on the morning of the 22nd.

The British photomosaic based on photos taken on 10 Dec 1917 – which is preserved in the Israel Antiquities Authority collection – probably represents part of the preparations for this operation. It shows the river from its confluence with Wadi el-Musrara – a point about 3 km from the river's mouth – and eastward. The Arab village of Jarisha is visible to the right (south) of the river, close to the confluence with the Musrara (which appears on British World War I maps as Nahr el-Baride); an earlier course of the Musrara – now a dry bed – can be discerned near the mosaics's lower margin. The fields to the left (north) of the 'Auja belong to the Arab village of Sheikh Muwannis. There are a few trees along the river's banks.

The RAF photo of 11 Dec 1944 shows, in addition to Jarisha at center, the Arab village of Jammasin in the lower right corner and parts of the Jewish town of Ramat Gan in the upper right one (the southern continuation of this area appears on pp. 100-101).

1917

1944

Our photo of 8 Feb 1997 shows the Tel Aviv-Haifa railway and the Ayalon Freeway crossing the Yarqon and Ayalon (that is Musrara) rivers near their confluence. The Roqah Boulevard runs north (to the left) of the Yarqon, and the Yarqon Park extends between the boulevard and the river. In the upper left corner appears the Ayalon Mall and the Ramat Gan Stadium.

1997

A memorial column set up by General Hill, the pro-Zionist commander of the 52nd Division, carrying inscriptions in English and Hebrew only. Hill demonstrated his opposition to the non-use of Hebrew by the British military authorities by dispensing with an Arabic translation of the inscription.

The memorial column today.

ON THE NIGHT
20TH–21ST DEC 1917
THE 155TH BRIGADE
52ND LOWLAND DIV
CROSSED THE AUJA
AT THIS SPOT BY
RAFTS AND A LIGHT
BRIDGE & TOOK THE
TURKISH POSITIONS
ON KH HADRAH

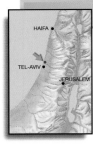

Sidna 'Ali – Herzlia-Pituah

The British northward advance on the coastal plain ended on 22 Dec 17 with the conquest of Arsuf, about 17 km northeast of Jaffa. Henceforward the front in that area remained basically stationary until Allenby's offensive in September 1918.

The Bavarian photo of mediocre quality, taken on 29 Dec 1917, shows the area a week after the conclusion of the British advance. A part of the crusader coastal town of Arsur, known in Arabic as Arsuf and razed by the Mamluks in 1265, is visible above the sea, near the photo's upper margin. The bright square building upon which several tracks converge is the shrine of Sidna [=Sayyiduna] 'Ali (our lord 'Ali), built around the tomb of 'Ali ibn 'Alim, who died in 1086. The dark triangle to the right of the shrine is the Arab village of El-Haram.

The RAF photo of 10 Dec 1944 shows a British police post between the ruins of Arsuf and the village of El-Haram. Kfar Shemaryahu, a village founded in 1937 by Jews from Germany, appears in the photo's lower right corner, and the scattered houses of HerzliPituah are visible in the lower left one.

The Arabs of El-Haram fled on 3 Feb 48. The Suvey of Israel photo of 3 Mar 1967 shows the quarter of Nof Yam, east of the shrine of Sidna 'Ali, and vastly expanded Herzlia-Pituah; the Tel Aviv-Hai highway runs between it and Kfar Shemaryahu.

◀ *Bedouin children, 1918.*

1995

A still more densely built up Herzlia-Pituah, with several hotels ong its beach, appears on our photo of 18 Dec 1995. Some elds south of Kfar Shemaryahu have given way to houses. The rine of Sidna 'Ali stands out near the upper margin's midpoint.

1967

1944

149

Ramallah and El-Bireh

Having completed their advance on the coastal plain north of Jaffa, the British proceeded to push back the Turks in the Jerusalem region as well. On 29 Dec 17 the 74th Division captured Ramallah, a village largely inhabited by Christian Arabs, and the 60th Division took El-Bireh, a mostly Muslim village. The two villages are situated about 15 km north of Jerusalem's Old City.

The Bavarian photo of the area was taken on 3 Jan 1918, five days after the British conquest. El-Bireh is the village in the foreground; some vestiges of the crusader village of Magna Mahumeria are discernible in the eastern part of El-Bireh, with threshing floors on the hilltops to the east and west of it. Ramallah appears close to the upper margin. The line linking points A and B is the main road from Jerusalem to Nablus, which passes along the western edge of El-Bireh. A secondary road, running roughly east to west, links El-Bireh with Ramallah; and a track from the eastern outskirts of Ramallah leads leftward (southward) to the Jerusalem-Nablus road. This track, together with a stretch of the Jerusalem-Nablus road and a stretch of the road leading to Ramallah, form an isosceles triangle, inside of which only a few houses are visible.

1918

1944

The photomosaic we formed from two RAF photos of 29 De[...] 1944 shows an enlarged El-Bireh and a significantly mo[...] widespread Ramallah. There is much more vegetation – on bo[...] sides of the road leading from El-Bireh to Ramallah, in the ne[...] parts of Ramallah, and elsewhere. A British police fortress stan[...] out north of the triangle.

The photo taken by the "Air Service" of the Haganah on 17 A[...] 1948 shows Ramallah from the north.

Population				
	1922	1945	1967	1996
Ramallah	3,104	5,080	12,134	20,561
El Bireh	1,479	2,920	13,037	33,539

1995

1948

Our photo of 10 Feb 1995 documents a further expansion of Ramallah-El-Bireh and shows, near the lower left corner, a part of the red-roofed Jewish settlement of Pesagot, founded in 1981 (pop. 864 in 1995).

The Israeli army evacuated Ramalllah and El-Bireh on 27 Dec 95.

1972

The Survey of Israel photo of 14 Jul 1972 shows the two West Bank towns, by now considerably larger, forming a single continuously settled area. All three sides of the triangle serve as main thoroughfares. The densely settled cluster on the southern outskirts of El-Bireh, west of the Jerusalem-Nablus highway, is the Al-Amʻari refugee camp set up in 1948 for refugees from Lydda, Jerusalem and Jaffa.

'Ein Siniya

On 9 Mar 18 the British, advancing northward astride the Jerusalem-Nablus road, captured the Arab village of 'Ein Siniya near a bend of the road; the frontline they established about 5 km north of the village remained stationary until the September offensive. The photo taken by British Squadron 14 on 25 Feb 1918*, which is reproduced at the bottom of this page, probably formed part of the preparations for the British advance. The Bavarian photo of 25 Apr 1918, which covers a much larger area than the British one, shows British columns marching along the Nablus road northeast of the village. The large house at the western end of the village belongs to the prominent Jerusalemite family of al-Husseini. Isma'il al-Husseini, Director of the Jerusalem Region Education Council under the Turks, built the oil-press that stands at the entrance to the village. In 1906 he leased the large house, the oil press and a mill to Jacob Chertok, a Jewish pioneer from Russia who lived there with his family for about two years (his son, Moshe Sharett, became Israel's second prime minister).

1918

1918*

▲ *A British balloon seen through the bracing wires of a plane; filmed by Frank Hurley during a flight from Jericho to Julis, Winter 1918.*

Population	
1922	114
1945	330
1967	333
1996	606

995

1967

C apt. John More of the 53rd (Welsh) Division, who took part in the March 1918 advance and later served in the area, wrote: "A most iverting episode took place on the 28th April. A Boche [German] irman made a spirited attack on one of our observation balloons at in Sinia. This had already happened on several occasions, so that he officer commanding the Balloon section laid a booby trap for the ext Hun [German]. He sent up an old balloon, filling its car with xplosives, which were connected by an electric cable to a switch on he ground. The enemy plane was to be allowed to approach as near s possible and then, at the psychological moment, the explosives were to be detonated electrically. The Boche opened fire at the balloon om a respectful distance at first, but noticing that our Archies took o interest, he boldly came nearer. He must have had the surprise of is life when, with a terrific report, the balloon burst into thin air, agments flying in all directions. His plane swayed and jolted and we nought he was coming down, but he recovered himself well and nade off home as fast as his legs, or rather planes, could carry him. o doubt he received an Iron Cross of the first Class for his prowess bringing down an English balloon. It is only fair to add that some ays later he returned and attacked a balloon in the same place and eally brought it down this time. The balloon caught fire, and unhappily he observer was killed. For this, no doubt the German pilot received bar to his Iron Cross (if there be such thing)."[90]

The Survey of Israel photo of 16 Jun 1967, taken after almost 70 years of British and Jordanian rule, shows a somewhat expanded village core and more than a dozen houses spread out in the valley to the south of it. Our photo of 10 Feb 1995 shows the progression of the village's growth under Israeli occupation.

1967

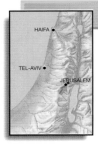

Roads from Jerusalem to Jericho

This photo by German Squadron 303, taken above the Judaean Wilderness on 10 Apr 1918, is reproduced from a manual for the tactical use of aerial photographs that was subsequently captured by the British; hence its mediocre quality. The meandering line linking points A and B is the old direct road that descends from Jerusalem to Jericho and the Jordan Valley. During World War I, German engineers facilitated transport along the steep descent into the valley by building a new graded section that branches off from the old road and runs first southeastward in the direction of An-Nabi Musa and then northeastward to Jericho.[91] On our photo, the new road starts near the point marked *Kaffeehaus* (coffee house) and winds its way to point C. The area was conquered by the British on 20 Feb 18, during their advance on Jericho and to the River Jordan.

◀ *A British automobile on the Jerusalem-Jericho road (one of Frank Hurley's color photographs).*

1993

An Australian soldier who used the pen name "Trooper Bluegum" wrote the following poem:

Palestine

A league-long line of mountains:
Some fertile plains:
Bright, rippling, purling fountains,
After the rains.
Vast valleys, lorn and lonely;
Smiling and green:
Dead cities, telling only
What might have been.

A weary, stricken people,
So long enslaved;
A spire and broken steeple,
By lanes ill-paved:
A thousand superstitions;
A hundred creeds;
The beggars' vain petitions
That no one heeds.

A field of poppies blazing:
Orchids new-born:
A wealth of flowers amazing
Fringing the corn:
A line of camels stringing
Across the brae:

The skylark sweetly singing
To welcome day.

A home of races, mingled
Gentile and Jew:
Women with veilèd faces:
Rogues, not a few.
A Sacred Land, and Holy:
Beersheba to Dan:
Where once a King so lowly
Lived as a man.

A land of milk and honey,
In Moses' day:
A place of paper money
Since Abdul's sway:
A prophets' land and sages',
By right divine:
The heir of all the Ages,
Poor Palestine!![92]

The Survey of Israel photo of 1 Aug 1969 shows the new road paved under Jordanian rule, which in general follows the course of the World War I road but is significantly straighter. In the left-hand third of the photo the road runs between the World War I road to its left and the road paved during the British Mandate to its right.

Our photo of 5 Dec 1993 shows the Jewish communal settlement of Mizpe Jericho, founded in 1978, to the right (east) of the road. By the end of 1995 it had 762 inhabitants.

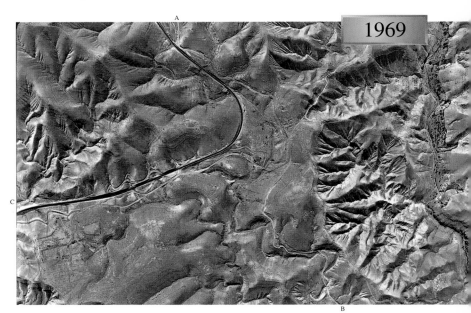

1969

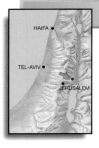

Jericho

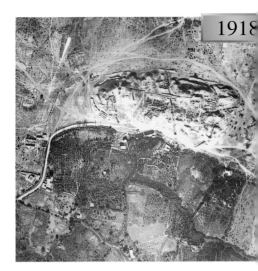

The Bavarian photo of 28 Mar 1918 shows the village oasis of Jericho from the southeast, with Wadi Qelt near the photo's center. South (left) of the wadi there are several British tent encampments and three planes cast their shadows westward. The new road from Jerusalem is the straight line that extends from point A rightward (northward); the old road descends from point B and joins the new one before passing the wadi. The road reaches a circle just west of the small, relatively densely built core of Jericho. From the circle, one road continues eastward (to point C) in the direction of the River Jordan and another leads northwestward (to point D), later running parallel to the Jordan all the way to Beisan and the Sea of Galilee. Beyond the photo's frame, this road passes the fringes of the tell of biblical Jericho. This tell, partially excavated by Ernst Sellin and Carl Watzinger in 1907-09, appears on a photo of 24 Apr 1918* taken by German Squadron 303 and preserved in the Rengstorf collection.

1918

1938

The area just north and northwest of Jericho's core appears in Kluger's oblique photo of 1938, taken from a low altitude. It shows a considerable increase in the number of houses, many of them with sloping roofs. There are many recently planted trees in the foreground.

Population	
1922	**1,029**
1945	**3,010**
1967	**5,312**
1996	**12,358**

1993

1967

The Survey of Israel photo of 7 Aug 1967 shows a notably extended Jericho. The entire area of the town's core is now built up and crisscrossed by lanes; the circle to the west of it has been replaced by a square. Just south of Wadi Qelt, near the road to Jerusalem, stands the large rectangular police fortress erected by the British. South of that, visible in the upper left corner of the photo, is one of Jericho's large refugee camps, 'Aqabat Jaber; most of its residents – refugees from what became Israel in 1948 – fled to the eastern bank of the River Jordan upon the Israeli conquest of this area in the Six-Day War of June 1967.[93]

Our color photo of 5 Dec 1993 renders clearly visible several water pools of the oasis. It shows a still more densely built up Jericho, especially south (left) of Wadi Qelt; in this area, several plastic-covered greenhouses stand out. The town's core, on the other hand, appears to have thinned out. The road from Jerusalem to Bet She'an (Beisan) and Tiberias now turns north near the new mosque and thus by-passes Jericho's center. The British-built police fortress, which the Jordanians had taken over in 1948, was used by the Israelis from 1967 on; about six months after this photo was taken, it started to serve the Palestinian Self-Government Authority.

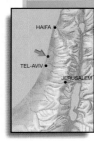

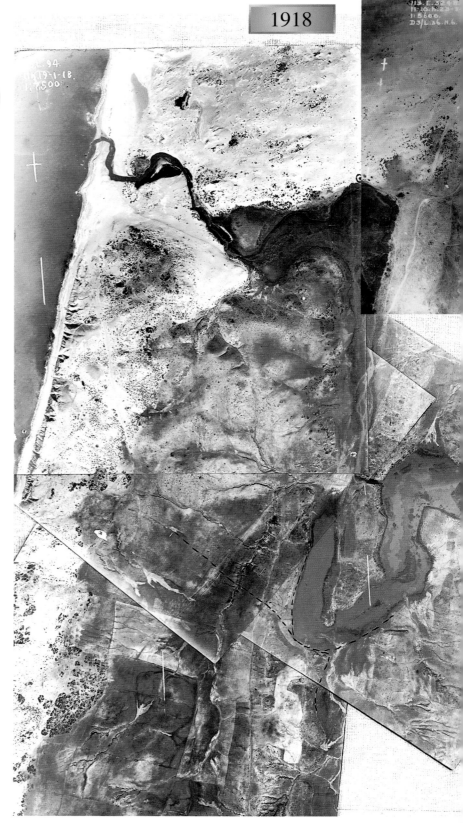

1918

The brook that flows into the Mediterranean about 25 km northeast of Jaffa reaches the sea after having crossed a limestone ridge through a deep artificial breach that was cut in antiquity – which explains its Arabic name: Nahr el-Faliq, "the stream that tears asunder." (The crusaders called it La Rochetaillée, "the cut rock.") In more recent times, with the decline of settlement in the coastal plain, the breach became partially silted up, so that only a portion of the brook's waters could reach the sea and the rest would form large swamps east and south of the breach, especially in the winter. These swamps appear near the right margin of the British photomosaic prepared from photos taken on 19 Jan 1918, which now forms part of the Israel Antiquities Authority collection.(We added to the mosaic's upper part a British photo of 23 Aug 18). The artificial breach is the short dark line that runs horizontally to the left (west) of the largest swamp. A British soldier hatched a line marking the limits of the swamp south of the breach. A road that parallels the coast runs west of the swamp's hatched perimeter and crosses the brook on a bridge situated north of the breach. Several Arab fields appear in the area southwest of the swamp.

On the morning of 19 Sep 18, when Allenby's decisive offensive began, the British front line ran some 5 km south of the Faliq. After a massive bombardment of the Turkish positions, five British infantry divisions (two of them composed of Indian troops) began to wheel northeastward across the coastal plain, opening the way for three cavalry divisions, which rushed northward in a bold attempt to break the Turkish-German hold on the Valley of Jezreel and Galilee at one fell swoop. The attempt succeeded. The offensive started at 04:30 hours, with the destroyers Druid *and* Forester *opening fire on the Turkish trenches north of the Faliq; at 07:20 hours British infantry overcame the Turks defending the bridge north of the Faliq breach; and at 08:00 hours, the leading cavalry regiment, having advanced along the beach, reached the mouth of the Faliq, wheeled to the coastal road and continued northward.*

A British war correspondent, Harry Ascalon, jubilantly reported at the time: "Overwhelmed by the devastating barrage and the tremendous onset of our troops who had advanced under its cover, the Turks were unable to hold the complicated and elaborate defences upon which they had so long and so fondly relied. The infantry came on irresistibly. The men were up to the vaunted Turkish line, into it, over it, through it. A feat often attempted in this war, and seldom accomplished, was triumphantly achieved. Infantry, by means of a frontal attack upon a long prepared and strongly held position, broke through and prepared a free passage for a thunderbolt of cavalry. The infantry, pivotting upon a position in the lower foothills, swung like a door on a hinge, first northward, then north-eastward, then eastward, across the Plain of Sharon, destroying, capturing or rolling up the Turks as it advanced. While this was happening the cavalry poured through the ever-widening gap and pressed forward to the north."[94]

In 1933 a Jewish development company, Ha-Noteʿa, urged upon the British government of Palestine to drain the Faliq swamps, which were causing malaria throughout the region. The drainage operations, partially financed by Ha-Noteʿa and the Supreme Muslim Council, which owned the swampy area, were begun in November 1934 and lasted three years.[95] In 1938-39, the Jewish villages of Bet Yehoshuʿa, Tel Yitzhaq and Kfar Netter were established east of the Faliq breach. In 1948 a fourth village was founded on its western side by Shoah survivors – hence its name, Udim (=brands from the burning).

Leef's photo of 16 Oct 1949 shows the houses of Udim on the hill northwest of the breach, some of the drainage channels of the Faliq, and the slightly changed location of its mouth. The unpaved coastal road, though in better shape than in 1918, is still little more than a track. In 1951 it was superseded by the Tel Aviv Netanya road, which runs slightly to the west of it.

1994

1949

Our photo of 30 Jun 1994 shows a still wider Tel Aviv-Haifa highway. North of the brook is Ramat Poleg, the southernmost quarter of the coastal town of Netanya. The artificial breach, now part of the Poleg Nature Reserve, parallels the photo's lower margin.

1967

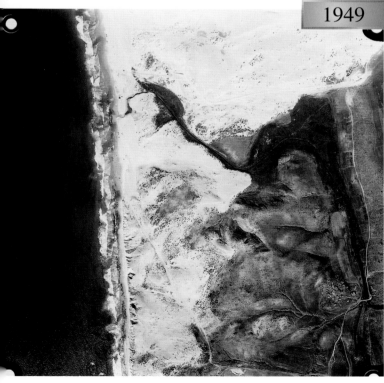

The Survey of Israel photo of 10 Mar 1967 shows that road ow part of the main Tel Aviv-Haifa highway) crossing the brook whose name has been Hebraized into Nahal Poleg – near the oto's center. Udim (pop. 486 in 1995) is now situated northeast the breach. In the lower left corner is the Orde Wingate Institute r Physical Education.

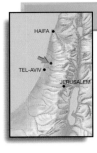

Kfar Sava

The few houses of the Jewish village of Kfar Sava, founded in 1903, appear at the center of the Bavarian photo of 17 Jan 1918. The tiny village absorbed many of the Jews whom the Turks had expelled from Jaffa, Tel Aviv and other southern localities with the advance of the British. The 1,500 or so refugees in Kfar Sava lived mostly in tents or in huts prepared from eucalyptus branches; 236 of them died of disease. From 22 Dec 17 on, with the British only some 3 km southwest of Kfar Sava, the village became part of the Turkish front. The Bavarian photo shows two tent encampments near the houses and several systems of trenches dug in the village's regular fields. Kfar Sava was repeatedly photographed from the air by both sides (see p. 28 above), and several inhabitants were killed by British shells. The last civilians were evacuated by the end of the spring.

Indian infantrymen of the 3rd (Lahore) Division conquered Kfar Sava at the outset of Allenby's offensive, on the morning of 19 Sep 18.

Population	
1914	100
1948	5,516
1995	69,000

1918

M enahem Klioner, a Jaffa merchant charged with administerin relief to the refugees in Kfar Sava, wrote in his memoirs publishe in 1920: "When the front came to be in Kfar Sava, two German batta ions came into the village, and as the rains were frequent in thos months and very torrential, they could not stay in their tents ar therefore entered the houses, the stables, and the tents [of the civ ians]. And indeed one must admit that they treated us in a qui humane manner, and protected us with all determination from Turkis assaults, and drove them away when they saw them drawing near some house to steal or to rob....They hated the Turks extremely, ar when they caught some of them coming to plunder, they would be them up severely, and so we were somewhat saved from assault. B the density became very great."[96]

Dov Skibin, one of the village's four original settlers, wrote: "When th rainy season was over, the British set up an observation post at th bottom of a balloon that was anchored to the ground somewhere ne Sarona [the German colony northeast of Jaffa]. The man in the bask

◀ *Refugees from Tel Aviv in their huts in Kfar Sava, 1917.*

1994

1949

f the balloon observed the moves of the Turks all the time....The [Turkish] commander who lived with us always cursed the balloon and wished its destruction. On a spring day his curses came true: a German plane passed opposite the balloon and set it alight with a spark of fire. The balloon immediately burnt up, the observer fell from the heights and was crushed. The commander went out, raised his hands and blessed Allah and his Prophet for this salvation. But it quickly turned out that his blessing was in vain. A few days later there was another balloon in the air. We then paid a high price for the burning of the first one."[97]

Leef's photo of 6 Oct 1949 shows a considerable part of Kfar Sava's area covered by houses; in many cases paths that in 1918 marked the limits of the village's fields are now streets.

Our photo of 9 Apr 1994 shows that almost all of Kfar Sava's original area has by now become urbanized. The line that runs upward from point A on the lower margin is Weizmann Street, the town's main thoroughfare. The red roofed building near the dense cluster of trees on the street's right (northern) side, is the town hall, originally the khan, Kfar Sava's first stone house, erected in 1906. On the Bavarian photo from 1918, the khan is the elongated building to the right and parallel to the village's main east-west track.

Nablus

Nablus, the largest inland town of central Palestine, served as headquarters of the Turkish 7th Army. Its commander was General Mustafa Kemal, the future founder of modern Turkey, whom posterity remembers as Atatürk (Father of the Turks). After the collapse of the Turkish front line on the coastal plain, three British infantry divisions and the 5th Australian Light Horse Brigade advanced eastward into the mountains; on 21 Sep 18, two days after the start of the offensive, the Australians, together with a light armored motor battery, captured Nablus and made contact east of it with the British troops who had advanced from the south along the Jerusalem-Nablus road. Mustafa Kemal retreated eastward to the River Jordan and succeeded in crossing it with a part of his army.

1918*

1918

AINN 3361 . 1500 h. 24.9.18. NABLUS . 1000 FT.

1948

On 24 Sep 1918, three days after its capture, aviators of the 1st Australian Squadron photographed Nablus from the west, from the low altitude of 1,000 feet. The photo shows the town nestling in a valley, with the slopes of Mt. Gerizim on its right and those of Mt. Ebal on its left. On the fringe of the densely built old core are numerous large buildings; one of them, above and to the right of point A on the left margin, is a hospital erected a few years before the war. Several minarets and a tall rectangular clock tower rise above the houses, many of which have sloping tiled roofs. There are some orchards along the borders of the town, and also within it. Beyond the town's far (eastern) end, at the narrowest point of the valley, stands a large, rectangular, flat-roofed structure: the Turkish barracks erected in 1875. The Turkish officers lived in the building that stands between the barracks and the town, partially concealed by trees. The Turkish railway from El-'Affule, completed in the spring of 1915, runs from point A rightward.

1994

A German photo of unknown provenance (see top left) which forms part of the Rengstorf collection, and probably dates from 1918*, shows the same area from the east. The large roofless building in the foreground is the partially rebuilt crusader church of Jacob's Well. The village behind it is Balatah, and the large structure to the right of the village is An-Nabi Yusuf, the traditional site of Joseph's tomb.

The photo taken by the "Air Service" of the Haganah on 11 Jan 1948 from the northwest shows that Nablus expanded considerably under British rule, both in the valley and on the mountain slopes. Under Jordanian rule the town grew still more markedly, especially toward the southeast, as evidenced in the Survey of Israel photo of 16 Jun 1967. An administrative and commercial center stands out on both sides of broad Hussein Boulevard, which leads to the Clock Circle at the northern edge of the town's original core.

Our photo of 9 Apr 1994 shows an increase in the number of high-rises near the town's commercial and administrative center. Nablus has continued to climb the adjacent mountain slopes, especially those of Mt. Gerizim to its south. A part of the Balateh refugee camp, established in 1950 for refugees from Jaffa, Lydda and elsewhere (pop. 8,904 in 1996), is visible beyond the northeastern slope of Mt. Gerizim.

The Israeli army evacuated Nablus on 11 Dec 95.

1967

Population			
1922	1945	1967	1996
15,947	23,250	61,053	102,462

The River Jordan

The undated photo from Erich Steiner's collection – probably of 1918 – shows, from the west, an 8-km stretch of the Central Jordan Valley about 30 km east of Nablus. The river winds and twists its way at the base of a valley that abounds with vegetation. Allied troops used to refer to this base as "the Ditch"; more generous observers have called it "the Jungle of the Jordan." There are barren, moonlike hills on either side of it. On the far, Trans-Jordanian, side extends a plain with some signs of cultivation: this is the upper part of the Jordan Valley. East of the plain rise the mountains of Trans-Jordan, seen near the photo's upper margin. The stream that runs down from these mountains and, upon reaching the plain, flows to the right (southwest) along the foothills, is the Nahr ez-Zerqa, the biblical Jabbok. On the near, Palestinian, side of the River Jordan there is no level ground in this sector between the mountains and the "Jungle," with the exception of the plain that starts beyond the cliff visible near the photo's lower right corner. The Jericho-Beisan road is the white line that traverses this plain from south to north and then continues among the hills above the river.

▲ *Armband worn by Palestinian Jews recruited locally, now in the Imperial War Museum.*

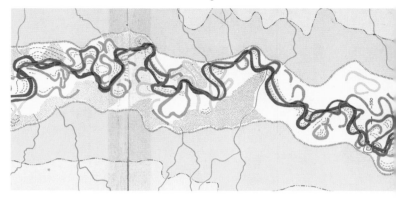

▶ *The Jordan's changing river channel*

▱	Old channel-parts.
▬	1928-35.
▬	Recent changes.

1918

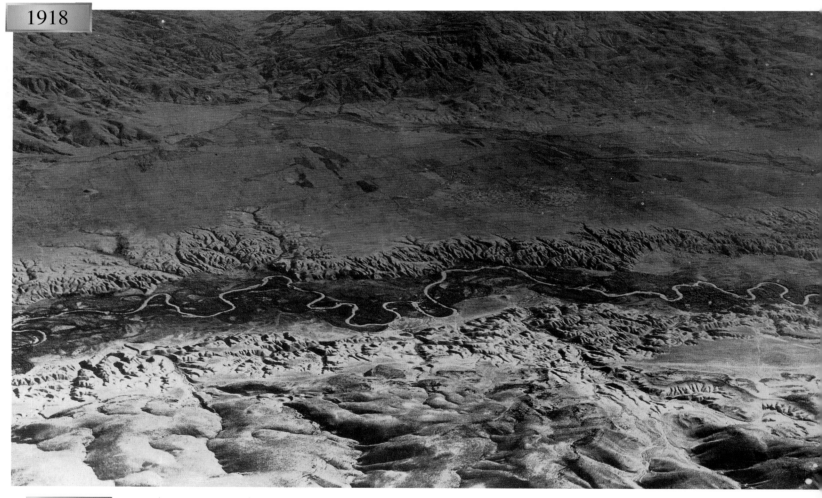

1918*

Our photo of 12 Apr 1997 shows a depleted River Jordan making its way southward between points A and B. The intensively cultivated and densely populated plain on the far side of the river is irrigated by the waters of the East Ghor Canal Project, the major Jordanian development scheme begun in 1958. The Jericho-Bet She'an road and the Israeli patrol way to its east stand out on the river's near side. The fields in the small plain visible near the photo's lower right corner belong to the Arab village of Marj Na`j.

About 20 km to the south, there is a ford across the Jordan at Umm esh-Shert; it appears on the photomosaic we put together from two photos taken by British 142 Squadron on 22 Jun 1918, now deposited at the Australian War Memorial (see left).

During the British push across the Jordan that formed part of Allenby's autumn offensive, this ford was captured on the night f 23 Sep 18 by the Jewish battalion that was officially known as the 3th Battalion of the Royal Fusiliers.

t. Vladimir (Ze'ev) Jabotinsky, who masterminded the creation of gular Jewish battalions within the British army (and later became e leader of Revisionist Zionism), took part in this action. Later he rote: "Malaria had robbed my company of all but three officers and ss than a hundred men. Lieutenant Barnes was in charge and I was mporarily second-in-command....Barnes and Abrahams occupied e rocks with seven of our eight Lewis guns. I was given the remain- g Lewis gun and was ordered to conduct the main operation. There

Col. Margolin and Lt. Jabotinsky on horseback.

was nothing praiseworthy about our work: the plan had been carefully worked out by the colonel and we just had to carry it out....

"At midnight we left the ridge and proceeded in marching order directly to Umm Esh Shert. We did not creep but marched upright along the wide Turkish road, for we had seen during the day that the ford, at any rate on our side of the river, was unoccupied. A hundred paces from the hills we halted and sent out scouts to reconnoiter. They returned with the news that the road was clear. We brought down our Lewis gun to the bank and took up our position on an elevated piece of ground opposite the ford. The gun was placed in a position covering both banks of the river. But the ford was clear on the other side as well. The Jordan at this point is about as broad as Park Avenue in New York; both approaches to the ford were clear of all vegetation. The night was not very dark and it was possible to see with our field-glasses that there was nobody at the stream. I left Sergeant Moskow with twenty men, and with the rest we went to comb the woods near our bank of the stream.

"This was more difficult. The trees are not tall, but they are close up to one another, and the ground is covered with all manner of thorns and similar vegetation. Two men....marched ahead; twenty paces behind them the party followed in a long, widely-spread line, reaching from the banks to the rocks which are the boundary of the Jordan 'ditch' on the west. The company was thus enabled to make a thorough search in the woods.

"Only once did we hear shots, but they came from the other side of the river. We did not reply. I signaled to Barnes, however, indicating the spot where the shots came from, and he opened fire with his Lewis guns. For five minutes the enemy replied; then there was silence. It was probably the rear-guard of the retreating Turks.

"Shortly before sunrise my scouts encountered the scouts of another of our companies, which had reconnoitered the upper portion of the 'ditch,' going in the opposite direction, southward. I signaled that the ford was free; the colonel telephoned to General Chaytor's Staff, and an hour later the dragoons could peacefully cross the Jordan and start pushing the retreating Turks away from the Land of Gilead."[98]

Caesarea

A crew of German Squadron 303 that flew over the ruins of Caesarea in the winter of 1917 observed broad bands that extend from the shore into the sea, surrounding a large underwater basin whose narrow opening faces north. One of the aviators had received a copy of Josephus Flavius' The Antiquities of the Jews *by military mail, and having read the description of the large harbor that Herod the Great constructed at Caesarea in the years 22-10 B.C., he was struck by its congruence with the observations made from the air and concluded that the underwater basin was King Herod's submerged harbor.*[99]

The aerial photograph of Caesarea that Lts. Holzhausen and Metzky took on 3 Dec 1917 – and which has recently surfaced in the Rengstorf collection – may well have been made during the flight in which the underwater basin was first observed: it appears very clearly in the photo's lower right corner. The long, narrow and vertically bisected field that stands out left of center, is Caesarea's hippodrome, with the town's Byzantine wall just to its left. The hill near the shore, at the edge of the sand dunes, hides Caesarea's theater; and the walled-in rectangle to the left of the submerged harbor is the ruined crusader town, fortified in 1251-52 by King Louis IX of France and destroyed by the Mamluk sultan Baybars in 1265. Within the crusader town are visible the houses of the village of Qisariya, established in 1878 by Muslim refugees from Bosnia (pop. 346 in 1922).

After the collapse of the Turkish front in the early hours of 19 Sep 18, the 5th Cavalry Division of the Desert Mounted Corps sped swiftly northward along the coast, and its leading regiment had reached the Jewish village of Hadera, just 7 km southeast of Caesarea, by 11:00 hours. The Turks beat a hasty retreat to the north and east.

An undated Bavarian photo, probably of 1918 , shows sever[al] houses of the Bosnian settlers standing on the ruined crusader wa[ll] with their fields extending on its both sides. All other houses a[re] confined to the space enclosed by the 13th-century walls. Th[e] southern crusader mole, with remains of the crusader citadel at[op] of it, extends into the sea near the photo's lower right corne[r.]

1996

1944

The RAF photo of 12 Dec 1944 shows some new houses in the Bosnian village (pop. 770 in 1945) and a few changes in the subdivision of its fields. The northern part of the Byzantine town wall and the two Roman aqueducts that run parallel to the shore stand out in the photo's lower left corner.

The inhabitants of Qisariya began to leave on 12 Jan 48; on 15 Feb 48 the Haganah conquered the village; and five days later the remaining 20 villagers were expelled and most of the houses were destroyed.

Our photo of 10 Jun 1996 shows the walls and moat of the crusader town which were cleared by Israeli archaeologists in the early 1960s. Much of the town's southern part was excavated in several campaigns. The sand dunes that appeared in the upper part of the 1917 photo are now largely covered by Kibbutz Sdot Yam, founded in 1940 (pop. 508 in 1995). The Roman theater, dug up by an Italian expedition in the 1960s, is visible on the shore just north of the kibbutz. The Herodian amphitheater, recently excavated by the Israel Antiquities Authority, extends along the shore between the theater and the crusader town. The hippodrome, near the photo's center, is surrounded by trees.

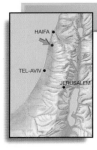

Zikhron Ya'aqov

Zikhron Ya'aqov, founded on the Carmel ridge in 1882 by Jewish pioneers from Romania, was originally called Zamarin, after the Arab village whose lands the founders had bought. It was later renamed by Baron Edmond de Rothschild – whose help was crucial for the survival of most early Jewish settlements, Zikhron Ya'aqov included – in honor of his father. During World War I the village was the center of the NILI spy ring, led by members of the local Aaronson family, which worked for the British. In the last phase of the war the village served as a refuge for Jews whom the Turks had expelled from Jaffa and other localities in the south.

The main feature of the undated photo probably taken in ▮1918▮ by aviators of German Squadron 300, which survives in the Groll collection, is the long Peasants' Street. It is intersected by a shorter one – the Street of the Officials – which originally housed members of Baron Rothschild's administration, and at whose left end stands the large building known as "Official-dom's House." To the left of the intersection is the village synagogue. The cemetery, partially obscured by trees, appears in the photo's lower left corner. (The village's winery is beyond the frame of this photo). The coastal plain stands out near the upper margin, and in the upper right corner, at the foot of the Carmel mountains, is the Arab village of El-Fureidis.

1918

1944

The RAF photo of 16 Dec ▮1944▮ shows a new street th parallels Peasants' Street on the west; the winery to the east of th village; the road that connects the village to the new coastal roa paved by the British; and the British police fortress at the junctic of those two roads. Our photo of 10 Jun ▮1996▮ shows th marked growth of both Zikhron Ya'aqov and El-Fureidis, with th first now spread out on several hills and the second forming single congested block. Many plastic greenhouses are visible in th plain below the two villages.

Population				
	1922	1945	1966	1995
Zikhron Ya'aqov	**1,302**	**1,302**	**4,000**	**9,080**
El-Fureidis	**335**	**780**	**2,550**	**7,750**

1996

r. Steuber, the chief medical officer of the Turkish-German forces in Palestine, visited Zikhron Ya'aqov in the fall of 1917. He wrote: "About noon I stop at Zamarin, the Jewish agricultural colony, and take coffee from the village head, swarmed from all sides by the community. The abundance of children is staggering. As if one would have shaken cockchafers from a tree, so they scrambled about me, climbed into my motor-car and curiously fingered my luggage. Surprisingly, all these Jewish colonists are peasants and wine-growers, and under the energetic protection of Baron de Rothschild and enjoy a genuine prosperity, but from a political point of view are considered highly unreliable."[100]

Ya'aqov Dushman wrote on the fate of the Jewish exiles from Jaffa and the south in Zikhron Ya'aqov: "Difficult and bad was the life of the exiles. A year and a half of wandering and sorrow had depressed their spirits to the utmost. A few found some work in the colony, but the rest passed their days in idleness. The support from the Emigration Committee did not suffice and they therefore had to rely on windfalls. At harvest-time the children and the elderly would go to glean in the fields. And when the yield was being transported to the threshing floor inside the colony, they would follow the carts, fighting over every ear of corn that fell. The peasants would not scold them, did not put them to shame, and even gave them some bundles and allowed them to glean from the sheafs. Their sons went even further: sitting on the carts they would sometimes let fall a handful of ears as if by accident and let the exiles gather them. The women would look through the windows and nod their assent. Their hearts were full of pity for the poor wretches who had been expelled from their homes. They were especially compassionate towards the elderly, who would tread with difficulty after the carts, unable to compete with the children, who would scamper like chickens from one cart to another, their little arms brimming with ears, while the hands of the elderly were almost empty and their faces expressed frailty and sorrow. Sometimes a door would open and the rebuke would be heard: 'Enough, you little ones! Let the old ones also gather!' Then the children would withdraw and the old ones would make use of their embarrassment, as long as the fear of the rebuke was on them."[101]

◄ *Villagers of Zikhron Ya'aqov regard the first British troops, Sep 18. The original caption says: "Simmarin - Scenes in a Delivered Jewish Village on Arrival of [Gen.] Chauvel's Troops".*

Tantura - Nahsholim, Dor

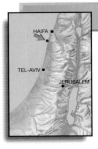

The undated German photo from the Rengstorf collection, probably of 1918, shows an 8 km stretch of the narrow plain between the Carmel mountains and the sea. Zikhron Ya'aqov is barely visible on the ridge near the midpoint of the photo's right margin; the irregular, dark block on the plain just below that ridge comprises some of its fields. The long narrow fields of the Arab villages of 'Ein Ghazal and Tantura appear at center. Tantura is the dark cluster standing out on the sands at lower right. Some fields of Tantura belong to the Bonstein family, which lived in the Arab village from 1886 to 1894 and then moved to Zikhron Ya'aqov. The dark area to the right (south) of it, parallel to the coast, is a part of the Kabara swamps.

1918

1949

Leef's photo of 25 Oct 1949 shows that Tantura somewhat expanded under British rule, especially northwards. The large rectangular building northeast of the village is the shell of the glass factory that Baron de Rothschild founded in 1892 and that functioned – under the direction of Meir Dizengoff, Tel Aviv's future mayor – only until 1894. (The factory is barely discernible on the World War I photo).

At the time the Leef photo was taken, Arab Tantura no longer existed. By the beginning of May 1948, the wealthier families had fled. As the remaining villagers refused to accept the Haganah's terms (that is, to hand over their weapons and the foreign irregulars), Battalion 33 of the Alexandroni Brigade conquered the village on the night of 22/23 May 48, and the inhabitants were either induced to leave or expelled. On 14 Jun 48 the founders of Kibbutz Nahsholim settled down in the village.

Population				
	1922	1945	1966	1995
Tantura	750	1,490		
Nahsholim			220	418
Dor			176	245

170

1996

The Survey of Israel photo of 6 Aug 1966 shows Kibbutz Nahsholim at left and the moshav Dor, founded in 1949, at right. Only a few of Tantura's houses are standing. Our photo of 10 Jun 1996 shows an expanded Nahsholim, with Rothschild's erstwhile glass factory – now a museum of nautical and regional archaeology – close to its center. Northwest of the kibbutz, ancient Dor is being excavated by a Hebrew University of Jerusalem expedition. West of the moshav Dor, just above the beach, are spread out the igloos and cottages of Dor Holiday Village; a Muslim shrine, one of the few remains of Tantura, may be discerned among the latter. Another vestige is the large rectangular building to the left of the Holiday Village's round promenade: its Arabic inscription attests that it was established in 1878 as a customs house.[102] The bright, densely built quadrangle in the photo's upper right corner is El-Fureidis; Zikhron Yaʻaqov spreads out to its right.

The glass factory that became a museum.

A Muslim shrine among the cottages of Dor Holiday Village. The strips of green cloth have been left by recent Muslim visitors as tokens of their respect for the saint buried there.

1966

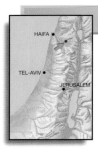

Nazareth

The undated, slightly damaged photo from the Steiner collection, probably of **1918,** shows the largely Christian town of Nazareth from the southeast. The large, rectangular, dark-roofed building that stands out near the lower left extremity of the town's original dense cluster of houses, is the Franciscan hospice of Casa Nuova which served as headquarters of the Turkish-German forces in Palestine from December 1917 to September 1918. (Alternatively, one may locate Casa Nuova with the help of the bright diagonal that runs from the photo's lower left corner to the town's dense cluster and appears to point at the hospice.) To the right of the Casa Nuova Hospice stands the Church of the Annunciation, which Franciscan friars erected in 1730 on the ruins of a much larger crusader cathedral. The large complex of buildings towering above the old cluster and connected to it by a zigzag path is the New French Orphanage. The pentagon-like building with an eastern entrance to its courtyard, which is situated near the right extremity of the old cluster, is the Russian teachers' seminary; Mary's Well is immediately to its right. The road from Haifa enters the photo's frame at point A; the road from El-'Affule at B; the one from Tiberias at C and that from Shafa 'Amr and Acre at D.

The photo taken from the southwest on 27 Jun **1948** by the young Israeli Air Force during the first Arab-Israeli truce shows almost the full extent of Nazareth's expansion under British rule. The large building in the photo's lower right corner is the British-built police fortress. After the British departure, it served as the headquarters of Fawzi el-Qawuqji's Arab Liberation Army, which at the time the photo was taken held most of Galilee. On 16 Jul 48 – three days before the start of the second truce – an Israeli armored column attacked Nazareth from the northeast; after some resistance the town surrendered. Some of the inhabitants fled, but most, including refugees from other localities, were allowed to stay put.

◀ *Funeral of two German aviators at the German military cemetery, Nazareth, with inhabitants of the town watching the scene from above.*

1994

The Survey of Israel photo of 4 Jun 1968 shows the new
ray-domed Church of the Annunciation whose construction was
egun in 1955. The Haifa-Tiberias road now by-passes the signifi-
antly enlarged town at some distance. Our photo of 9 Apr 1994
ocuses on the central part of an expanding Nazareth; the stretch of
he old Haifa-Nazareth road that runs near the Church of the An-
unciation is now called Pope Paul VI Street.

1948

1968

Population	
1922	**7,424** (4,885 C, 2,486 M)
1945	**14,200** (8,600 C, 5,600 M)
1967	**30,900**
1995	**54,900**

173

Kluger's photo of **1937** focuses on the Church of the Annunciation. Casa Nuova is to its left and the Franciscan monastery to its right. The photo – which encompasses only part of the town – shows its expansion on both sides of the Haifa-Tiberias road (that runs below the Church of the Annunciation) as well as on the slope above the Russian seminary and elsewhere. In the days of the British Mandate, Nazareth was the administrative center of Galilee.

▲ *The entrance to the German military cemetery at Nazareth. (On the reverse side of the photo, Steiner refers to the place as* Heldenfriedhof, *Heroes' Cemetery.)*

▶ *Scene on the Nazareth road after the advance of the 13th British Cavalry Brigade.*

▶ *The German military cemetery today.*

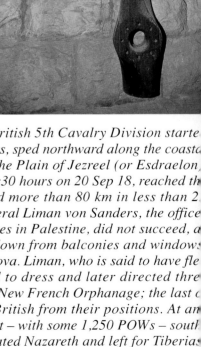

◀ *A group of* mukhtars *(village heads) after an interview with the British military governor of Nazareth.*

▶ *A plane's propeller that served as a German aviator's monument, now in the tower of the German military cemetery.*

The 13th Cavalry Brigade of the British 5th Cavalry Division started its advance on 19 Sep 18 at 07:00 hours, sped northward along the coastal plain, crossed the Carmel ridge into the Plain of Jezreel (or Esdraelon), ascended the hills of Galilee and at 04:30 hours on 20 Sep 18, reached the outskirts of Nazareth, having covered more than 80 km in less than 22 hours. Their intention to capture General Liman von Sanders, the officer commanding the Turkish-German forces in Palestine, did not succeed, as German clerks and orderlies, firing down from balconies and windows, blocked their advance on the Casa Nuova. Liman, who is said to have fled at first in his night clothes, returned to dress and later directed three counterattacks from the heights of the New French Orphanage; the last of these, he maintained, dislodged the British from their positions. At any rate, the British were ordered to retreat – with some 1,250 POWs – southward to El-'Affule; Liman then evacuated Nazareth and left for Tiberias, and when on the following day the 13th Brigade returned to the town, it did not encounter any resistance.

◄ *A close-up of the Church of the Annunciation and its immediate surroundings, 12 Apr 97*

D r. Paul Range, a German officer who served in Nazareth from March to September 1918, wrote: "The old town with its narrow, crooked, steep, ascending and descending lanes offers picturesque scenes. Many of the rich private houses are nicely built, and all are stately, constructed as they are from hewn stones. The streets are only 2-3 m wide, with a gutter in the middle, and all are paved. Centuries of use have made the lime cobblestones very smooth and in rainy weather quite dangerous....Around the old town, climbing along the hills or atop them, are grouped several new monasteries and other religious institutions that tower above the townscape. Once the gardens that belong to them have grown, the townscape will become still friendlier. At present, the often 3- to 4-m-high bare walls mar the picture. To walk through the streets of the town at noon between the high stone walls is not exactly a pleasure."[103]

Dr. Steuber, who served as chief medical officer at the Nazareth headquarters, had a different impression. "Nazareth," he wrote, "is a dirty town in the mountains, half-crumpled and in ruins like all Turkish places in Palestine. A certain contrast to this is presented by the numerous, in part ostentatiously built, Christian hospices and orphanages....With the exception of the main street, Nazareth's streets and lanes are narrow, crooked and dark, and because of their steepness do not allow cart traffic....In Nazareth, too, accommodating the headquarters caused some difficulties. There was no dearth of large stone buildings; but these had served as Turkish military hospitals and were bug-ridden to an extent that defies any description. The flight from the bugs repeatedly rendered necessary a change of quarters. The commander in chief was not spared; he suffered with a philosophical equanimity the ravages of this higher authority."

"In Palestine we often asked ourselves: How might the soil of the Holy Land, the memory of that great event that took place 2,000 years ago, affect our simple German soldier?....It would appear that the impression....differed quite substantially from one man to another. Thus I recall a brief conversation between two gunners of the battery attached to [German Infantry] Battalion 701, which, passing by, I overheard in the latitude of Nazareth: 'Look, Emil, here did the star of Nazareth rise!' The other retorted: 'Don't talk rot, comrade, here we are going to be deloused!'".[104]

◄ *The Jewish town of Nazerat 'Illit (Upper Nazareth), founded in 1957 - a view from the south, 12 Apr 97. In 1995 the town had 40,000 inhabitants, including 4,400 'Arabs and others'. The Arab village in the distance is Er-Reine (pop. 10,500 in 1995).*

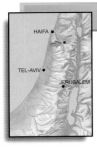

El-'Affule – 'Afula

The photo of El-'Affule taken by the Bavarian Squadron on 20 Jan <u>1918</u> demonstrates the crucial military importance of the place during the war. The large railway station, with several trains on its tracks, lies on the line that from 1905 on linked Damascus – via Der'a, Samakh and Beisan – with Haifa. The tracks that turn southward are part of the railway that from 1915 on led to Lydda and Beersheba, and in 1916 reached the eastern edge of the Sinai Desert in preparation for an attack on the Suez Canal. The bright line that runs from the lower to the upper margin is part of the vital road, improved during the war, that linked Damascus with Beersheba via Tiberias, Nazareth, El-'Affule, Nablus, Jerusalem and Hebron. The Arab village of El-'Affule stands to the left (west) of this road.

Population	
1922	56?
1945	2,31(
1995	35,00(

1918

◀ *19 Sep 18: The British bomb El-'Affule.*

▲ *El-'Affule during Wo War I.*

1997

1937

On 19 Sep 18 at 01:15 hours, shortly before the beginning of Allenby's offensive, a huge Handley Page plane, flown by an Australian crew, dropped 800 kg of bombs on El-'Affule and hit the central telephone exchange of the Turkish-German forces in Palestine. On the following morning El-'Affule was bombed twice; one of the attacks was photographed from the northeast by one of the aviators (see photo on previous page). On 20 Sep 18 at 07:15 hours, the Deccan Horse of the 14th Cavalry Brigade captured El-'Affule.

The lands of El-'Affule were bought in 1924 by a group of American Zionists, who endeavored to establish there an urban center for the Valley of Jezreel. Kruger's photo shows the place – now known as 'Afula – in 1937. The railway station and the road from Nazareth, at center, are the only features that have not changed. 'Afula's water tower, central boulevard, and synagogue stand out in the foreground. North of 'Afula are visible, from right to left, Balfouria (founded in 1922), Tel 'Adashim (1913), Kfar Gideon (1923) and Yizra' (1923). A part of Nazareth is discernible near the mountains, toward which the arrow-straight road, partially lined with trees, appears to point.

Our photograph of 12 Apr 1997 shows a major part of the present-day town.

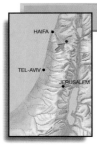

Merhavya

In the upper left corner of this Bavarian photo, probably taken in 1918, can be seen the encampment of Bavarian Squadron 304 near the Jewish settlement of Merhavya, whose houses form an incomplete rectangle near the lower margin's midpoint; the structure within the rectangle, casting a shadow leftward, is Merhavya's water tower. Between the encampment and the settlement are visible the mound and the moat of the crusader castle of La Fève, with some remains of the Arab village of El-Fuleh and two large wooden shacks of Merhavya perched atop the medieval remains. The straight line near the photo's left margin is the Turkish railway that links nearby El-'Affule with Beisan, Samakh, Der'a and Damascus.

Merhavya (God's expanse, after Psalms 118:5) was founded in 1911 on the site of the Arab village of El-Fuleh, which had been purchased by Joshua Hankin and transferred to the Jewish National Fund. The plan was to set up in Merhavya a "cooperative settlement," according to the ideas of the Zionist economist and sociologist Franz Oppenheimer. Upon the arrival of the Bavarian Squadron in November 1917, the settlers had to hand them two of their four houses. Yet the presence of the Bavarians was beneficial for the settlement: they repeatedly intervened with the Turkish authorities on behalf of the settlers, treated their sick, and once menac-

ingly overflew the neighboring Arab village of Sulam and threw a bomb near it to make the villagers hand over to justice a thief who had come to blows with one of Merhavya's guards. The settlers and the Bavarians held common festivities.

The Deccan Horse reached Merhavya and the (largely evacuated) Bavarian encampment on the morning of 20 Sep 18, a short while after having taken El-'Affule.

After the war, the cooperative settlement broke up and the place was settled by other Jewish groups until, in 1929, it was taken over by Kibbutz Merhavya.

1997

1946

Kluger's photo of 1946 shows most of the kibbutz, with the original rectangle and water tower at its
center. The mound of the medieval castle is now – to
the chagrin of archaeologists – largely de-lapidated,
covered by new buildings and planted with trees.

Our photo of 12 Apr 1997 shows the expanded
kibbutz in its entirety; the original rectangle is right of
center, the water tower concealed by trees. The mound,
with a lane drawing a whitish half-circle to its left, is
barely discernible. The kibbutz factory stands out near
the right margin's midpoint.

Population	
1922	135
1935	350
1995	588

*German soldiers, a camel and horses near the
water tower.*

*German planes that the British captured at
Merhavya, and amongst them a British plane. The
leftmost German plane bears a painted swastika - a
quite common emblem on German and French World
War I planes. (The German-Jewish pilot Fritz
Beckhardt, too, adorned his plane with this sign.)*[105]

Beisan – Bet She'an

The Arab village of Beisan appears on this British photomosaic, prepared from Australian photos taken on 3 Sep 1918 and preserved in the Israel Antiquities Authority collection. Seventeen days later – and less than 36 hours after the start of the British offensive – the 4th Cavalry Division, advancing from El-'Affule, captured Beisan, having covered some 115 km.

The large uninhabited tell of ancient Bet She'an (Scythopolis) appears near the upper margin of the part of the photomosaic we chose to reproduce; the dark line between it and the margin is Wadi Jalud (Nahal Harod). The only visible vestige of Roman Scythopolis is the outer rim of the theater: it assumes the form of a bright half-circle that opens toward the tell. The bright quadrangle at the southern end of the Arab village is the Turkish khan.

Kluger's photos of 1937 and 1939 face eastward; the tell does not appear on them. The 1937 photo concentrates on the khan, with the letters BN on its roof. The large quadrangular building below and to the left of it is a school built over the remains of a crusader fort. The 1939 photo, taken at a greater distance from the khan, shows that the rectangle to the west of it has in the interim been razed. A comparison with the mosaic of 1918 indicates an expansion of the village to the south and southwest. The RAF photo of 25 Jan 1945, which like the mosaic covers the entire area, shows more accurately Beisan's considerable growth under the British Mandate.

Apprehensive lest Arab Beisan might support the expected invasion by Trans-Jordan's Arab Legion, the Haganah captured the tell on 12 May 48 and called for the town's capitulation. Units of the Arab Liberation Army and most of the inhabitants fled before the surrender took place; the remainder were later expelled to Trans-Jordan or Nazareth.

The Survey of Israel photograph of 16 Jun 1967 shows Israeli Bet She'an and its main tourist attraction, the Roman theater excavated by Israeli archaeologists in the early 1960s. The rectangle west of the khan, razed sometime between 1937 and 1939, is now a municipal garden. Several houses of Arab Beisan remain standing in the vicinity of the khan, especially to the northwest of it. The isolated bright building to the right of the Roman theater is Beisan's mosque, now Bet She'an's museum.

1918

1937

1939

1994

Our photo of 9 Apr 1994, focusing on Bet She'an's north-eastern part, highlights the ongoing excavations of Roman and Byzantine Scythopolis, mainly between the theater and the tell. The almost completely uncovered oval amphitheater stands out to the left of the green rectangle of the municipal garden, north of which the crusader fort is being excavated.

1945

1967

Population	
1922	1,941
1945	5,180
1967	12,500
1995	14,900

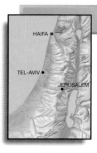

The undated photo from Adolf Schreiber's album, probably taken in 1918, shows the northwestern end, or "nose," of the Carmel ridge. The photo is taken from the northeast. The coastal plain can be glimpsed on the far side of the ridge. The small cluster of houses on the ridge itself, close to the photo's left margin, is the quarter of Karmelheim (see p. 186). The substantial building at the right end of the ridge, overlooking the Mediterranean, is the Carmelite monastery, originally built around 1770. The terminal of the Turkish railway that reached Haifa in 1905 is seen in the photo's lower left corner; to the right of it is the mole of Turkish Haifa's harbor, with a broad, bright strip of sand to its right. Haifa's old town, founded in the mid-18th century by the powerful Bedouin sheikh Daher el-'Omar, is the densely built rectangle along the shore, on the far side of the bright strip of sand. To the left of the old town, above the railway terminal, are some extensions of Haifa. The large isolated block above them, at the foot of the mountain, is the Hebrew Technion, whose foundation stone was laid in 1912. There are other extensions to the right of the old town. The regularly laid out streets and fields on their right are those of the German Temple Colony of Haifa, founded in 1869.

1918

▲ *Jodhpore and Mysore Lancers of the 5th Cavalry Division entering Haifa, 23 Sep 18.*

On 22 Sep 18, with El-'Affule, Beisan and Nazareth in the hands, the British moved on Haifa along the main road from Nazareth, but were repulsed about 5 km southeast of the town. On the following day elements of the 5th Cavalry Division moved in. squadron of Mysore Lancers, reinforced by a squadron of Sherwood Rangers, climbed Mt. Carmel and captured the Turkish guns near Karmelheim, while the Jodhpore Lancers charged the Turkish machine-guns on the slopes above the main road and speared the gunners. The way into Haifa was now open and the town was soon taken.

The RAF photo of 7 Jan 1945 shows the new large harbor the British erected between 1929 and 1931, whose construction entailed the reclamation from the sea of a sizable area. The coastal railway from Lydda, paralleling the harbor, reached Haifa in January 1919. The Jewish quarter of Bat Galim stands on the shore northwest of the harbor. The dense cluster of the old town stands out in the photo's lower left corner, quite far from the shore because of the massive reclamation of land from the sea that took place during the harbor's construction. The area between the German Colony and the old town is almost continuously built up.

1997

1945

dome, completed in 1958, stands out. Left of the lower end of the colony's main street stands the Dagon grain silo, its 70-m height deducible from the huge shadow it casts leftward. There are many new houses, and several empty plots, in the area of the old town.

Our color photograph of 18 Jan 1997, taken from the same angle as the World War I photo preserved in Schreiber's album, allows to perceive accurately Haifa's expansion along the Carmel ridge and its slopes, the extent of the area reclaimed from the sea, and the demolition of much of the old town.

1970

By the time this photo was taken, the inhabitants of the German Colony had been either interned or deported.

In Haifa, too, hostilities started a few days after the UN partition resolution of 29 Nov 47, and perhaps as many as 25,000 Arabs fled during the ensuing four months. British withdrawal of troops stationed between the Jewish and Arab areas on 21 Apr 48 triggered a swift Haganah operation that, within 24 hours, ended in a complete Arab collapse. The remaining Arab leaders refused to sign a British-mediated cease-fire surrender and decided instead to call on Haifa's Arabs to leave the town. The exodus took place in the days that followed, with British assistance; in its initial phase, Jewish civilian leaders called on the Arabs to remain.

The Survey of Israel photo of 26 Jul 1970 shows the entire area northwest (right) of the former German Colony built up. In the Bahai garden above the erstwhile colony the shrine's new

Population		
1922	**24,634**	(9,377 M, 8,863 C, 6,230 J)
1945	**138,300**	(35,940 M, 26,570 C, 75,000 J)
1967	**209,900**	(incl. 12,200 Arabs and others)
1995	**252,300**	(incl. 26,700 Arabs and others)

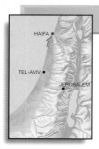

Haifa - Downtown

This aerial photo from Schreiber's album also appears to date from 1918. Taken from the northwest at a very low altitude, it focuses on the houses and fields of the German Temple Colony at Haifa. The short, sickle-like mole at the end of Carmel Avenue – the colony's straight, tree-lined main street – was erected in 1898 on the orders of the Turkish sultan to facilitate Kaiser Wilhelm II's landing. The large tripartite building overlooking the colony from the right is the convent of the Dames de Nazareth. The group of substantial houses to the left of the road that runs upward and to the right of the convent is the Jewish quarter of Herzlia, founded in 1909.

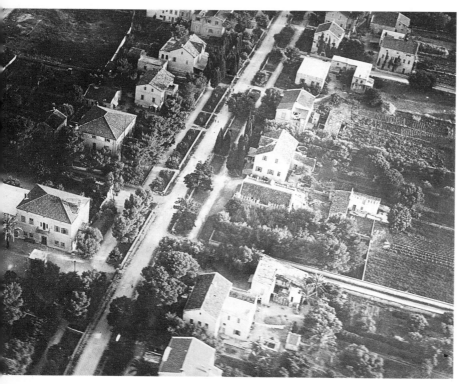

▲ *The Hebrew Technion overlooking the Turkish harbor, c.1918*

◄ *Carmel Avenue, c.1918.*

1996

Nahum Goldmann, the future Zionist leader who visited Haifa in 1913, wrote: "...I had to take up quarters in the German hotel as there was no room left in the Jewish one. This gave me the opportunity to admire the great civilizing qualities of these German colonists. In Haifa they established a very pretty settlement that, in its scrupulous cleanliness and neat, pretty layout contrasts in this respect favorably with several Jewish ones. The inclination to the tiny, the love for modest, natural adornment, and beyond that the deep civilizing sense of order are virtues that in Palestine, too, Jews are still often lacking. The skill to beautify one's house for a few pennies, to lay out a splendid garden for a few dimes, is unfortunately something the Jewish colonist still does not know. Yet I believe that this is a shortcoming that time will overcome. After all, these Germans brought these qualities from their Swabia; the Jewish colonist must, on the other hand, make them his own only here. They could not have developed in Berditshev and Kremenchug. Already today one sees them emerging among diverse colonists. And some gardens in Tel Aviv or Petah Tiqva can already match those of the German Colony at Haifa."[106]

On 24 Sep 18, the British military correspondent F.J. Ferguson filed the following report: "The few hundred Turks left behind at Haifa resisted our advance. The configuration of the ground, with a marsh on one side of the road and the slopes of Mount Carmel on the other, prevented our troops from deploying on a line of any width. The Turks were thus able to concentrate their fire on a narrow front, but our men gradually worked their way forward and drove the Turks out of their positions. They held out, however, till they had fired the last round from their field-guns, because I saw two guns surrounded by empty shell-cases, while a little further down the road a waggon bringing up a fresh supply was overturned, a lucky shot having killed the horses. The population gave our men a most enthusiastic reception, the German colonists even participating in this welcome. These Germans are mostly quiet emigrants from Wurttemberg who came to Palestine on conscientious grounds. They complained bitterly of Turkish exactions and the lack of security. Their settlement is one of the most successful in Palestine."[107]

Kluger's photo of 1937 shows much of the same area from the southwest. Carmel Avenue, with sloping-roofed houses on either side, stands out in the photo's left part; the Bahai shrine is clearly visible in the garden above that street's upper end; the Turkish mole, eclipsed by the new, much larger breakwater, appears at upper right. In the area the British reclaimed from the sea are seen the port offices, the new railway station, and Kingsway — the main thoroughfare of the new commercial center — with large rectangular buildings on its northern side. In our photo of 10 Jun 1996, the entire area that appeared in Schreiber's photo is densely built up. The former German Colony's Carmel Avenue, later renamed Carmel Boulevard, is now known as Ben-Gurion Boulevard, its houses bereft of their patches of front lawn. The British-built Kingsway is now Independence Road.

1937

The Bavarian photo of 10 Mar 1918 shows the quarter of Karmelheim, founded in 1890 by members of the German Temple colony of Haifa. The lane from the colony proper, paved by the colonists by 1887, runs toward the quarter from the photo's upper right corner. At the entrance to the quarter is a rectangular grove with a water reservoir in its upper part. The sloping-roofed house next to the grove's short side is the Hotel Pross, apparently completed in 1893. The large hospice established by Pastor Schneider is seen near the lane leading from Haifa, near the photo's right margin.

In the fall of 1917 Dr. Steuber turned Schneider's hospice into a convalescent home for German soldiers. Lorries would convey them to and from the beach. When Turkish soldiers attempted to cut trees in Consul Keller's nearby garden, the Germans stepped out, arms in hand, and stopped them.

From a Hebrew-written report by Joseph Lishansky, leading member of the pro-British NILI spy ring: "10th of Adar 5677, Zikhron Ya'aqov, 4.III.1917. On Mt. Carmel there are patrols that keep watch over the sea and, when the [British] planes are flying, notify by phone all army posts in the Valley of Jezreel so that they may ready the guns and [cause] the army to disperse in the fields. The [British] ships should be notified to take great care with their wireless tele-graphs (or perhaps they allow people to come ashore who are [in reality] spying for the Turks), for [the Turks] boasted in my presence that a long time before the ships are seen, and even long before the appearance of the planes, they know when they are coming. Let them be careful and check carefully their doings lest, God forbid, they cause our downfall as well."[108]

1989

Our photo of 23 Nov [1989] shows Moriah Boulevard, the main artery on the crest of the Carmel, winding its way along the same course that the German lane had taken at the beginning of the century. The rectangular grove extends to the right of central Carmel's gray auditorium. The red-roofed building to the left of the auditorium, which houses the James de Rothschild Cultural Center, was originally the Hotel Pross. Some red roofs of erstwhile Karmelheim may be discerned left of the grove.

▲ *General Liman von Sanders and Major Prigge (far right) with members of the Aimann family, Karmelheim, 1918.*

◄ *General of the Cavalry Otto Liman von Sanders, commander in chief of the Turkish-German forces on the Palestinian front as of March 1918, at the entrance to the Hotel Pross.*

The "Air Wagon," propelled by a plane's engine, used by German aviators on the El-'Affule-Haifa railway. It was put together by the Jewish engineer Barukh Katinka (seen here standing to the right of the engine).

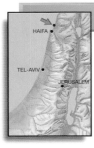

Acre

The photo from Schreiber's album, probably dating from 1918, shows from the southeast the town of Acre, at the northern end of the Bay of Haifa. After the Mamluk destruction of Crusader Acre in 1291, the place was largely in ruins until, in the mid-18th century, Daher el-ʿOmar rebuilt a smaller town on the promontory jutting out into the Mediterranean. The massive walls with their triangular outer works, which stand out in the photo, date from the 19th century; they postdate the earlier, slighter fortifications that in 1799 withstood Napoleon Bonaparte's siege. The large quadrangle on the inner side of the northern wall is the Turkish citadel; to its right is the town's main mosque, founded in 1781 by Jazzar Pasha, who was to defend the town successfully against Bonaparte. The islet in the small bay east (right) of the walled-in town, is the medieval Tower of the Flies, which marked the southern end of the now submerged eastern breakwater of Acre's harbor. On the beach to the right of this islet stands the Turkish railway station, the terminal of a line from Haifa that was completed in 1913. A few houses are seen north and northeast of the walls; most of these are built along streets that, being perpendicular to the coastline, testify to a central plan for the area outside the walls. A large swamp extends north of these streets.

On 23 Sep 18, while one column of the 5th Cavalry Division advanced on Haifa, another moved on Acre by way of Shafa ʿAmr, and captured it without encountering serious resistance.

1918

The RAF photo of 4 Jan 1945 shows the growth of New Acre along a regular gridiron of streets north and northeast of the walled-in town; the largest of its buildings is the British police fortress on the shore north of the walls. A rectangular municipal garden extends north of the Turkish railway station; the British coastal railway to Beirut by-passes New Acre from the east. The northern swamp is only slightly smaller than at the end of World War I. The Turkish citadel now serves as the central prison of British Palestine.

◄ *A close-up of the main mosque and its surroundings, c.1918.*

Population	
1922	**6,420** (4,883 M, 1,344 C, 78 J)
1945	**12,360** (9,890 M, 2,330 C, 50 J)
1967	**32,800** (incl. 8,450 Arabs and others)
1995	**45,300** (incl. 10,800 Arabs and others)

1994

1945

The Survey of Israel photo of 7 Jun 1968 shows the major part of a significantly expanded Acre, now predominantly Jewish, partially built on what was the northern swamp. The larger part of the Turkish citadel now serves as a hospital for the mentally ill; a fishermen's wharf covers the remains of the southern mole of the medieval harbor.

Our photo of 26 Apr 1994 concentrates on Old Acre. The activity at the fishermen's wharf has intensified; numerous tourist buses are parked near the western waterfront; excavations in the citadel's courtyard are uncovering parts of the 13th-century head-quarters of the Knights Hospitaller.

1968

After the UN partition resolution of 29 Nov 47, the Arabs of [A]cre, aided by irregulars from neighboring countries, succeeded [in] disrupting communications with the isolated Jewish settlements [n]orth and northeast of the town. After the fall of Arab Haifa many [r]efugees arrived in Acre, and with Haganah mortar fire hitting the [t]own, many of the local inhabitants began to flee. An outbreak of [ty]phus on 5 May 48 intensified the exodus. On the night of 16/17 [M]ay the Haganah went on the attack, and a night later the town [s]urrendered. The Arab irregulars were taken captive; 5,000 to [6],000 local inhabitants chose to remain.

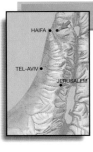

Shafa 'Amr (Shefar'am)

The small Galilean town of Shafa 'Amr – populated by Christians, Muslims, Druze and until 1920 also by a few Jews – appears on this oblique Bavarian photo taken from the southwest, probably in 1918. The line linking points A and B on the margins is the track that ascends from Acre to Nazareth. There are threshing floors on both sides of the hill on which the town is situated. The large building on the hill's summit is the citadel that 'Othman, a son of Daher el-'Omar, erected in about 1761. The small dome of the town mosque may be discerned on the high ground to the left of the citadel. A large building with a bright roof that has a small dome in its midst, stands out in the town center; it is the Greek-Catholic Church of Sts. Peter and Paul, built in 1904. The trapezoid complex near the spot where the track forks, at the far end of the town, belongs to the Dames de Nazareth, who settled there in 1866 and built a convent and a girls' school.

1918

1945

The RAF photo of 26 Jan 1945 shows some growth of the town, especially on the northern slope; the Acre-Nazareth road is now paved, and so is the road that runs through the town. The undated, oblique photo taken by the Haganah's Air Service – apparently in 1948 – shows the town from the opposite direction.

From early March 1948 Shafa 'Amr was under the control of a Druze battalion, recruited in Syria, which in mid-April attempted to attack Kibbutz Ramat Yohanan, southwest of Shafa 'Amr. A month later the battalion moved to Upper Galilee. In mid-July local Druze emissaries reached an agreement with Israeli liaison officers according to which the Druze, upon an Israeli attack, were to surrender after a semblance of resistance. On 14 July, after an artillery barrage aimed at Shafa 'Amr's Muslim quarter, Israel's 7th Brigade captured the place. Most of the Muslim inhabitants fled beforehand; a considerable number were allowed to return a few weeks later.

1995

The Survey of Israel photo of 7 Jun 1968 shows a markedly larger Shafa 'Amr (known in Hebrew by its ancient name,
Shefar'am), one of Israel's Arab towns. Our photo of 15 Nov
1995 focuses on that part of Shafa 'Amr (now still more expanded) that is congruent with the area appearing in the World War
photo.

1948

1968

Population			
1922	**2,288** (1,263 C,	623 M,	402 D)
1945	**3,640** (1,560 C,	1,380 M,	690 D)
1968	**10,000**		
1995	**24,200**		

191

Sea of Galilee (Lake Kinneret)

The undated photo from Rengstorf's collection, apparently taken in 1918, is of less than mediocre quality; but since it is the only World War I photo that allows a glimpse of the Sea of Galilee almost in its entirety, with a snow-capped Mt. Hermon looming on the horizon, it is reproduced here.

Our photo of 12 Apr 1997 shows most of the Sea of Galilee, with the River Jordan winding its way from the lake, through the densely settled valley, to point A on the lower margin. The snow-covered peak of Mt. Hermon is visible above the haze.

The photo from Groll's collection, probably taken by aviators of German Squadron 300 in 1918,* shows the southwestern shore of the Sea of Galilee from a low altitude. The Jordan leaves the lake at left; the Jewish settlement Deganya and its orchard are on the river's near bank; the encampment with several parked lorries on the lake's shore is a German military infirmary.

Deganya was founded in 1909; in 1911 it became the first collective settlement in the country. During the war it had about 30 inhabitants. In November 1917, upon the arrival of Squadron 300, the settlement's members and their children – among them the 2-year-old Moshe Dayan – had to hand over their houses to the German aviators and move into storage rooms. When the squadron commander, Hellmuth Felmy, was asked to clear a room for a sick child, he refused; but a German medical officer ministered to the child. The Germans defended the members from Turkish exactions and supplied electricity to their makeshift dwellings.

1997

1989

In our photo of 10 Dec 1989, the Jordan and the original houses of eganya are largely hidden by trees. The main road to Tiberias runs along the ke's shore.

H einrich Schmittdiel, an NCO with Squadron 300, described his involuntary hosts in his still unpublished diary: "About 20 young people, mostly from Russia, are accommodated here as agricultural workers; in addition a dozen girls. Among themselves they talk only Hebrew, as they wish to revive this language. To be sure, they are Zionists. They take turns at work, so that always one part goes to the fields while the other idles in smart clothes. The buildings are new and quite usefully furnished. In the summer, the entire community, with their girls, sleep in tabernacles in the garden. Behind the house and to the side of it a pretty orange grove extends down to the Jordan....Among the Jew girls is a Russian student, Sonia, a violin virtuoso. We often listen when she plays in the evenings. Her playing is marvelous. The Jew girls wear their hair short, while that of our lads flows down to their shoulders. All behave very reservedly and are friendly only when they need our help."

Reminiscing in 1934, Devorah Dayan wrote: "We live in wartime. The German army is in the kitchen and in the other buildings, and we crowd together in the cowshed's upper storey, in the machines' storage rooms, in every roofed corner. As if it were natural that planes should fly every day over our heads, that the proud *Hauptmann* (captain) should watch out from the window, that the *Stallmeister* should groom his horses in the court; as if it were natural for German sounds to be heard in our court, and for their drunken officers to sing, on their festive nights, like in a tavern."[109]

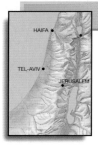

This photo from the Munich War Archives, probably dating from 1918, is a copy the Bavarian aviators prepared from a no longer extant original, hence its mediocre quality. It shows the Golan Heights, the River Yarmuk coming down from the mountains (near the midpoint of the photo's right margin), the southern part of the Sea of Galilee, and a 5-km stretch in which the River Jordan, having left the lake, twists its way southward. The bright area at the lake's southern end is the Arab village of Samakh; Deganya is visible immediately to the east (right) of the Jordan's exit from the lake; the Jewish colony of Kinneret is the grouping of bright dots on the lake's near shore, at the photo's left margin; the dark cluster to the left of the Jordan's large loop, close to the photo's lower right corner, is the Arab village of El-'Ubeidiya. Considerable cultivation is visible in the Jordan Valley, and some also on the Galilean plateau to the southwest of the lake and on the Golan Heights to the east.

Samakh - partial view.

1918

After the conquest of Nazareth, Liman von Sanders attempte to establish a line along the Yarmuk and the western shore of th Sea of Galilee; Samakh, the weak link in this new front, was to t held at all costs. On 24 Sep 18 the 4th Australian Light Hors Brigade advanced on Samakh from Beisan and on the followin morning, after a fierce battle, overcame the Germans, who defende Samakh's railway station "with exceptional boldness and stubbor ness, their courage stimulated by an abundance of rum" – accorc ing to the official Australian history of the campaign. Turks an Germans dug in south of Deganya's courtyard were overpowere as well. German Squadron 300 had already left for Der'a on 2 Sep 18; their retreat triggered a Bedouin raid on Deganya, whos members fled to Kinneret. On their return a day later, they foun the settlement thoroughly looted.[110]

◀ *The Jordan's exit from the lake and Deganya on a postcard of 1921.*

1994

1938

Kluger's photo of **1938,** which covers much of the same area, shows in the lower left corner the communal settlement of Kinneret (to be distiguished from the colony of Kinneret on the lake's shore), which was founded in 1913. An extended Deganya appears to the west of the Jordan's outlet; it is now called Deganya "A," to distinguish it from Deganya "B" to the south (right), founded in 1920. The line that runs from the right margin's midpoint to Samakh and thence southeastward to the gorge of the Yarmuk River is the (originally Turkish) railway linking Haifa with Der'a (and Damascus). On the shore northeast of Samakh is the Arab village of Es-Samra. The line dividing the fields of the two Deganyas from those of Samakh is easily discerni-ble. The two kibbutzim Massada and Sha'ar ha-Golan, both founded in 1937 southeast (right) of Samakh, are barely visible near the photo's right margin.

The Arabs of El-'Ubeidiya, Es-Samra and Samakh fled in March-April 1948. On 18 May 48 Syrian armor conquered Samakh; Massada and Sha'ar ha-Golan were evacuated under pressure of other Syrian forces. On 20 May five Syrian tanks, several armored cars, and an infantry company attacked Deganya "A," de-fended by about 70 men. At the height of the battle a tank penetrated the Deganya's perimeter defences, but was hit by one or more Molotov cocktails and anti-tank rounds. The Syrians began to retreat; a few hours later their attack on Deganya "B" was repulsed as well. Later that day Israeli artillery shelled the Syrian col-umns, upon which they evacuated Samakh and the two kibbutzim to the southeast of it, after having wrecked them.

Our photo of 9 Apr **1994** shows, in addition to the two Deganyas, Kibbutz Bet Zera' (founded 1927) near the large loop of the Jordan at lower right, a part of Kibbutz Afiqim (founded 1932) near the right margin, and the rebuilt Massada and Sha'ar ha-Golan in the upper right corner. An industrial zone and a park occupy the site of erstwhile Samakh; to its east and northeast are the kibbutzim Ma'agan, Tel Qatzir and Ha-On, all founded in 1949. The site of erstwhile El-'Ubeidiya is slightly beyond the lower margin.[111]

Kinneret

The oblique photo from Groll's collection, probably taken in 1918, shows from a very low altitude the northern part of the colony Kinneret, founded in 1909 about 2 km northwest of the Jordan's outlet from the Sea of Galilee. The houses of the settlers – originally eight in all – form a line that parallels the lake (which does not appear on the photo). The much larger, two-storied house that stands apart belongs to the Treidels, a Zionist family from Koblenz, Germany.

▲ *The outle of the Jordan from Lake Kinneret, c. 1918.*

1918

H einrich Schmittdiel, NCO with German Squadron 300, writes in his diary that while in general Jews were reserved in their relations with the German aviators, there was one exception, "a German Jewish owner of a nice farm beyond [west of] the Jordan. A brother of his studied in Germany....and was in 1916 and 1917 a sergeant in our squadron. I have conversed with him – his name is Treidel – often and gladly about the local conditions. Our meteorological station is now located at the Treidel farm."[112]

Kluger's photograph from 1937 shows the small colony in its entirety, its western and northern sides protected by a stone wall. The Treidel house is now partially hidden by trees. The road along the shore leads from Samakh to Tiberias. The RAF photo of 2 Jan 1945 offers a vertical view of the same scene.

1937

1994

The Survey of Israel photo of 28 Jun 1968 shows a considerably larger village. The protective stone wall, pierced at two
points, is no longer Kinneret's western limit; in addition, there are
houses on the fields between the original street and the lake, and
there is a new street to the south.

Our photo of 9 Apr 1994 shows Kinneret's further expansion on both sides of the original street, and the continued oblitera-
tion of the protective wall. A son of one of the three Treidels from
Coblenz lives in the house they built.

1945

1968

Population	
1922	**149**
1945	**220**
1967	**180**
1995	**376**

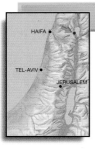

Tiberias

The photo of Tiberias taken by the 1st Australian Squadron from the direction of the Sea of Galilee on 22 Oct 1918 (and preserved in the aerial photographs unit of the Geography Department of the Hebrew University of Jerusalem) shows almost all of the town's buildings as situated within the walls that the Bedouin chieftain Daher el-'Omar and one of his sons erected in the mid-18th century. The round towers at the end of the northern and southern walls stand in the waters of the lake; the town's citadel is only partially seen, near the midpoint of the photo's right margin. The broad bright line linking points A and B is the Turkish road from Damascus to Nazareth; the grayish line leading to point C is the road to Samakh. The large tripartite building with a projecting central segment, near which the road from Damascus passes upon entering the town, is the hospital of the Scottish Mission, inaugurated in 1894. The large building standing where that road turns right toward Nazareth is Hotel Tiberias, the town's first modern hotel, built in 1896 by a member of the German Temple Society. To its left is the town's main mosque, erected by Daher el-'Omar. A large Greek Orthodox monastery stands on the shore, at the town's southeastern extremity. The enclosure to the left of point B contains the traditional tomb of Maimonides. The three houses in the enclosure standing out in the photo's upper left corner were erected in 1911 in an attempt to establish Jewish farms in the town's immediate vicinity.

1918

1937

On 25 Sep 18 a squadron of the 4th Australian Light Horse Brigade moved from Samakh to Tiberias and together with a squadron of the 3rd Australian Light Horse Brigade and a light armored motor battery that advanced from Nazareth, captured the town after overcoming slight Turkish opposition.

Kluger's photo of 1937 shows a substantial growth of Tiberias outside the walls. The old town itself is cut into four parts by three wide west-to-east streets. The straight embankment or "Lido," constructed by the British after the great flood of 1934, has placed the town's easternmost houses at some distance from the waterfront. The RAF photo of 4 Jan 1945 shows the Jewish quarter of Qiryat Shmuel along the road to Nazareth, and the British police fortress.

1994

The Survey of Israel photograph of 28 Jun 1968 shows the growth of the new town; most of the old one has been razed.

By the time we took our photo on 9 Apr 1994, much of the old town had been taken over by large hotels and parking lots. A major crusader structure stands unearthed, surrounded by lawns, in a large rectangle near the old town's southwestern corner.

1945

In 1948 Tiberias was the first town with a mixed Arab and Jewish population to come entirely under Jewish control. Hostilities erupted in March, with the Jews of the old town isolated and with Jewish traffic barred from passing through it to northeastern Galilee. Haganah forces countered on 12 Apr 48 by capturing Nasir ad-Din, a village on the ridge overlooking the town, thereby isolating Arab Tiberias from its hinterland; five days later they attacked the Arab-held area in a coordinated drive from Qiryat Shmuel downward and from the old town upward. The Arab leaders decided to evacuate Tiberias under British protection. Much of the old town was destroyed in late 1948-early 1949.

1968

Population	
1922	**6,950** (4,427 J, 2,096 M, 422 C)
1945	**11,310** (6,000 J, 4,540 M, 760 C)
1967	**23,500**
1995	**37,300**

▲ *German lorries near the wall of Tiberias. The town's main mosque is at the left.*

▶ *Tiberias, 26 Sep 18: Transport of the Australian Mounted Division entering the town from the northwest the day after it had been captured from the Turks.*

▼ *A road sign in Tiberias, reading in Turkish and German: "To Damascus," "To Samakh," "To Transport Base 505." Above: Parts of the road sign now in the Imperial War Museum, London. Below: The road sign as appearing in a contemporary film on the Australians in Sinai and Palestine.*

▼ *Tiberias, 25 Sep 18: Australian cavalry entering the town from the west. At right, Hotel Tiberias.*

Die heißen Schwefelquellen am See Genezareth.

◄ *The hot baths south of Tiberias and the tomb of Rabbi Meir.*

▼ *A lane in Tiberias.*

Muhammad Rafiq and Muhammad Bahjat, two Turkish officials who made a tour of the country in an early phase of World War I, reported: "Tiberias is undoubtedly a dull and even suffocating little town. It was once enclosed by a wall that began in the north, continued eastward, and finally southward. It was always forbidden to build houses outside the walls. Therefore Tiberias is imprisoned within them. After the year 1324 [=1906-07] they began to build outside of them. Only 15 houses were built, and all the other houses of Tiberias are for the time being within the walls.

All of the houses and even sidewalks are built of black basalt....More than one half of the buildings have one storey, and the rest have two or even three storeys. All merge one into another. One may say that all are constructed in the same manner: all are quadrangular or rectangular, and a few have tiled roofs. All roofs are built of earth or plaster. The house walls are all of stone."[113]

▼ *Women washing clothes at the lake.*

▼ *The Muslim shrine of Sitt Sakineh south of Tiberias.*

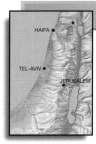

Safed

Shot from the northeast, this Bavarian photo – probably dating from 1918 – shows the central part of Safed, the capital of Upper Galilee. The ruined walls of the oval Crusader/Mamluk castle stand out in the center. The Jewish quarter occupies the photo's upper right quarter; parts of the Muslim quarters appear in the photo's left third. The large, C-shaped Rothschild Hospital stands out in the lower left corner; the buildings of the Scottish Mission are seen between the hospital and the lower margin.

Australian patrols reached Safed on 26 Sep 18 and found it empty of Turkish troops.

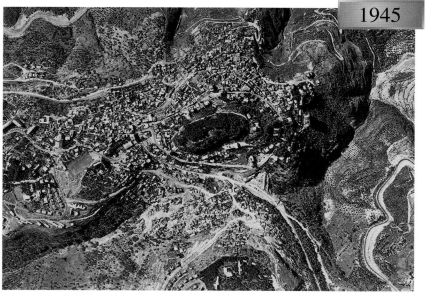

The RAF photograph of 7 Jan 1945 shows all of Safed. A straight staircase divides the Jewish quarter from the Arab one to its left. The British police fortress on Mount Canaan is partially visible at the lower margin.

From 29 Dec 47 on, the Jews of Safed – heavily outnumbered by their Arab neighbors – came under repeated sniper attacks. On 16 Apr 48 the British handed over the police fortress on Mount Canaan and other crucial positions to the Arabs, and left. The Jewish quarter came under siege. On 1 May two companies of the Palmah Galilee Battalion captured two Arab villages north of town and opened a corridor through which the battalion made its way into the Jewish quarter. On 6 May one of its platoons attacked the castle area but was repulsed; later, guns of the Arab Liberation Army shelled the Jewish quarter. A unit of Trans-Jordanian volunteers left town shortly before the start of a second, three-pronged attack by the Galilee Battalion during the night of 10/11 May. After a fierce battle, in which the attackers made use of a homemade

1994

imprecise but noisy mortar (named davidka, *after its inventor*), *all* ~~m~~ain Arab positions were captured. Many Arab civilians left town ~~fr~~om 2 May onward; in the wake of the Jewish victory all foreign ~~v~~olunteers and most civilians fled. The remaining 130 civilians ~~w~~ere later deported to Lebanon or Haifa.

The Survey of Israel photo of 15 Jan 1966 shows the Cita~~d~~el Garden covering the oval area of the medieval castle. Some of ~~S~~afed's new suburbs are visible south and east of the old center. A ~~p~~art of the erstwhile Arab quarter southeast of the castle area is in ~~r~~uins.

Our photo of 9 Apr 1994 concentrates on the old center of Safed. The bus station stands out near the midpoint of the lower margin. Little remains of the former Arab quarter to the left of the station. Parts of a new quarter are visible in the upper left corner.

1966

Population	
1922	**8,761** (5,431 M, 2,986 J, 343 C)
1945	**11,930** (9,100 M, 2,400 J, 430 C)
1968	**13,100**
1995	**22,800**

List of Abbreviations

AWM	Australian War Memorial, Canberra
CZA	Central Zionist Archives, Jerusalem
DGA	Department of Geography - Aerial Photographs Unit, the Hebrew University of Jerusalem
F	Hellmuth Felmy's collection, in possession of his son, Helmut Felmy, Bad Soden
G	Fritz Groll's album deposited by author in JNUL (shelfmark: TMA 4390)
G-1	Fritz Groll's albums in the Municipal Archives, Jerusalem
G-2	Photographs from Fritz Groll's collection in author's possession
GPO	Government Press Office, Jerusalem
IAA	Israel Antiquities Authority collection of aerial photographs
IAA [DGA]	IAA collection of World War I British mosaics of aerial photographs, deposited in DGA
IWM	Imperial War Museum, London
JNUL	Jewish National and University Library, Jerusalem
L	Zalman Leef's collection, Jerusalem (Copies in MAgr)
M	Bayerisches Hauptstaatsarchiv, Munich, Abt. IV: Kriegsarchiv
MAgr	Soil Survey, Land Evaluation and Remote Sensing Department, Ministry of Agriculture, Tel Aviv
PRO	Public Record Office, Kew
PS	Palestine Survey: RAF photos of 1944-45, deposited in MAgr, DGA, and SI
R	Prof. Karl Heinrich Rengstorf's collection deposited by author in DGA
S	Erich Steiner's collection deposited by author in DGA
Schr	Adolf Schreiber's album, in possession of Susanne Kolmar and David Rüegg, Munich
SI	Survey of Israel, Tel Aviv
V	Heeresgeschichtliches Museum (Militärwissenschaftliches Institut), Vienna
YBZ	Yad Izhak Ben-Zvi, Jerusalem
- Vil	Ze'ev Vilnay's collection
- Bir	Hillel Birger's collection

Data on the Photographs

Page numbers are printed in **bold** type. The entry '**42** *1918*: S, 26 Aug, 11:00, 2,000 m' means that on page 42, the photo from 1918 – extant in the Steiner collection – was taken on 26 August of that year, at 11:00 hours, from an altitude of 2,000 meters. The entry 'AWM B-1430 + B-1431' means that we combined two photos, preserved at the Australian War Memorial, Canberra, into a mosaic. '*1945*: PS 40/6005, 17 May. [SI]' means that the RAF photo of 17 May 1945, the shelf mark of which is P[alestine] S[urvey] 40/6005, has been reproduced from the copy owned by the Survey of Israel, Tel Aviv. - Unless otherwise indicated, the new photos are by Moshe Milner.

1-41 All data are given in the captions. **42** *1918*: S, 26 Aug, 11:00, 2,000 m; *1945*: PS 40/6005, 17 May [SI]. **43** *1956*: SI 14/9124, Nov, 12:30, 5,200 m; *1995:* 26 Feb, 10:30, 5,000 ft. **44-45** S - all photos and the telegram. **46** *1917*: G 203 (no details); *1949*: L 1/3286, 24 Sep, 14:50. **47** *1968*: SI 155/3957, 19 Jul, 10:35, 3,100 m; *1994*: 26 Feb, 12:00, 3,000 ft. **48** G 82 + G 199; M 494 o; JNUL TMA 4185, No. 34; G 201. **49** G 210; G 207. **50** *1918*: M 970, 13 Jul, 06:30, 3,000 m; *1917*: R, 2 Nov, 07:30, 600 m; AWM B-1791. **51** *1945*: PS 16/6180, 16 Jan. [DGA]; *1967*: SI 126/6005, 18 Jun, 13:55, 3,200 m; *1994*: 26 Feb, 11:45, 3,500 ft. **52** *1917*: JNUL Phot. 258, No. 532 (no details); *1945*: PS 29/6083, 14 Mar [DGA]. **53** *1949*: L 49/6322, 26 Oct, 16:35; *1966*: SI 112/9151, 23 Jul, 12:50, 1,900 m; *1994*:

26 Feb, 14:30, 4,000 ft. **54** JNUL TMA 4185, Nos. 26, 118, 46, 42a, 55. **55** AWM B-1628; V R-12155; G 188; G-2, No. 7. **56** *1918*: M 463 (section), 28 May, 12:30, 4,500 m; *1945*: PS 15/6043, 10 Jan [DGA]. **57** *1967*: SI 129/7750, 10 Jul, 14:20, 3,800 m; *1993*: 11 Dec, 10:00, 3,000 ft. **58** *1918*: M 452 (section) + M 454 (section), both of 15 Apr, 08:45, 4,000 m; *1945*: PS 15/5049, 10 Jan [MAgr]. **59** *1947*: CZA Album 147, 7706/1; *1967*: SI 129/7506, 10 Jul, 12:40, 1,900 m; *1994*: 26 Feb, 14:50, 2,500 ft. **60** *1917*: S, 25 Nov, 3,000 m; *1918*: M 429 (section), 21 Jan, 14:15, 3,800 m. **61** *1945*: PS 20/5008, 27 Jan [DGA]; *1966*: SI 112/9771, 23 Jul, 13:35, 1,950 m; *1994*: 26 Feb, 15:10, 3,000 ft. **62** *1918*: M 426 (section), 21 Jan, 14:15, 4,000 m; *1949*: L 44/5218, 23 Oct, 15:30. **63** *1966*: SI 110/8537, 18 Jun, 11:25, 4,800 m; *1994*: 26 Feb, 15:10, 3,500 ft. **64** *1918*: M 462 (section), 16 Jun, 06:00, 4,200 m.; AWM B-2132. **65** *1945*: PS 12/6130, 5 Jan [DGA]; *1966*: SI 112/9554 + 9555, 23 Jul, 12:15, 1,900 m; *1994*: 26 Feb, 10:50, 4,000 ft. **66** *1918*: M 365 h (section), 29 Jan, 14:30, 3,100 m; *1917*: PRO Air 1/2287/209/75/55 (Part D, No. 111), 30 Nov, 3,000 m; AWM B-1542. **67** *1949*: L 37/3227, 19 Oct, 14:40; *1968*: SI 152/3094, 12 Jul, 14:50, 1,800 m; *1994*: 26 Feb, 10:30, 3,500 ft. **68** AWM B-1751; AWM B-1686. **69** AWM B-1654; AWM B-1687. **70** *1917*: M 379 (section), 25 Nov, 13:30, 2,800 m; 1944: PS 7/5009, 29 Dec [DGA]; ground photo - autho. **71** *1990*: 8 Apr, 14:10, 3,500 ft. **72** *1918*: AWM B-2059 (no details); AWM B-1509; AWM B-5. **73** *1949*: L35/2784, 16 Oct, 11:20; *1990*: 8 Apr, 13:50, 3,500 ft. **74** M 307 b, 19 Mar 18, 15:00; AWM B-1612.

75 AWM B-1684; AWM B-1665; AWM B-4. **76** *1917*: G-1, No. 39 (no details); JNUL TMA 4183, No. 45. **77** *1949*: L 18/7879, 6 Oct, 15:00; *1994:* 26 Feb, 15:50, 3,000 ft. **78** *1917*: S, 3 Dec, 2,500 m; *1918*: M 184 (section), 08:15, 4,500 m. **79** *1944*: PS 2/5142, 10 Dec [DGA]; *1997*: 7 Feb, 12:20, 3,500 ft.; G-2, No. 11. **80** AWM B-1748; G-2, No. 3; G 219; G 228. **81** G 216; AWM J-5707. **82** *1918:* M 161, 24 Jul, 15:00, 5,100 m; AWM B-1430 + B-1431, both of 26 Jan 18. **83** *1949*: L 19/8176, 6 Oct, 16:20; *1997*: 7 Feb, 12:10, 3,500 ft. **84** *1918*: M 159 a (section), 14 Feb, 08:30, 3,400 m; *1949*: L 49/6489, 26 Oct, 11:25. **85** *1969*: SI 178/8200, 10 Jun, 15:25, 3,200 m; *1997*: 7 Feb, 12:00, 3,500 ft. **86** *1917*: M 107(section), 12 Dec, 13:30, 3,200 m.; CZA 6910; CZA 3328. **87** *1949*: L 33/2142, 14 Oct, 10:30; *1968*: SI 152/2643, 12 Jul, 11:10, 2,100 m; *1994*: 26 Feb, 16:00, 3,500 ft. **88** *1918*: M 84, 10 Jan, 14:30, 3,700 m. **89** *1997*: 8 Feb, 13:00, 6,000 ft. **90** AWM B-1744; AWM J-3154. **91-92** *1918*: M 93 a (section), 12 Jan, 10:30, 2,200 m. **93-94** *1997*: 8 Feb, 12:50, 3,500 ft. **95** AWM B-1754; AWM J-950; JNUL TMA 4183, No. 24. **96** *1917*: G 125 (no details); *1937*: CZA Keren Ha-Yesod Collection, Tel Aviv album 203/7722. **97** *1949*: L 33/2200, 14 Oct, 10:55; *1997*: 8 Feb, 11:00, 2,000 ft. **98** *1917*: M 93 d (section), 27 Nov, 12:00, 2,000 m; *1944*: PS 3/5071, 11 Dec [MAgr]. **99** *1956*: SI 7/5764, Aug, 13:40, 3,100 m; *1997*: 8 Feb, 10:40, 6,000 ft. **100** *1918*: M 98 (section), Mar 08:15, 4,500 m; *1949*: L 33/2151, 14 Oct, 10:30; postcard - S Narinsky's series, No. 14. **101** *1969*: SI 177/8033, 21 Apr, 13:50, 3,200 m; *1997*: 8 Feb, 13:15, 3,500 ft. **102** *1917*: M 664 (section), 16 Dec, 12:15, 3,000 m; AWM B-1697. **103** *1945*: PS 9/5012, 3 Jan [DGA]; *1969*: SI 186/0294, 2 Sep, 2,080 m; *1997*: 7 Feb, 10:50, 5,000 ft. **104** *1917*: M 684, 29 Nov, 12:30, 3,000 m; *1944*: PS 7/5025, 29 Dec [DGA]. **105** *1967*: SI 126/5954, 18 Jun, 13:35, 3,100 m; *1995*: 6 Apr, 11:00, 3,000 ft.; *1997*: 7 Feb, 11:00, 4,000 ft. **106** *1917*: M 736 (section), 4 Dec, 11:30, 3,700 m; *1968*: SI 148/2643, 21 Jun, 13:50, 2,500 m; AWM B-2364. **107** *1990*: 7 May, 13:10, 3,500 ft.; *1997*: 7 Feb, 11:10, 4,000 ft. **108** *1918*: M 744 a, 15 May, 13:45, 5,000 m; YBZ Vil (unnumbered); *1948*: YBZ Bir 8/1/1/40, 4 May. **109** *1994*: 2 Aug, 10:30, 4,000 ft. **110** *1917*: IWM Q-108358, 28 Nov, 13:00; YBZ Vil 1858; YBZ Vil 1861. **111** *1970*: SI 211/4228, 8 Jun, 14:00, 1,800 m; *1995*: 10 Feb, 10:40, 6,000 ft. **112** *1918*: M 964 (section), 4 Sep, 11:30, 4,000 m; *1944*: PS 16/5146, 16 Dec [DGA]. **113** *1967*: SI 126/5700, 18 Jun, 13:50, 3,450 m; *1994*: 26 Feb, 11:00, 5,500 ft. **114** *1917*: S, 23 Nov, 3,000 m; *1939*: CZA Album 93, 7523/2. **115** *1967*: SI 126/5457, 18 Jun, 12:50, 3,300 m; *1993*: 5 Dec, 10:45, 4,000 ft. **116** *1918*: M 823, 18 Jul, 06:45, 4,500 m; YBZ Vil 1831; surrender sheet in IWM - author. **117** *1944*: PS 1/5006, 7 Dec [DGA]; *1967*: SI 125/5391, June 16, 12:20, 3,400 m; *1995*: 10 Feb, 10:35, 6,000 ft. **118** *1918*: M 820 (section), 4 June, 06:15, 5,000 m. **119** *1944*: PS 1/5005, 7 Dec [DGA]; *1967*: SI 125/5390, June 16, 12:20, 3,400 m; *1994*: 2 Aug, 11:10, 6,500 ft. **120** *1918*: M 803 b, 29 Apr, 13:30, 4,000 m. **121** *1945*: PS 30/5028, 15 Mar [SI]; *1967*: SI 5391 (= p. 117); *1995*: 10 Feb, 10:00, 6,000 ft. **122** *1918*: M 785 a, 3 Jun, 12:45, 4,300 m; *1945*: PS 26/5105, 20 Feb [DGA]; signpost in IWM - author. **123** *1967*: SI 125/5391 (= p. 117); *1995*: 10 Feb, 10:35, 6,000 ft. **124** *1918*: M 906, 11 Jul, 06:15, 4,400 m; *1945*: PS 26/5105, 20 Feb [DGA]. **125** *1967*: SI 125/5391 (= p. 117); *1994*: 2 Aug, 11:40, 6,000 ft. **126** *1918*: M 795, 15 Sep, 08:30, 5,000 m. **127** *1945*: PS 30/5028 (= p. 121); *1967*: SI 125/5391 (= p. 117); *1995*: 10 Feb, 10:10, 6,000 ft. **128** *1918*: M 796 (section), 15 Sep, 08:30, 5,000 m; *1945*: PS 30/5028 (= p. 121). **129** *1967*: SI 125/5390 (= p. 119); *1994*: 2 Aug, 11:50, 6,000 ft. **130** *1945*: PS 30/5028 (= p. 121). **131** *1967*: SI 125/5390 (p. 119); AWM J-1220; AWM J-5679. **132-133** *1917*: M 779, 2 Nov, 08:45, 1,800 m. **134-135** *1995*: 10 Feb, 09:50, 5,000 ft. **136** *1917*: R, 11 Dec; S. **137**: *1995*: 10 Feb, 10:15, 6,000 ft. **138** *1918*: M 835, 22 Jun, 06:45, 4,500 m; CZA 12027. **139** *1937*: CZA Album 44A, 7737/5; *1995*: 10 Feb, 10:15, 6,000 ft. **140** *1918*: M 649, 15 Aug, 13:30, 4,800 m; YBZ Vil B-405. **141** *1944*: PS 7/5038, 29 Dec [DGA]; *1967*: SI 125/4674, 16 Jun, 09:45, 2,350 m; *1995*: 10 Feb, 10:45, 5,000 ft. **142** *1918*: M 133, 17 Dec, 14:30, 3,000 m; Archiv der Tempelgesellschaft, Stuttgart, No. 57. **143** *1949*: L 19/8188, 6

Oct, 16:20; *1990*: 4 Feb, 13:30, 3,500 ft. **144** *1918*: M 149, 15 Jan, 15:00, 2,000 m; *1949*: L 49/6499, 26 Oct, 11:25. **145** *1956*: SI 7/5719, Aug, 13:20, 2,900 m; *1966*: SI 113/0217, 30 Jul, 11:20, 1,900 m; *1994*: 2 Aug, 10:10, 4,000 ft. **146** *1917*: IAA [DGA] F-35 (section), 10 Dec, 11:00; *1944*: PS 3/5073, 11 Dec [MAgr]. **147** *1997*: 8 Feb, 13:20, 3,500 ft; YBZ Vil 2105; column today - author. **148** *1917*: M 20, 29 Dec, 12:00, 3,000 m; M 1272. **149** *1944*: PS 3/6036, 10 Dec [MAgr]; *1967*: SI 121/4130, 3 Mar, 13:00, 3,150 m; *1995*: 18 Dec, 14:00, 4,000 ft. **150** *1918*: M 596, 3 Jan, 14:15, 3,000 m; *1944*: PS 7/6003 + PS 7/6005, both of 29 Dec [MAgr]. **151** *1948*: YBZ Bir 8/1/2/60 (No. 2), 17 Apr; *1972*: SI 321/0348, 14 Jul, 16:05, 5,200 m; *1995*: 10 Feb, 11:00, 5,000 ft. **152** *1918*: M 558, 25 Apr, 12:30, 3,900 m; *1918**: AWM Aerial Photos Palestine, No. 5105A, 25 Feb, 11:25; balloon: reproducd from AWM 42/2 (a film on the Australians in Sinai and Palestine). **153** *1967*: SI 125/5376, 16 Jun, 12:15, 3,400 m; *1995*: 10 Feb, 11:10, 5,000 ft. **154** *1918*: PRO Air 1/2287/209/75/55 (Part C), 10 Apr, 09:30, 4,700 m; AWM B-1648. **155** *1969*: SI 180/8581, 1 Aug, 15:10, 2,100 m; *1993*: 5 Dec, 09:15, 3,000 ft. **156** *1918*: M 1028 (section), 28 Mar, 07:00, 3,500 m; *1918**: R (section), 24 Apr, 08:00, 4,000 m; *1938*: CZA, Album 92, 7733/1. **157** *1967*: SI 130/8048, 7 Aug, 13:50, 2,500 m; *1993*: 5 Dec, 09:30, 2,500 ft. **158** *1918*: IAA [DGA] H-4 (section), 19 Jan, 11:00 + photo of 23 Aug, 11:10 (copy of AWM unnumbered photo made at DGA). **159** *1949*: L 35/2653, 16 Oct, 14:15; *1967*: SI 122/4311, 10 Mar, 13:05, 3,200 m; *1994*: 15 Jun, 11:30, 3,500 ft. **160** *1918*: M 22 (section), 17 Jan, 14:30, 3,900 m; Wilson family collection, Petah Tiqva. **161** *1949*: L 18/7920, 6 Oct, 15:10; *1994*: 9 Apr, 09:00, 3,500 ft. **162** *1918*: AWM B-3486, 24 Sep, 15:00, 1,000 ft; *1918**: R (no details); *1948*: YBZ Bir 8/1/1/78, 11 Jan. **163** *1967*: SI 125/5314, 16 Jun, 13:53, 3,370 m; *1994*: 9 Apr, 10:20, 2,200 ft. **164** *1918*: S (no details); *1918**: AWM Aerial Photos Palestine, Nos. 5263 + 5264; armband in IWM - author; map - Map Collection, Department of Geography, the Hebrew University of Jerusalem. **165** *1997*: 12 Apr, 14:50, 4,000 ft; ground photo - Archives of the Jabotinsky Institute in Israel, Tel Aviv. **166** *1917*: R, 3 Dec, 11:00, 2,000 m; *1918*: M 14 (section; no details). **167** *1944*: PS 4/6095, 12 Dec [DGA]; *1996*: 10 Jun, 18:05, 5,000 ft. **168** *1918*: G-1, No. 26 (no details); *1944*: PS 6/5053, 16 Dec [DGA]. **169** *1996*: 10 Jun, 18:00, 5,000 ft; villagers: reproduced from AWM 42/3 (a film on the Australians in Sinai and Palestine). **170** *1918*: R (no details); *1949*: L 46/5523, 25 Oct, 11:25. **171** *1966*: SI 114/0634, 6 Aug, 10:45, 1,800 m; ground photos - author. **172** *1918*: S (no details); funeral - S. **173** *1948*: YBZ Bir 8/1/1/1, 27 Jun; *1968*: SI 144/1651, 4 Jun, 15:12, 2,120

m; *1994*: 9 Apr, 15:30, 5,000 ft. **174** *1937*: CZA Album 181, 7818/4; entrance to cemetery - S; mukhtars - AWM B-274. **175** Church of the Annunciation - 12 Apr 1997, 15:20, 3,000 ft; scene on Nazareth road, 1918 - AWM B-270; Nazerat 'Illit - 12 Apr 1997, 15:22, 3,000 ft. **176** *1918*: M 526, 20 Jan, 15:00, 2,500 m; bombing - IWM Q108360; houses - Schr. **177** *1937*: CZA Album 73, 7883/1; *1997*: 12 Apr, 14:15, 4,000 ft. **178** *1918*: M 527 (section, no details); water tower - M 1257; planes - AWM B-2480. **179** *1937*: CZA Album 187, 7787/3; *1997*: 12 Apr, 14:00, 3,000 ft. **180** *1918*: IAA, unnumbered mosaic (original number: AINN 2495), 3 Sep; *1937*: CZA Album 59, 7525/1; *1939*: CZA Album 163, 7525. **181** *1945*: PS 18/6021, 25 Jan [MAgr]; *1967*: SI 125/5029, 16 Jun, 11:37, 3,270 m; *1994*: 9 Apr, 10:40, 2,000 ft. **182** *1918*: Schr (no details); lancers - IWM Q12335. **183** *1945*: PS 14/5131, 7 Jan [MAgr]; *1970*: SI 221/1605, 26 Jul, 08:30, 1,720 m; *1997*: 18 Jan, 11:15, 6,000 ft. **184** *1918*: Schr (no details); Carmel Avenue - Prof. Alex Carmel's collection; Technion - S. **185** 1937: CZA Album 106, 7672/2; *1996*: 10 Jun, 17:45, 2,500 ft. **186** *1918*: M 11 (section), 10 Mar, 15:00, 3,000 m; air wagon - E. Berghaus, *Auf den Schienen der Erde. Eine Weltgeschichte der Eisenbahn*, Munich 1960, opp. p. 225. **187** *1989*: 23 Nov, 13:10, 4,000 ft; ground photos - S. **188** *1918*: Schr (no details); mosque - M 7 (no details). **189** *1945*: PS 11/6068, 4 Jan [DGA]; *1968*: SI 143/0881, 7 Jun, 11:55, 1,700 m; *1994*: 26 Apr, 17:00, 3,000 ft. **190** *1918*: M New number 2912 (section; no details); *1945*: PS 19/6006, 26 Jan [DGA]. **191** *1948*: YBZ Bir (no details); *1968*: SI 143/1116, 7 Jun, 13:37, 2,000 m; *1995*: 15 Nov, 14:30, 4,000 ft. **192** *1918*: R (no details); G-1, No. 32 (no details). **193** *1989*: 10 Dec, 13:10, 2,500 ft; *1997*: 12 Apr, 15:20, 4,000 ft. **194** *1918*: M 974 (section; no details); Samakh - M 1296 (no details); postcard - S. Narinsky's series, No. 15. **195** *1938*: CZA Album 88, 7605/10. **196** *1918*: G-2, No. 10 (no details); *1937*: GPO 34/K-1861; Jordan outlet - S. **197** *1945*: PS 8/5097, 2 Jan [MAgr]. **198** SI 150/1909, 28 Jun, 13:42, 2,000 m; 1994: 15:10, 1,000 ft. **198** *1918*: DGA (original number AINN 'M' 242), 22 Oct, 10:25, 2,000 ft; *1937*: CZA Album 152, 7693/4. **199** *1945*: PS 11/5137, 4 Jan [DGA]; *1968*: SI 155/1995, 28 Jun, 14:17, 2,110 m; *1994*: 9 Apr, 11:45, 2,000 ft. **200** lorries - M 1292; transport - AWM J 932; cavalry - American Colony Album, Jerusalem; road sign in IWM - author; in film - AWM 42/3. **201** Tiberias from the lake - M 1293; lane - G 141; Sitt Sakineh - G-2, No. 15; women washing clothes - G 144. **202** *1918*: M 520 (section, no details); *1945*: PS 14/5012, 7 Jan [DGA]. **203** *1966*: SI 107/7558, 15 Jan, 13:30, 2,430 m; *1994*: 9 Apr, 14:20, 5,000 ft.

Notes on the Maps

1. The map on p. 29 showing the deployment of German and British air squadrons on the Palestine front (Summer, 1918) is based on (a) the map in Holzhausen, "Die deutschen Fliegerstreitkräfte an der Sinai-und Palästinafront 1916-1918," *Orient-Rundschau* 18 (1936), 38; and (b) on the diagram in H.A. Jones, *The War in the Air: Being the History of the Part Played in the Great War by the Royal Air Force*, vol. 6, Oxford 1937, p. 209.

2. Maps on pp. 38-39:
(a) War of Independence, 1948: The delineation of the areas under Israeli control on 24 May 1948 is based on J. Wallach and M. Lissak, eds., *Carta's Atlas of Israel: The First Years, 1948-1961*, Jerusalem 1978, map 51 [in Hebrew].
(b) 1997: The delineation of the areas under Palestinian responsibility is based on Map 2 and on the 'Consolidated Map of the West Bank' attached to the *Israeli-Palestinian Interim Agreement on the West Bank and the Gaza Strip. Washington, D.C., September 28, 1995*, Jerusalem, Ministry of Foreign Affairs, n.d. 'Area C'–defined as "areas of the West Bank outside Areas A and B, which, except for the issues that will be negotiated in the permanent status negotiations, will be gradually transferred to Palestinian jurisdiction in accordance with this Agreement"–appears on our map in white. Reasons of scale have precluded a full display of the territorial arrangements agreed upon.

Demographic Data

The following sources were used:

1918: Palestine Office of the Zionist Organization, *Census of the Jews of Palestine*, 1: Judea, 2: *Samaria and Galilee*. Jaffa 1918-19 [in Hebrew].

1922: Government of Palestine, *Report and General Abstracts of the Census of 1922 taken on 23rd of October, 1922*, compiled by J.B. Barron. Jerusalem 1922.

1945: Government of Palestine, Office of Statistics, *Village Statistics, April 1945*. Jerusalem 1945.

For the 1922 and 1945 data on religious affiliation I use the abbreviations C for Christians, J for Jews, and M for Muslims.

1967:
(a) Israel Central Bureau of Statistics, *List of Settlements, their Population and Codes, 31. XII. 1967*, Technical Publications Series 28. Jerusalem 1968.
Publications in this series give data on the total population of a locality as well as on 'Arabs and others' included in the totals.
(b) Israel Defence Forces, *Census of Population conducted by the Central Bureau of Statistics, 1: West Bank of the Jordan, Gaza Strip and Northern Sinai, Golan Heights*. Jerusalem 1967.

1995: Israel Central Bureau of Statistics, *List of Localities, their Populations and Codes, 31. XII. 1995*, Technical Publications Series 68. Jerusalem 1996.

1996: Palestinian Central Bureau of Statistics, *Small Area Population: Revised Estimates for 1996*. Ramallah, April 1996. [The estimates are for 'Midyear 1996'].

The grand totals appearing in these publications add up as follows for the Land between the River Jordan and the Mediterranean:

	1922	1945	1967		1995-96
Palestine (British Mandate)					
-Muslims	590,890	1,061,270			
-Jews	83,794	553,600			
-Christians	73,024	135,550			
-Others	9,474	14,100			
Israel			2,773,900		5,619,000[bc]
-Jews				2,383,600	4,549,500[c]
- Arabs and others				390,300[a]	1,069,500[c]
West Bank			598,637		1,571,575[d]
- Muslims				565,904	
- Christians				29,446	
- Others				3,287	
Gaza Strip			356,261		963,028[d]
- Muslims				352,532	
- Christians				2,305	
- Others				1,424	
Total	757,182	1,764,520	3,728,798		8,153,603[e]

[a] Of these, 65,857 were counted in the 1967 Census of East Jerusalem.

[b] Of these, 138,600 are defined as "Israelis in Jewish localities in Judea, Samaria and Gaza Areas."

[c] Estimates for 31 Dec 95.

[d] Estimates for 'Midyear 1996.'

[e] This grand total is certainly inflated, as the 174,400 'Arab and other' inhabitants of Jerusalem, included in the total for Israel in the Israeli publication, must overlap to a considerable extent with the 254,387 inhabitants of the 'Jerusalem District,' included in the West Bank total of the Palestinian publication. On the other hand, the Israeli estimates relate to the end of 1995, the Palestinian to mid-1996.

Transliteration

For the transliteration of Arabic place-names I relied on the British maps of Palestine (scale 1:100,000). For the transliteration of Hebrew place-names I followed mostly the *List of Localities* published by the Israel Central Bureau of Statistics (but I decided to write, for instance, Rishon le-Zion, not Rishon Leziyyon).

Foothotes

1. On maps and aerial photographs, see for instance J. K. S. St. Joseph, "The Scope of Air Photography," in J. K. S. St. Joseph (ed.), *The Uses of Air Photography: Nature and Man in a New Perspective*, London 1966, p. 15. For Marcel Griaule's emphatic endorsement see for instance his "Aviation and Scientific Research," *Nature* 157 (1946), 848-849, and *Méthode de l'ethnographie*, Paris 1957, pp. 83-85; for a more restrained view see J. Clifford, *The Predicament of Culture: Twentieth-Century Ethnography, Literature, and Art*, Cambridge, Mass., and London 1988, pp. 68-70.

2. See Dalman's remarks in his autobiographical account in E. Stange (ed.), *Die Religionswissenschaft in Selbstdarstellungen*, vol. 4, Leipzig 1928, pp. 1-29 (the quotation appears on p. 25).

3. B.Z. Kedar and D. Pringle, "La Fève: A Crusader Castle in the Jezreel Valley," *Israel Exploration Journal* 35 (1985), 164-179.

4. S. Freud, *Civilization and its Discontents*, transl. J. Strachey (New York and London 1989), p. 18. [The essay was originally published in 1930].

5. The passage is most readily available in Ahad Ha-'Am, *'Al parashat drakhim*, vol. 1, Berlin 1930, pp. 27-28. For an authorized German translation see "Die Wahrheit aus Palästina," in Achad Haam, *Am Scheidewege. Gesammelte Aufsätze*, vol. 1, Berlin 1923, pp. 86-87. (In early Zionist literature, the Hebrew Eretz-Israel [=Land of Israel] was routinely rendered into English as Palestine, into German as Palästina, etc.).

6. Cf. A. Y. Brawer, "On the Collection of Aviators' Photographs in the National Library," *Teva' va-Aretz* 4.9 (April 1937), 458 [in Hebrew]. Brawer remarked that "many areas of our country that had been desolate during the War, were turned by us into blooming gardens. A comparison of the German photographs with those taken [at the time of writing] by British aviators, which can be obtained from the British headquarters for scientific purposes, [constitutes] an important historical source of great practical-political value": ibid. - The Potsdam collection was destroyed during World War II.

7. Upon my suggestion to Amir Drori, director of the Israel Antiquities Authority, the material was subsequently deposited at the Aerial Photographs Unit, Department of Geography, the Hebrew University of Jerusalem.

8. Mrs. Schraffenberger accepted my invitation to come to Israel and deposit the main part of the Groll Collection in the National Library in Jerusalem, but she died in the spring of 1990. Her niece, Mrs. Ruth Schell, kindly entrusted me with conveying the material to Jerusalem. Its shelfmark in the National Library is TMA 4390.

9. On General Felmy's activities during World War II and his subsequent conviction for war crimes in the Balkans, see R. Hampe, *Die Rettung Athens im Oktober 1944*, Wiesbaden 1955, and H. W. Neulen, *Feldgrau in Jerusalem: Das Levantekorps des kaiserlichen Deutschland*, Munich 1991, p. 289.

10. Some photographs of the Schreiber and Rengstorf collections are rather mediocrely reproduced in R. Koeppel, *Palästina: Die Landschaft in Karten und Bildern*, Tübingen 1930.

11. J. Otterman, "Baring High-Albedo Soils by Overgrazing: A Hypothesized Desertification Mechanism," Science 86 (1974), 531-533. Otterman was not aware of the fact that the difference was already visible on the famous photograph of the Sinai Peninsula, Israel, and parts of Saudi Arabia, Jordan, Syria and Lebanon, taken by the Gemini astronauts and published in 1967.

12. An earlier version of this chapter appeared under the title "Aerial Israel - a Historian's Infatuation," *Ariel. A Review of Arts and Letters in Israel* 63 (1986), 58-71.

13. On aerial activity on the Sinai-Palestine front see [H.] Felmy, "Sinaifront und Palästina," in G. P. Neumann (ed.), *Die deutschen Luftstreitkräfte im Weltkriege*, Berlin 1920, pp. 519-531; Holzhausen, "Die deutschen Fliegerstreitkräfte an der Sinai- und Palästinafront 1916-1918," *Orient-Rundschau* 18 (1936), 31-33, 37-42; H. A. Jones, *The War in the Air: Being the Story of the Part played in the Great War by the Royal Air Force*, vol. 5, Oxford 1935, pp. 160-166, 177-189, 191-249; vol. 6, Oxford 1937, pp. 175-238; and F. M. Cutlack, *The Australian Flying Corps in the Western and Eastern Theatres of War 1914-1918*, The Official History of Australia in the War of 1914-1918, vol. 8, Sydney 1938, pp. 29-171. The role of French sea planes is described at some length in P. Chack, *On se bat sur mer*, Paris 1927, pp. 141-257. See also H. Henkelburg, *Als Kampfflieger am Suez-Kanal, Berlin 1917; H. Eisgruber, Krieg in der Wüste. Der tollste und seltsamste Feldzug des Weltkriegs*, Berlin 1934. On aerial photography on both sides see D. Gavish, "Aerial Photographs of Palestine by World War I Aviators," *Cathedra* 7 (April 1978), 119-150 (in Hebrew). On the utilization of aerial photographs in the preparation of maps see H. H. Thomas, "Geographical Reconnaissance by Aeroplane Photography, with Special Reference to the Work done on the Palestine Front," *Geographical* Journal 55 (1920), 349-370; Holzhausen, "Die Tätigkeit der Vermessungsabteilung 27 in Palästina," *Orient-Rundschau* 19 (1937), 52-55; D. Gavish and G. Biger, "Innovative Cartography in Palestine: Initial Use of Aerial Photography in Town-Mapping (1917-1918)," *Cathedra* 20 (July 1981), 207-216 [in Hebrew]. On aerial photographs of archaeological sites taken during the war see T. Wiegand, *Sinai. Wissenschaftliche Veröffentlichungen des deutsch-türkischen Denkmalschutzkommandos*, vol. 1, Berlin 1920; Holzhausen, "Deutsche Flieger im Dienst der Archäologie," *Luftwelt* 2 (1935), 487-489; and C. Watzinger, *Theodor Wiegand: Ein deutscher Archäologe, 1864-1936*, Munich 1944, pp. 290-293.

14. The feats were described by Felmy and his observer; see Oberlt. [G.] Felmy and Oberlt. Falke, "An der Sinai-Front," Wir *Luftkämpfer: Bilder und Berichte deutscher Flieger und Luftschiffer*, Sonderheft der Berliner Illustrirter Zeitung, Berlin 1918, pp. 42-44. The photograph appears in Fritz Groll's main album.

15. *Notes on the Interpretation of Aeroplane Photographs Taken on the Palestine Front*, 2nd edition issued by General Staff, Intelligence, G.H.Q., Egyptian Expeditionary Force, June 1918. The handbook is stored in the box containing photos 5817-6263 of the series 'Aerial Photos Palestine.'

16. *Taktisches Lichtbild-Buch der Stabsbildabteilung des Kommandeurs der Flieger Jildirim*, PRO Air 1 2287 209/75/55.

17. *Kriegstagebuch der Bayer. Flieger-Abt. 304b, 24. Juli 1917 - 3. April 1919*, geführt von Oberlt. Fritz Berthold [hereafter cited as *Diary of Squadron 304*]. The diary's shelfmark in the Bavarian War Archives is *Luftschiffer u. Flieger*, Nr. 48.

18. The diary of the Australian squadron reveals that eight pilots who took off from the airfield near Julis participated in the attack and threw 56 bombs. Five of them believed to have obtained good results; two - fair; one - very good. AWM, *War Diary of No. 1 Squadron, Australian Flying Corps*, for January 1918: Entry for 3.1.18, and Appendix 3 - Bombing.

19. *Diary of Squadron 304*, entries for 3 and 4 January 1918.

20. Munich, Bavarian War Archives, *Luftschiffer u. Flieger.*

21. The Palestine News. The Weekly Newspaper of the Egyptian Expeditionary Force of the British Army in Occupied Enemy Territory, 18 April 1918, p. 8.

22. The shelfmark of the weekly reports is *Luftschiffer u. Flieger*, Nr. 50.

23. AWM, *War Diary of No. 1 Squadron, Australian Flying Corps*, February to September 1918.

24. *Diary of Squadron 304*, entries for 6 and 7 June 1917.

25. Liman von Sanders, *Fünf Jahre Türkei*, Berlin 1920, p. 343.

26. *Diary of Squadron 304*, entries for 12-18 September 1918.

27. *Diary of Squadron 304*, entry for 19 September 1918.

28. Jones (note 13 above), vol. 6, pp. 224-226, with the quote appearing on p. 225. See also C. Falls and A.F. Becke, *Military Operations Egypt and Palestine. From June 1917 to the End of the War*, London 1930, pp. 502-503.

29. Kluger's photographs are deposited in the Central Zionist Archives and in the Government Press Office, both in Jerusalem. For some data on Kluger's biography see S. Sheva, "The Man Who Created a Style Despite himself," *Devar ha-Shavu'a*, 5 June 1970, pp. 20-21, 35 (in Hebrew). For a discussion of Kluger's work, with an emphasis on his ground photographs, see O. Yeda'yah, "Toward Social Functioning: On the Photographs of Zoltán Kluger from the 'Tower and Stockade' Period," *Kav* 10 (July 1990), 12-19 (in Hebrew).

30. Copies of these photographs are deposited in the archives of the Survey of Israel and the Ministry of Agriculture, both in Tel Aviv, and at the Aerial Photographs Unit of the Hebrew University of Jerusalem. Some original negatives are extant in Britain at the Joint Air Reconnaissance Intelligence Centre. On the 1944-45 survey see D. Gavish, *Land and Map: The Survey of Palestine, 1920-1948*, Jerusalem 1991, pp. 258-259 (in Hebrew).

31. This collection is deposited in the archives of Yad Ben-Zvi, Jerusalem.

32. Zalman Leef, a surveyor by profession, attended an advanced course on the use of aerial cameras in photogrammetry, in Switzerland in 1938. While serving as a member of the Israeli delegation at the 1949 Lausanne peace talks with the Arab states, he purchased the equipment for his new institute. See N[imrod] L[eef], "The Life and Work of the Late Zalman Leef," in *Eretz-Israel*, vol. 2: *The Zalman Leef Book*, Jerusalem 1953, pp. 1-3 (in Hebrew). The Leef survey of 1949 is kept by Mr. Nimrod Leef, Jerusalem; copies of most photographs may be consulted at the Ministry of Agriculture in Tel Aviv.

33. This sketch is based on Steiner's *Kriegsranglisten-Auszug* and other official papers, most of which were generously placed at my disposal, together with his Levantine photographs, by his daughter Nanna Steiner of Munich and by his son Knud U.K. Steiner of Espoo, Finland. The photographs will be ultimately deposited with the Aerial Photographs Unit, Department of Geography, the Hebrew University of Jerusalem.

The shooting down of the British airplane is documented also in the *Diary of Squadron 304* and on the back of Steiner's photo showing the wreckage of B-3594. A Polish translation of Steiner's death certificate was obtained from Muzeum Stutthof, Sopot, Poland.

34. I am indebted to Knud Steiner for having graciously given me his father's copy of the German translation of *The Revolt in the Desert*. On subsequent pages Steiner gives the names of aviators killed or wounded during two incidents mentioned by Lawrence.

35. H.E. von Tzschirner-Tzschirne, *In die Wüste. Meine Erlebnisse als Gouverneur von Akaba*, Berlin n.d., p. 114; T.E. Lawrence, *Seven Pillars of Wisdom: A Triumph*, Garden City, NY 1938 [1926], p. 314.

36. For accounts of the British conquest of Palestine in 1917-18 see A. P. Wavell, *The Palestine Campaigns*, 3rd ed., London 1931; Falls and Becke, *Military Operations* (note 28 above); H. S. Gullett, *The Australian Imperial Force in Sinai and Palestine, 1914-1918*, The Official History of Australia in the War of 1914-1918, vol. 7, Sydney 1923; C. G. Powles, *The New Zealanders in Sinai and Palestine*, Auckland 1922; also, the lavishly illustrated volume by D. L. Bullock, *Allenby's War: The Palestinian-Arabian Campaigns 1916-1918*, London 1988. Several German participants left behind personal accounts. The most informative of these are F. Frh. Kress von Kressenstein, *Mit den Türken zum Suezkanal*, Berlin 1938; Liman von Sanders, *Fünf Jahre Türkei*, Berlin 1920; J. Drexler, *Mit Jildirim ins Heilige Land. Erinnerungen und Glossen zum Palästina-Feldzug 1917-1918*, Ravensburg 1919; [W.] Steuber, *"Jildirim." Deutsche Streiter auf heiligem Boden. Nach eigenen Tagebuch-aufzeichnungen und unter Benutzung amtlicher Quellen des Reichsarchivs*, Schlachten des Weltkrieges, vol. 4, 2nd ed., Oldenburg and Berlin 1925; H. Guhr, *Als türkischer Divisionskommandeur in Kleinasien und Palästina: Erlebnisse eines deutschen Stabsoffiziers während des Weltkrieges*, Berlin 1937; P. Range, *Vier Jahre Kampf um das Heilige Land*, Lübeck 1939; and F. von Papen, *Der Wahrheit eine Gasse*, Innsbruck 1952. For general accounts from the German viewpoint, see the well-documented book by C. Mühlmann, *Das deutsch-türkische Waffenbündnis im Weltkriege*, Leipzig 1940, and the recent book by Neulen (note 9 above), with an exhaustive bibliography.

37. The most detailed account, in English, of the War of 1948 presents the Israeli point of view: N. Lorch, *The Edge of the Sword: Israel's War of Independence, 1947-1949*, 2nd ed., Jerusalem 1968; the account should be read alongside the chapters in the author's autobiography that describe its difficult genesis: N. Lorch, *Late Afternoon: My First Seventy Years (and what preceded them)*, Tel Aviv 1997, pp. 174-204, 366-375 (in Hebrew). On the fate of the Arabs in the areas that became Israel see B. Morris, *The Birth of the Palestinian Refugee Problem, 1947-1949*, Cambridge 1987 (I use the revised and expanded Hebrew translation, Tel Aviv 1991).

38. Ahmed Djemal Pasha, *Erinnerungen eines türkischen Staatsmannes*, Munich 1922, p. 302.

39. S. Hedin, *Jerusalem*, Leipzig 1918, pp. 140-141. See also C.I. Hoffer, "Der Kampf um das heilige Land," *Volk und Heer* 2.7-9, Vienna and Leipzig 1918, pp. 10-11.

40. R.M.P. Preston, *The Desert Mounted Corps. An Account of the Cavalry Operations in Palestine and Syria, 1917-1918*, Boston and New York 1921, pp. 34-35. For a favorable description that nevertheless contrasts the 'European' public and simple private buildings, see the Hebrew account in *Be-Sha'ah zo* 3, Jaffa 1916, p. 91. See also the descriptions in W.S. Kent Hughes, *Modern Crusaders. An Account of the Campaign in Sinai and Palestine up to the Capture of Jerusalem*, Melbourne 1921, p. 124, and R. Skilbeck Smith, *Subaltern in Macedonia and Judaea, 1916-17*, London 1930, p. 134.

41. T. Canaan, *Mohammedan Saints and Sanctuaries in Palestine*, Jerusalem 1927, pp. 97-98.

42. J. More, *With Allenby's Crusaders*, London c.1923, p. 95.

43. E. Blackwell and E.C. Axe, *Romford to Beirut via France, Egypt and Jericho*, London 1926, p. 110.

44. See M. Larkin, *The Hand of Mordechai*, New York and South Brunswick 1968.

45. The expulsion of one of these villages inspired S. Yizhar, the noted Israeli author, to write his "Story of Khirbet Hiz'eh," published in 1949. For data on this and other Arab villages see W. Khalidi, ed., *All That Remains: The Palestinian Villages Occupied and Depopulated by Israel in 1948*, Washington, D.C. 1992. (The book, whose very motto tendentiously truncates a sentence by Moshe Dayan, should be used with care).
For a study of aerial photos of 1918, 1945, and 1972 of the region of Barbara, an Arab village about six km northeast of Deir Suneid, see W. Richter, *Israel und seine Nachbarräume. Ländliche Siedlungen*

und Landnutzung seit dem 19. Jahrhundert, Wiesbaden 1979, plates 31, 32, 34. The volume contains juxtapositions of aerial photos of various rural areas taken between the mid-1940s and the early 1970s.

46. The war diary is kept at the Australian War Memorial, Canberra.

47. "Nasser's Memoirs of the First Palestine War," trans. W. Khalidi, *Journal of Palestine Studies* 2/2 (Winter 1973), 23-27. The memoirs were originally published, in Arabic, in 1955.

48. See M. Ben-Hillel Hacohen, *War of the Nations: A Diary,* ed. S. Rubinstein, vol. 1, Jerusalem 1981, p. 153 (in Hebrew); and E. Belkind, *This Is How It Was...,* Tel Aviv 1979, p. 89 (in Hebrew). On the construction of the railway see Steuber (n. 36 above), p. 109; and W. Pick, "Der deutsche Pionier Heinrich August Meissner-Pascha und seine Eisenbahnbauten im Nahen Osten, 1901-1917," *Jahrbuch des Instituts für Deutsche Geschichte der Universität Tel Aviv* 4 (1975), 293.

49. Gullett (n. 36 above), pp. 454-455.

50. Dov Gavish utilized aerial photos of 1917, 1945, and 1987 to study the changes that had taken place in the area of Qastina, an Arab village about six km northwest of the Sawafirs: "Aerial Perspectives of Past Landscapes," in Ruth Kark, ed., *The Land that became Israel. Studies in Historical Geography*, New Haven, London and Jerusalem 1989, pp. 308-319. But fascination with aerial photos should not have led to the implanting (on p. 309) of the word "aerial" into a quotation from Susan Sontag's *On Photography*.

51. "Bericht über die Räumung des Flugplatzes Arak el-Manchije," Bavarian War Archives, Munich, *Luftschiffer u. Flieger,* Nr. 54; Gullett (n. 36 above), pp. 448, 457-458; Jones (n. 13 above), vol. 5, pp. 241-242.

52. Gullett (n. 36 above), p. 470.

53. Powles (note 36 above), p. 154.

54. R.N. Salaman, *Palestine Reclaimed. Letters from a Jewish Officer in Palestine,* London c.1920, pp. 46-47. In a footnote, the author explains that *rahamonus* is "a Hebrew word denoting a characteristic type of charity and kind-heartedness, divorced from all system, common amongst Jews."

55. Hughes (note 40 above), pp. 133-135.

56. Rifki's war memoirs were published in 1932 in Turkish. Several passages appear in English translation in G. Lewis, "An Ottoman Officer in Palestine, 1914-1918," in D. Kushnir (ed.), *Palestine in the Late Ottoman Period: Political, Social and Economic Transformation,* Jerusalem and Leiden 1986, pp. 402-415 (the quoted passage appears on p. 408).

57. M. Meirowitz, "Pages from a World War I Diary," in D. Yudelowitz (ed.), *Rishon le-Zion 1882-1941*, Rishon le-Zion 1941, p. 404 (in Hebrew).

58. J. Klausner, "A World Coming About," *Ha-Shiloah* 28 (1913), 163-164 (in Hebrew).

59. K. Baedeker, *Palestine and Syria,* Leipzig 1912, p. 12.

60. Gullett (note 36 above), p. 479.

61. R. Meinertzhagen, *Middle East Diary 1917-1956,* New York 1960, p. 7.

62. Palmah: the elite units of the Haganah, the main Jewish militia under the British Mandate.

63. *The Letters and Papers of Chaim Weizmann,* vol. 8, series A: *November 1917 - October 1918,* ed. D. Barzilay and B. Litvinoff, New Brunswick, NJ and Jerusalem 1977, Letter 181, p. 172. (The original letter was written in Russian.)

64. J. B. Glubb, *A Soldier with the Arabs,* London 1957, p. 142.

65. Falls and Becke (note 36 above), p. 184; S. Tolkowsky, *A History of Jaffa,* Tel Aviv 1926, pp. 135-136 (in Hebrew). This is one of the first books on the country's history that utilizes aerial photographs.

66. A. Ruppin, *Memoirs, Diaries, Letters,* trans. from the German by K. Gershon, New York 1971, p. 90.

67. N. Goldmann, *Erez-Israel: Reisebriefe aus Palästina,* Frankfurt/M 1982, p. 22.

68. *Weizmann Letters* (note 63 above), Letters 163, 213, pp. 132, 211. (The original letters were written in Russian.)

69. *Ha-Shiloah* 27 (1912), 308 (in Hebrew).

70. Ruppin (note 66 above), pp. 93, 122-123.

71. Ahmed Djemal Pasha (note 38 above), p. 305.

72. Ruppin (note 66 above), pp. 90, 94.

73. See D. Gavish, "The Old City of Jaffa, 1936: A Colonial Urban Renewal Project," *Eretz-Israel* 17, Jerusalem 1984, pp. 66-73 (in Hebrew); Gavish includes also some of the RAF aerial photos that document the demolition. For a brief English version see Gavish, "Aerial Perspectives" (n. 50 above), pp. 315-319.

74. Skilbeck Smith (note 40 above), p. 151.

75. On this place see Canaan (note 41 above), pp. 14, 18, 39.

76. E. Grant, *The Peasantry of Palestine: Life, Manners and Customs of the Village,* Boston 1907, pp. 14-15.

77. See H. Goren, "Early 20th Century Christian Institutions in Abu Ghosh," *Cathedra* 62 (December 1991), 80-106 (in Hebrew).

78. For a detailed account see B. Morris, "The Case of Abu Ghosh and Beit Naqquba, al-Fureidis and Jisr az Zarka in 1948 – Or Why Four Villages Remained," in idem, *1948 and After: Israel and the Palestinians,* revised and expanded edition, Oxford 1994, pp. 257-284.

79. Kh. al-Sakakini, *Kadha ana, ya dunya,* Jerusalem 1955, pp. 92-94 (translated by Daniella Talmon-Heller).

80. G. Levy, "At the Tomb Holy to All," *Ha-Aretz – Weekly Supplement,* 7 Oct 94, p. 17 (in Hebrew; based on an interview with Maj.-Gen. [Res.] 'Uzzi Narkiss, OC Central Command in 1967).

81. von Papen (note 36 above), p. 100.

82. Powles (note 36 above), p. 227.

83. *Proclamations, Ordinances and Notices issued by O.E.T.A. (South) to August 1919,* Cairo 1920, p. 41.

84. *Standing Orders and General Instructions for the Information of Officers,* Jerusalem, October 1918, p. 112.

85. *Weizmann Letters* (note 63 above), Letter 163, pp. 132-133.

86. *The Palestine News,* 9 May 18, p. 8.

87. *Standing Orders* (note 84 above), p. 104.

88. Quoted from the text as printed in the 8 Aug 18 issue of *The Palestine News*. On the problem of establishing the authentic version of Weizmann's speech see my "Laying the Foundation Stones of the Hebrew University of Jerusalem, 24 July 1918," in *The History of the Hebrew University of Jerusalem: Origins and Beginnings,* ed. S. Katz and M. Heyd, Jerusalem 1997, pp. 107-119 (in Hebrew).

89. Steuber (note 36 above), pp. 125-126.

90. More (note 42 above), p. 185.

91. Gullett (note 36 above), p. 537; Powles (note 36 above), map opposite p. 176.

92. H.S. Gullett and C. Barrett, eds., *Australia in Palestine,* Sydney 1919, pp. 123-124.

93. For a comparative study of aerial photos of Jericho taken in 1918, 1945, and 1974, see Richter (note 45 above), pp. 350-363.

94. *The Palestine News,* 26 Sep 18, p. 6.

95. See especially File M 107/37 of the British Chief Secretariat, now kept in the Israel State Archives. I intend to deal with this little-known British project, and its like, in a future article.

96. M. Klioner, *The Kfar Sava Scroll: The History of the Exiled 1917-18,* Jaffa 1920, p. 39 (in Hebrew).

97. D. Skibin, *The Memoirs of a Kfar Sava Man,* Herzlia 1947, pp. 139-142 (in Hebrew).

98. V. Jabotinsky, *The Story of the Jewish Legion,* transl. S. Katz, New York 1945, pp. 137-138.

99. Holzhausen, "Deutsche Flieger im Dienst der Archäologie," *Luftwelt* 2 (1935), pp. 488-489.

100. Steuber (note 36 above), p. 101.

101. J. Dushman, "In the Winery (Notes from the Time of the Expulsion)," *Ha-Aretz,* 18 Oct 29, p. 6.

102. The *hijra* year is 1295. The inscription is to be published by Moshe Sharon in his *Corpus inscriptionum arabicarum.*

103. P. Range, *Nazareth,* Leipzig 1923, pp. 12-13.

104. Steuber (note 36 above), pp. 95-96, 134-135, 148-149.

105. F. A. Theilhaber, *Jüdische Flieger im Weltkrieg,* Berlin 1924, pp. 49-50.

106. Goldmann (note 67 above), p. 103.

107. *The Palestine News,* 3 Oct 18, p. 11.

108. J. Nedavah, ed., *Joseph Lishansky, Man of 'Nili.' Writings, Letters, Memoirs,* Tel Aviv 1977, p. 154 (in Hebrew). After the ring's exposure in October 1917, Lishansky was captured by the Turks; he was hanged in Damascus on 16 Dec 17.

109. H. Schmittdiel, 'Mein Kriegstagebuch,' part 2, pp. 61-63. My thanks to Dr. Ernst Schmittdiel, Erlangen, for permitting me to utilize the manuscript of his father's diary. D. Dayan, *In Happiness and Sorrow,* Tel Aviv 1957, p. 23 (in Hebrew).

110. Gullett (note 36 above), pp. 730-734, with the quotation appearing on p. 733; S. Dayan, *On the Banks of Deganya and Kinneret,* Tel Aviv s.d., pp. 205-230 (in Hebrew).

111. For a comparative study of aerial photos of this area taken c. 1918 and 1976, see Richter (note 45 above), pp. 342-350. (The photo of c. 1918 is erroneously dated to 1915).

112. Schmittdiel (note 109 above), p. 61.

113. M. Rafiq and M. Bahjat Bek, *Beyrut Vilayeti,* vol. 1, Beirut 1335 [1916-1917], p. 377. I would like to thank Dr. Avner Levy for having translated this passage from the Turkish original.